THE CANNABIS KITCHEN COOKBOOK

THE CANNABIS KITCHEN COOKBOOK

FEEL-GOOD EDIBLES, FROM TINCTURES
AND COCKTAILS TO ENTRÉES AND DESSERTS

ROBYN GRIGGS LAWRENCE

PHOTOGRAPHS BY **POVY KENDAL ATCHISON**

FOREWORD BY JANE WEST

Skyhorse Publishing

Copyright © 2015 by Robyn Griggs Lawrence
Photographs copyright © 2015 by Povy Kendal Atchison, unless otherwise noted
New Skyhorse paperback edition 2019

All rights reserved. No part of this book may be reproduced in any manner without the express written consent of the publisher, except in the case of brief excerpts in critical reviews or articles. All inquiries should be addressed to Skyhorse Publishing, 307 West 36th Street, 11th Floor, New York, NY 10018.

Skyhorse Publishing books may be purchased in bulk at special discounts for sales promotion, corporate gifts, fund-raising, or educational purposes. Special editions can also be created to specifications. For details, contact the Special Sales Department, Skyhorse Publishing, 307 West 36th Street, 11th Floor, New York, NY 10018 or info@skyhorsepublishing.com.

Skyhorse® and Skyhorse Publishing® are registered trademarks of Skyhorse Publishing, Inc.®, a Delaware corporation.

Visit our website at www.skyhorsepublishing.com.

10 9 8 7 6 5 4 3 2

Library of Congress Cataloging-in-Publication Data is available on file.

Cover design by Brian Peterson
Cover photo by Povy Kendal Atchison

Print ISBN: 978-1-5107-4988-7
Ebook ISBN: 978-1-5107-0059-8

Printed in China

DEDICATION

To Dennis, who nurtured me through this process from seed to flower with humor, intuition, and love. You're the man.

This book is also for anyone who has died, been imprisoned, or persecuted because of a sacred plant. I wrote much of it on my laptop, sitting on a sofa that I bought on Craigslist from a mom whose son was tasered to death near his illegal cannabis growing outside of Boulder, Colorado, in 2007—just as medical marijuana was blossoming into a legitimate business. There's no justice in a town, in a world, when I can sink into that sofa and write about a plant—a vegetable—that cost Ryan Wilson his life.

TABLE OF CONTENTS

Entrees 177

Sides 214

Desserts   230

Savory Snacks   256

Sweet Snacks 266

Cocktails 278

Through her catering company, Edible Events, Jane West creates artfully choreographed events that enhance guests' cannabis experience.

FOREWORD

When marijuana prohibition ended, cannabis came to mainstream America. By many estimates, cannabis will be federally legal by 2020. Most American states have laws on the books or ballot initiatives in line to legalize. We've reached a point where we can not only consider but also celebrate the merits and virtues of a plant that's been vilified and propagandized for most of our lifetimes. It will take several more decades of advocacy to end the drug war on a global scale, but we're moving exponentially in that direction.

This shift in public perception and legislation has launched a cultural revolution in homes and kitchens nationwide, and this movement goes beyond normalizing cannabis use. This is about fully embracing cannabis as a sacred herb, and my friend Robyn Griggs Lawrence encapsulates it in this book—a cannabis culinary journey written from the right side of history.

The world-renowned chefs featured in this cookbook are the innovators and pioneers in cannabis culinary arts, and they share with us their carefully crafted, globally inspired recipes. Robyn's insider tour of these artisans' kitchens provides a truly unique understanding of their nuanced, craft recipes. Steeped in the rich flavors and aromas of gourmet cannabis, these recipes are a fine taste of the future of culinary arts.

Welcome to the modern kitchen—where the health, wellness, and psychotherapeutic benefits of one sacred plant can be harnessed with simple adherence to the wisdom of the culinary arts. With the right cannabis ingredients, culinary knowledge, and skill, any chef can also achieve the plant's benefits—relaxation for some, serious medicine for others. We are empowered to manifest wellness from our own stovetops.

Normalization is integral to ending prohibition. *The Cannabis Kitchen Cookbook* is leading the way. Robyn Lawrence can see into the future, to the modern kitchen, where cannabis is an herb, handled akin to rosemary or sage. This is how Americans will come to understand that cannabis in the kitchen is not a conversation about "psychedelic drugs." This is a journey into the culinary arts, a whole new world of oils, butters, tinctures, infusions, simple syrups, juices, and all the endless possibilities that this plant brings to our kitchens and homes.

—Jane West
Founder, Edible Events Co.
Cofounder, Women Grow
International Business Times 20 Most Influential People in Cannabis, 2015

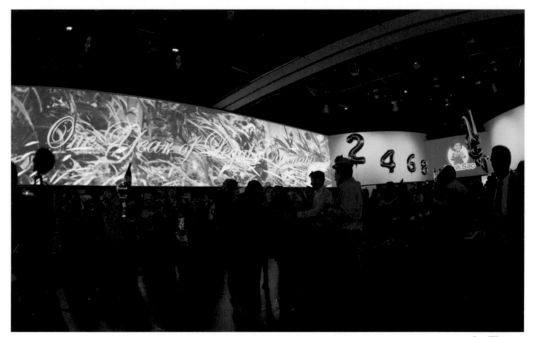

JaneWest.com

INTRODUCTION

I grew up in a Midwestern town where the sweet stink of corn sugars being processed into syrup was a daily reminder of the industry our region was built on—the price we paid for prosperity. Today I live in Boulder, Colorado, where the tropical aroma of cannabis plants releasing volatile oils—difficult for warehouse walls to completely contain—hovers over certain areas. Herbaceous and far more pleasant than my hometown's fragrance, this new smell is also a by-product of prosperity.

Boulder is one of a handful of places in the world where cannabis can be legally produced, sold, and consumed, and the industry is booming as people discover the plant's culinary and medicinal value. Cannabis is part of many Coloradoans' fanatically healthy lifestyles, a source of inspiration and pleasure for a diverse group of professionals, carpenters, outdoor enthusiasts, yogis, and soccer moms. It has brought tax and tourism dollars, worldwide attention, and a deep responsibility.

If we do this right, the world will follow. People will no longer rot in jail for possessing a plant, and the plant will no longer need to be hidden behind warehouse walls. Fields of cannabis could surround Boulder—and cities around the world—like the cornfields that ring my Midwestern hometown. And if we do this right, we will never modify or adulterate this herb to make anything resembling high-fructose corn syrup.

***

I became part of the cannabis economy in 2009 when my gynecologist prescribed medical marijuana to ease the symptoms of dysmenorrhea. I wasn't unaware that it could round my corners when stress and hormones threatened my symmetry. I'd self-medicated before I'd had kids, but I was a newbie when Doctor Joe's recommendation (and registration with the state of Colorado) unlocked the gates to my neighborhood medical marijuana dispensary, where shelves were lined with as many varieties of cannabis as there are cheeses at Dean & DeLuca. (And how do you know how many types of cheese—or cannabis, wine, chocolate, coffee—there can be until you see them all in one place?)

The deep green herbs in this wonderland had names ranging from mouthwatering (Plushberry) to scary (Green *Crack*?). After a short consultation about my needs and usage (polite and discreet), the "budtender" pulled down a few jars for me to look at and sniff. When he opened those jars, the essential oils from those nuggets filled my nostrils—oaky eucalyptus, cheesy lemon, musky blueberry—the way garlic hits your nose when you walk into Rao's. The genie was out of the bottle. Cannabis revealed itself to me as food—to be simmered, sautéed, and savored rather than smoked.

Trouble was, I didn't have a *Joy of Cooking* or *Better Homes & Gardens* (the two cookbooks on my counter) to tell me how to utilize the flavor of this complicated herb while also extracting its psychoactive chemical compounds—which were key to my doctor's orders. I went online and found everyone's opinions about how to cook with cannabis, and I ended up a little bit terrified: *I could burn up three hundred dollars worth of cannabis in butter or send a friend on a bad trip!*

And I actually knew nothing about how this new ingredient was grown, processed, and delivered to me. The budtender said it was "organic hydroponic" and had a list of chemicals that weren't used in its cultivation, but what about the nutrients and fertilizers that *were* used to grow it in warehouses around Boulder? And why did it all have to be hydroponically grown, anyway? Most kale isn't grown that way.

The answers weren't online, so I turned to experts—real people who know the plant from years of study and experimentation. Matt Davenport, consultant and sustainable cannabis grower who's introducing permaculture principles and techniques to the industry, schooled me on how to buy (and eventually grow) the healthiest, safest, and most sustainable cannabis. Medicine hunter and ethnobotanist Chris Kilham gave me his primer, based on decades of tracking cannabis around the world and finding ways to incorporate it into exquisite food. And chefs from coast to coast—masters of flavor who share my passion for organic, nutritionally balanced food as medicine—taught me foolproof techniques for infusing butter and oil, how to pace myself (and friends) with cannabis food, and how to find personal dosage levels (*very slowly*).

They gave me the tools I needed to cook with cannabis—safely, responsibly, and elegantly. They helped me fill my kitchen with the nutty bite of herbs slow-roasting into winter squash and simmering into mushrooms, and the fresh, green smell (so *Boulder*) of leaves from heirloom plants (grown from seeds that my sweetheart, Dennis, has been saving for decades, nurtured among the tomatoes and zucchini in his mountainside garden) being ground up into pesto. Friends gather for insightful, memorable, hilarious evenings around plates of Pottanesca sauce made with peppery cannabis-infused olive oil and wild-caught salmon with cannabis cream. Mixologist Rabib Rafiq taught me to shake up a mean cannabis cocktail—the limit is one, only one—and caterer Jane West shared secrets for making everyone comfortable at cannabis-infused dinners and parties, learned from years of throwing such events in Denver.

Learning to cook with and share cannabis is a great gift—empowering, enlightening, elevating—and one that must be shared. The chefs encouraged me to compile their wisdom and recipes in this cookbook because they've seen cannabis work miracles on themselves and others, and they're doing everything they can to ensure that everyone who wants them has these tools. They sent me iPhone photos of recipes scribbled on napkins between lunch and dinner shifts, flew to Colorado for photo shoots (and feasts), and made themselves available to answer technical questions and look over recipes, even when they had a full house for Valentine's Day.

They made this cookbook happen. And as it crescendoed into existence, with a publishing deadline looming, chef and caterer Andie Leon (who had just stepped away from the chaos in the kitchen at her new restaurant to answer a recipe question) summed up for me why everyone did it. "God put this plant on the planet for a reason," Andie said. "I'll do everything I can so that everyone, everywhere, can use it in their own healing journeys."

This book is a roadmap for yours. Live long and prosper.

THE CHEFS

This cookbook is a compilation of twelve chefs' and one barkeep's wisdom, honed after decades of experimenting with cannabis. These chefs have seen cannabis and good food heal people time and time again. They understand the plant's power, and they're making it possible for everyone to incorporate that power into a healthy lifestyle.

Leslie Cerier

Harvest Time Oil de Mary Jane Leaf

Raspberry, Apple, and Pear Cannacrisp with Almonds, Cashews, and Walnuts

Teff Cannabis Waffles

Cannabis, Ginger, and Arame Eggrolls with Goji Berries

Eggplant, Lentil, and Cannabis Curry

Bok Choy, Cashews, and Scallions Stir Fried in Cannabis-Ginger Red Palm Oil

Cannabis Sweet Potato Fries with Hemp Seeds and Kelp Flakes

Leslie Cerier, a.k.a. The Organic Gourmet, teaches "seed-to-table" cooking, her way of celebrating the earth's bounty by adapting meals to what's freshly picked and plentiful, at some of the world's finest spas and wellness centers. Leslie's art is teaching people to make vegetarian, gluten-free food for health and pleasure. For Leslie, it's all about the *yum*! Through six cookbooks, including *Gluten-Free Recipes for the Conscious Cook* and *Going Wild in the Kitchen;* sold-out classes at Rancho La Puerta, Esalen Institute, and Kripalu Center for Yoga and Wellness, among others; and chef trainings across the globe, Leslie is teaching people to appreciate and maximize the garden's culinary gifts.

Leslie sees cannabis as one of those gifts. She first realized its potential when she ate a pot brownie at a party in western Massachusetts in the 1970s, well before she opened her farm-to-table catering and personal chef business in Amherst. Once she realized she could eat cannabis, Leslie started mulling over tastier, healthier ways to get it into food. Layering oil infused with cannabis into recipes packed with fresh, whole foods and big flavors, Leslie found that cannabis works with everything from stews to crisps. She considers cannabis an important addition to her repertoire of healthy ingredients, with a bonus.

"I'm always experimenting, capitalizing on what's local and in season, and I'm always willing to make something new," Leslie says. "That's how I cook with cannabis, and I want everyone to feel that freedom."

www.lesliecerier.com

Mike DeLao

Cannabis, Hemp, and Coconut Oil
Glycerin Tincture
Green Detox Juice
Cannabis, Cucumber, and Lime Juice
Sweet Chard and Cannabis Juice
The Green Standard
Sunshine and Citrus Cannabis Juice
Mellow Shrimp Cappellini Finished with Cannabis Oil

Jack Herer (the cannabis activist, not the cultivar named after him) changed the way Mike DeLao makes cannabis food. Mike was churning out sweets for patients at a cannabis collective he cofounded in Orange County, California, when he tried to give Jack cookies during a NORML conference in Berkeley in 2008. The emperor of hemp couldn't touch the cookies because he was diabetic. Mike, a founding member of the California Medical Marijuana Association, invited Jack and his wife for a cannabis-infused barbecue, Jack became a mentor, and Mike stopped cooking with sugar.

Mike was head chef at the Irvine, California, Embassy Suites, steeped in heavy French food, when he got a doctor's recommendation for medical marijuana and registered a grow. He left the stressful corporate job to help found OCC Collective, linking caregivers (people who grow and prepare cannabis and cannabis products) with patients. As he worked with patients, Mike became convinced that all the cannabis in the world couldn't overcome unhealthy eating habits and attitudes. He cut out processed food and started juicing raw Colombian Gold flowers from his backyard and apprenticing at raw food restaurants.

Today Mike grows enough cannabis to take care of his family and give to patients, but only if they're willing to detox and change the way they eat. "If people don't take care of their bodies," he says, "no matter how much cannabis they juice or eat, they won't feel good."

Mike has repeated that message several times during his spots on *Cannabis Planet*, a thirty-minute television program that airs in local markets and online. "Take as much care of yourself as you do your plants," Mike says. "You feed the plants organic nutrients; you flush them for two weeks. And then you take yourself to *McDonald's*?"

www.ChefMike420.com

Scott Durrah

Sativa Onion Soup with Ginger and Lemon
Fresh Cannabis Flower Guacamole
Mixed Greens, Mango, and Pineapple with
*   Cannabis-Curry Vinaigrette*
Smoked Apple-Glazed Roast Pork Loin with
*   Walnut and Cannabis Leaf Stuffing*
Spinach, Potato, and Cannabis Curry
Jamaican Chicken Stir-Fry with Curry Coconut Milk
Pumpkin Praline Mousse Cups with Cannabis Coconut Nectar
Super Lemon Haze Banana Rum Surprise

Scott Durrah is a master at growing, cooking with, and teaching people how to fortify their bodies and minds with cannabis by combining it with whole, healthy food. A veteran chef who has run award-winning restaurants in Los Angeles, Denver, and Jamaica, Scott learned good food from his Italian grandmother in Boston, where he grew up, and owes much to the Rastafarians he cooked with in Jamaica. Scott and his wife, Wanda James, were instrumental in getting cannabis legalized in Colorado and have helped build a thriving industry in the state.

Scott and Wanda ran Apothecary of Colorado, a ten-thousand-square-foot grow facility and dispensary in Denver, and Simply Pure, which offered organic, vegan, gluten-free cannabis food. (They were forced to close the edibles company in 2012 because they couldn't get banking services.) Today they own Jezebel's Southern Bistro and Bar in Denver and Simply

Pure Cooking School, offering cannabis culinary excursions to Jamaica, chef certification, and cooking classes in Denver. Scott, a former Marine, is on the Board of Directors for Safer Alternative for Enjoyable Recreation (SAFER), a group that educates people about the relative safety of cannabis compared with alcohol.

Through his classes, demonstrations, and national media appearances, including *The Daily Show,* CBS, and CNBC, Scott is teaching people how to maximize cannabis's flavor and health benefits in gourmet cuisine. "You have to understand food and cannabis and how they work together on your body," Scott says. "Because cannabis is a great healing plant, but if you eat like crap, you're not going to feel good."

www.facebook.com/simplypurechefs

Joey Galeano

Cannabis-Roasted Chicken with Onions, Carrots, and Fennel
Seared Wagyu New York Strip with Cannabis Rub
Sesame-Crusted, Cannabis-Seared Ahi Tuna with Wasabi, Soy, Cannabis and Citrus Sauce
Kushie Tomato Soup with Grilled Boursin and Gruyere Croutons
Cinnamon-Cannabis Roasted Sweet Potatoes
Black Chinese Heirloom Rice with Coconut Milk and Cannabis

Joey Galeano grew up cooking next to his Italian mother and grandmother in Brooklyn and started working in restaurants when he was fourteen. A former chef for restaurants and private clients as well as a bartender, Joey now has his dream job as executive chef for MagicalButter, a Seattle-based company that makes microprocessor-controlled botanical extraction machines and runs the world's first and only cannabis food truck, The SAMICH Truck.

"We offer over-the-top, gourmet food made from fresh local ingredients and artisan breads because we want to show people that cannabis food is not just brownies and cookies," Joey says.

After years of trying to get cannabis-infused oil and butter right, Joey started using the MagicalButter machine, which controls temperature and stirring to churn out perfect extractions every time. Now he can consistently deliver between 75 and 100 milligrams of THC to every plate, which he says is enough to make diners "feel great without feeling like they've just been hit with a tranquilizer dart that could knock out a black rhino."

Even with a magical machine, cooking with cannabis humbles Joey. "I've been cooking professionally for more than thirty years," he says, "and this is the hardest way to cook because potency and taste have to be balanced at all times."

Joey has appeared in national media, catered VIP parties at the Cannabis Cup, and cooked at Michael Jordan's Steak House in Chicago (one of his personal highlights). He lives in the Tampa Bay, Florida, area and tours the country with The SAMICH Truck (SAMICH is for Savory Accessible Marijuana Infused Culinary Happiness), a bright pink former school bus that MagicalButter parks at festivals and conventions as a way to educate people about the benefits of eating cannabis through gourmet cannabis food.

www.magicalbutter.com

Rowan Lehrman

Simple Cannabis Butter
Cannabis Cream
Wild Mushroom, Cannabis, and Hazelnut Pate with
    Apple, Bacon, and Sage
Hemp Seed–Crusted Chinook Salmon with Cannabis
    Cream
Kheer with Green Cardamom, Mango, and Pistachios
Matcha and Cannabis Crème Brûlée
Popcorn with Cannabis Butter and Spicy Hemp Furikake

Rowan Lehrman is an accidental chef. Her father was the executive chef at Maharishi International University in Fairfield, Iowa, and her mother cooked in the University kitchens, which served thousands of Ayurvedic meals a day to Transcendental Meditation students. When Rowan was eight, her family moved to the Oregon coast and built a cabin with no electricity in the tiny town of Neskowin. Rowan helped her family by gathering wood for the cooking fire and foraging for wild ingredients like mushrooms, mussels, and blackberries.

Rowan's childhood, a "twenty-year-long culinary school," taught her reverence for seasonal, local food. In 2000, she opened Panini Bakery, specializing in sourdough breads, rustic pastry and pizza by the slice, with her (now ex) husband in Newport, Oregon. One day she looked over the pizza, soup, and bread she'd just made for the daily lunch rush at Panini and realized, *Oh ****, I'm a chef!* Now a co-chef at Tables of Content, an oceanfront restaurant at the Sylvia Beach Hotel in Newport, Oregon, she can't imagine being anything else.

Rowan is also an accidental cannabis chef. After she divorced and sold Panini (still a hip local spot), Rowan went to a "trim camp," a month-long, seasonal work camp in Mendocino County, California, where workers trim cannabis leaves and manicure flowers. That particular operation was a "challenging, miserable, lawless place," Rowan says, and NYC Sour Diesel—literally bales of it—was her only source of culinary inspiration. She appointed herself unofficial camp cook and threw the citrusy sativa's leaves into salads and sautéing them in butter. Her campmates thought she was crazy until they tried—and loved—the experimental dishes.

Now a backyard beekeeper and culinary bookworm, she has fantasized about sitting on her porch and eating homemade sourdough bread with honey from her bees and cannabis butter from plants in her garden. In 2014, Oregon voters legalized cannabis, making her dream possible. "Growing up, I had neighbors and friends who went to jail over this plant," Rowan says. "I'm really glad about the new freedoms people have here in Oregon."

Andie Leon

Cannabis-Infused Coconut or Olive Oil

Shaman's Tincture

Cannabis Agave

Cannabis Milk

*Cannabis-Wheel Buns with Goji Berries and
    Chia Seeds*

Hemp Protein and Blueberry Muffins

Cannabis Hemp Seed Scones

Fresh Fan Leaf Pesto

*Salmon and Rice Cheese Risotto with Sesame
    and Chia Seeds*

*Flourless Superfood Cannabis Chocolate
    Cake*

*Cannabis, Chia, Almond, and Goji Berry "Pot
    Brownie" with Cranberry, Chocolate, and
    Red Wine Sauce*

Green Tea, Cannabis, and Coconut Brownies

Cannabis Coconut Mojito

Through love, good food, and cannabis, Andie Leon overcame an eating disorder that started when she was thirteen years old (around the time she got her first job, at McDonald's) and was destroying her physical and emotional health. Now a caterer delivering healthy, gourmet cannabis food to clients in Los Angeles's Laurel Canyon and the chef/owner of C2 Organics: The Super Foods Café, in the heart of Hollywood, Andie's mission is to share the gift of local, organic, non-GMO food and nutritious superfoods with as many people as possible.

Andie binged and purged for years until she discovered cannabis's ability to ease the anxiety and negative thoughts behind her actions about six years ago. Combined with a diet of antioxidant-rich whole foods and other healing herbs such as turmeric for pain and saffron for her mood, cannabis helped Andie heal.

"I can't eat highly processed edibles from dispensaries because they trigger my weight obsession and craziness," Andie says, "but I can eat as much of my flourless chocolate cake as I want because it's made with healing foods and cannabis. We must refuse to be poisoned blindly."

Andie, who studied holistic nutrition at the Institute of Integrative Nutrition and raw nutrition with superfoods expert David Wolfe, completed her pastry chef course at Escoffier culinary school. She teaches superfoods classes at Whole Foods Markets in Los Angeles. "Cooking is a great creative art," Andie says. "The more you let go, the greater your creative instincts become. I tell people in my classes to take my platform and dive into a world of amazingness. We're not followers. We're explorers."

www.c2organics.com

Catjia Redfern

Cannabis Ghee
Gin or Vodka Infusion
Bhang Ki Thandai
Fromage Fondue Infusee
Buttermilk Panna Canna
Pemmicannabis
Alice B. Toklas Carrot Cupcakes
Buzzy Bee's Knees

Denver, Colorado–based artist and chef Catherine (Catjia) Redfern learned long ago that cannabis could calm and stimulate her, providing both relief and inspiration. (She recently learned that cannabis's ability to make some people "smell" colors and "see" sounds and feelings is called *synaesthesia*.) Catjia creates high-quality finishes, Venetian plaster surfaces, and murals for upscale homes throughout Colorado and works as a private chef, preparing organic, gluten-free meals for a Denver bio-dentist and his staff and patients.

In 2009, Catjia cofounded Medamints, a cannabis-infused, xylitol-based pressed tablet mint with alkalizing organic herbs and spices that delivers ten milligrams of THC in controlled, consistent doses. Catjia's been active in anti-prohibition efforts and medical marijuana advocacy since Colorado took the lead in cannabis reform nearly a decade ago. "I'm a suffragette in the crusade to end prohibition and stigma," Catjia says. "I'm a foot solider ready to march in the victory parade when the War on Drugs is ended."

A Renaissance woman, Catjia studied art in Massachusetts and was a New England Patriots cheerleader for a season. She's the mother of an amazing teenaged son, a certified yoga teacher, and a gospel choir singer. She's learning to tango, "a delicious frustration."

Incorporating elements of the Paleo Diet and Ayurveda, the ancient Indian healing system, into her mostly gluten-free cooking, Catjia's goal is to introduce cannabis as an important part of a healthy, balanced diet. "I've been using cannabis all my life, and it's so freeing that it's now legal," she says. "I love being able to make healthy cannabis food for people who are sick and bring treats to parties and events."

www.redferndesign.biz

Herb Seidel

Beginner's Oil
Beginner's Butter
Baked French Toast with Cannabis, Honey, and Pecan Sauce
Baked Artichoke, Crab, and Cannabis Dip
Cannabis Ceviche
Olive and Cannabis Tapenades
Grilled Romaine Hearts with Olive Cannabis Dressing
Dijon and Cannabis Green Beans with Pecans
Broccoli, Bacon, and Almonds in Cannabis Mayonnaise Vinaigrette
Spring Vegetables Sauteed in Cannabis Butter
Smokin' Grilled Corn
Red Beans and Ricely Yours
Roasted Garlic, Cannabis, and White Bean Dip
White Chocolate, Walnut, and Cannabis Bars

Herb Seidel (a.k.a. Mota) combines what he learned as a restaurant chef and health care consultant in Chicago with his experience as a longtime cannabis smoker to create healing cannabis food that helps him cope with aches and pains from hours in the kitchen. One of the first chefs to step out and publicly teach people to make great-tasting cannabis food in the early 2000s, Herb is driven to share what he's learned with everyone. Now living in Los Angeles, Herb serves fine cannabis cuisine to private clients, caters special events, travels the cannabis convention circuit, and sells a tutorial video series, *Cook with Herb*.

For Herb, who trained at one of Chicago's signature culinary arts schools, the biggest challenge in making cannabis food is creating recipes as tasty as they are effective. It's all about how you infuse the oil and butter, Herb says, and he starts with that solid foundation. "When I started cooking with cannabis, I looked at all the cookbooks and information out there, and no one was being nice to the oil and butter," Herb says. That inspired him to create his gourmet butter and oil recipes for beginners, which are impossible to screw up and have less green flavor.

"When people eat good food, they get healthy," Herb says. "That was part of my decision to get into this. I'm not a pharmacist or a doctor, but I can help people understand how to cook and medicate with cannabis."

www.cookwithherb.com

Donna Shields

Southwestern Breakfast Buzz with Spicy Black Beans

Magic Herb Mushrooms Stuffed with Garlic-Herb Goat Cheese

Winter Squash Roasted in Cannabis Oil with Pomegranate Seed and Dried Cherry Stuffing

Trippy Trail Mix

A registered dietitian, nutritionist, recipe developer, and writer who's spent more than twenty-five years working with the world's largest food brands and media outlets, Donna Shields, MS, RDN, discovered cannabis's healing properties when it helped her through breast cancer treatment and recovery. She was frustrated, however, by the lack of information—and inventory—for people like her, who don't want to ingest cannabis through their lungs or in sweets. Realizing there is a need for health practitioners to be better informed about the therapeutic value of cannabis, Donna and a partner are developing an online holistic education portal geared for health professionals. Focusing on the synergy between integrative nutrition and cannabis, they will offer a certification in cannabis nutrition, with plans to bring an organic, healthy line of edibles to the marketplace.

Donna, a former faculty member at the Culinary Institute of America in New York and author of the *Caribbean Light* cookbook and *The Pregnancy Cookbook*, layers cannabis into food that delivers health benefits along with a high. Her simple recipes require only a few (usually plant-based) ingredients, but her way of mixing contrasting flavors and textures makes food jump off the plate. "Cannabis is like any other ingredient; you work with it or against it," she says. "If people can think of it like that, it doesn't feel weird and scary."

The bottom line, for Donna, is that cannabis integrated with a good diet is an optimum route to wellness. "Food is incredibly powerful," she says. "It's information for our cells. We can turn on and turn off the genes for disease by using food as medicine."

HolisticCannabisNetwork.com, www.donnashields.com

The Boulder Bakers

These women, who work at Sweet Mary Jane, a Boulder, Colorado-based edibles company, make incredible sweets—and their skills extend well beyond dessert.

Grace Gutierrez

Lemon, Poppy Seed, and Cannabis Pancakes
Crab and Mahi-Mahi Sliders with Cannabis, Turmeric, and Garlic Sauce

Lemon Candy Cannabis Cake
Lemon Lavender Champagne

Colorado native Grace Gutierrez has been baking for as long as she can remember and cooking since she left home to attend art school in Denver. In 2012, she jumped at the opportunity to learn a new trade as head baker at Sweet Mary Jane. Grace is all about beautiful presentation and making people say wow when they see her food. "I love making colorful, creative dishes, and I can never pass up trying something new in the kitchen," she says.

Lucienne Bercow Lazarus

Cannabis Honey
Grilled Potato Salad with Cannabis-Marinated Oranges and Olives
Crunchy Kumquat Salad with Sweet Cannabis-Garlic Dressing

Cannabis Avocado Mousse with Cashews and Lavender
Cannabis Sugar Cookie Stacks with Orange, Kumquat, and Ginger Confit
Go Phish! Deconstructed Brownies

Lucienne Bercow Lazarus is Sweet Mary Jane's office administrator in Boulder, Colorado. Lucie graduated from George Washington University in 2012 and has a background in food styling and recipe development. She feels very lucky to live in Colorado, where she is witnessing first-hand how budding entrepreneurs are bringing economic growth to the state and how the cannabis industry as a whole is shaping both the state and the country at a pivotal time in history.

Emily Sloat

Hash Hive Cookies

Third-generation baker and Colorado native Emily Sloat has been baking cannabis-infused cookies and brownies for friends for a long time and began baking for Sweet Mary Jane in 2014.

The Mixologist: Rabib Rafiq

Cannabis Gin Tincture

Green Cannabis Chartreuse

Cannabis Simple Syrup

Melamine

Central Park North

Mary Jane Daiquiri

Green Rush

High Monk Swizzle

Pine Forest Fizz

Dutch Pilot

Internal Combustion Collins

Twentieth of April

Rabib Rafiq approaches cocktails from the ground up, with no sacrifices. When he becomes entranced with a flavor profile or a spirit, his journey begins. Rabib uses various lab equipment and unorthodox tools at his bar, along with a very distinctive Japanese style to achieve results with which he is never satisfied. "If you think you've achieved perfection, you're halting your own growth, thus limiting yourself and those around you," he says.

In Rabib's world, the shape of an ice cube, the sugars and acids in fruit, and the age and fizziness of a carbonated liquid are all ingredients to be measured, tested, and tweaked. He's never satisfied with his end product, driving him to go on and on. When creating cocktails, Rabib's goal is to control variables as much as possible (consistent cannabis can be a challenge) so he can observe and test the results.

Born in Bangladesh, Rabib traveled through Europe and Asia before getting to the United States. He worked at some of the top cocktail bars in New York, as well as doing interior design for speakeasies and pre-Prohibition cocktail bars. He has recently moved to Amherst, Massachusetts, where he, along with his brother, owns and operates Bistro 63 at the Monkey Bar, a restaurant and a cocktail bar that he worked at while studying Physics at the University of Massachusetts.

www.bistro63.com

The Ethnobotanist: Chris Kilham

20-Minute Cannabis Olive Oil
Bonzo Butter
Highland Yogi Smoothie
Good Morning Sativa Chai
Ganja Java Go-Juice
High Ho Pottanesca
Holy Mole!
Majoon Love Balls

CNN calls ethnobotanist, author, and educator Chris Kilham "the Indiana Jones of natural medicine." As explorer in residence for Naturex, the world's largest botanical extraction company, Chris travels the globe seeking out traditional plant-based food and medicinal products to bring to market—and he's always on the lookout for the best indigenous foods, as well.

Chris is on the Medical Advisory Board for *The Dr. Oz Show* and writes frequently about cannabis in his weekly *Fox News* column. A regular adviser for *Fox News Health, Woman's World,* and various industry and trade publications, Chris has been featured in major media outlets including the *New York Times, Newsweek,* and *Natural Health* magazine, among others. The author of fourteen books, including *Hot Plants, The Five Tibetans,* and *The Ayahuasca Test Pilots Handbook,* Chris lectures throughout the world on holistic health and botanical medicines and teaches at the University of Massachusetts-Amherst. Chris and his wife, Zoe Helene, travel on Medicine Hunter expeditions to promote plant medicines, environmental protection, and cultural preservation.

Chris considers cannabis a sacred plant, along with coffee, chocolate, chiles, and kava. He's been tracking and researching cannabis in northern Asia, southern Siberia, the Himalayas, Nepal, China, and Jamaica and incorporating what he's learned about preparing and cooking with the plant in his own kitchen since the 1980s. Chris has drunk *bhang* with Indian *sadhus* and picked cannabis flowers along the Silk Road.

"I think we're about to see a real blossoming of cannabis cookery in this country," Chris says. "People are taking this culinary aspect of cannabis very seriously. These are the earliest days of the great wide world of cannabis cuisine."

www.medicinehunter.com

Permalos Consulting

THE PLANT

Cannabis grows from seeds in living soil, producing leaves and flowers from sun and rain. For thousands of years, she grew wild and free, on high plains and mountaintops, in gullies and fields. The earliest humans discovered and nurtured her, and she gave people fiber and medicine for centuries. Prohibition drove cannabis underground, but she found ways to survive without sunlight or healthy living soil. Sadly, the methods used to keep her alive compromised her very integrity.

In hidden warehouses, shipping containers, and suburban basements deep underground, prohibition-era cannabis growers have developed elaborate systems for cultivating large amounts of cannabis in small spaces. Synthetic cultivation systems that "force feed" plants concentrated forms of nitrogen-phosphorous-potassium (NPK) fertilizer are poor substitutes for the natural nutrients in a healthy growing environment. And though most growers "flush" the plants with plain water a few weeks before harvest, heavy metals, pesticides, plant growth regulators, and hormones from synthetic NPK systems can linger.

Indoor grow operations are now the foundation of the medical cannabis industry. Secure and climate-controlled, grow warehouses can churn out five to six harvests a year to meet dispensary and patient demands. Indoor-grown cannabis now accounts for more than a third of the cannabis grown in the United States, says *Mother Jones*.

Much of the cannabis that's grown outdoors is cultivated in California's Emerald Triangle, a rural region comprising Mendocino, Humboldt, and Trinity Counties, where families have been farming cannabis for generations. Though the legal market is mitigating the situation, some is still cultivated for the black market in massive illegal grows in northern California's public parks, polluting the soil and water. Patches can be found in rural fields, woods, and public lands throughout the country. Less than 4 percent of the cannabis in America is grown in people's backyards, according to the National Survey on Drug Use and Health.

That is changing. As the cannabis industry moves out of prohibition's shadow and consumers concerned about their health and well-being demand organic, nontoxic, more sustainable options, interest in sun-grown varietals is rising. Dispensaries in California are touting organic sun-grown cannabis as a better value that's safer for the environment. Grow It In the Sun, a group of residents in the Bay Area and Humboldt County, educates people about the benefits of sun-grown herbal medicine and environmental impacts of cannabis grown under artificial conditions. Encouraged by law reforms, medical cannabis patients and adults in states where cannabis is legal are bringing the plant back into their gardens and incorporating it into functional, ornamental landscapes (check local regulations about cannabis visibility and accessibility before considering this idea).

CANNABIS AND PERMACULTURE

Permaculture is a design science based on systems thinking that mimics natural patterns and ecosystems, rejects industrial farming practices such as monocultures and chemicals, and embraces biodiversity and self-sufficiency. Developed by Australians David Holmgren and Bill Mollison in the 1970s, permaculture has received more attention as a solution for sustainable and regenerative food production during the last decade.

Through his company, Permalos Consulting, Matt Davenport is bringing the ethics and principles of permaculture to organic no-till soil cultivation and the commercial cannabis industry, making it possible to grow without bottled NPK fertilizers, commercial bagged potting soil, synthetic pesticides, plant growth regulators and hormones, herbicides, insecticides, fungicides, GMOs, or other adulterations (yes, all of those typically go into cannabis production).

"Eliminating all of these harmful agents from the cultivation process ensures that the cannabis produced is the safest available and most regenerative product on the market," Matt says. "Based on a set of ethics and principles, permaculture is a lens through which we can model our gardens, our businesses, our lives, and everything in between. By viewing cannabis cultivation through this lens, we are able to turn a traditionally wasteful cultivation process into a regenerative one that benefits the environment, the producer, the community, and the end user alike."

Visit www.permalos.com for more information.

WHAT IS CANNABIS?

Cannabis (cane-like) *sativa* (sown or planted) is an annual with long, toothy leaves and flowers containing trichomes, hairs covered with sticky crystal resin glands. The flowers bloom on branches from a woody central stalk that grows from one foot high to twenty feet high. (These "trees," which can be found growing under hoop houses along Colorado's fertile Western Slope and in northern California, are worth seeing if you get the chance.)

Rising Moon Seeds

Parts of the Plant

Apical or Terminal Bud (Cola): Cluster of female flowers that can grow up to a foot or more in length.

Bud Site (Flower): Egg- or conical-shaped clusters of blooms that grow up to several inches long.

Trichome: Tiny hairs with sticky crystal resin glands on leaves, stems, calyxes, and flowers.

Calyx: Pear-shaped nodule underneath sugar leaves with high concentrations of trichomes.

Pistil: Tiny red-orange hair that collects pollen.

Fan Leaf: Large, pointy leaves, mostly devoid of trichomes, removed at harvest.

Sugar Leaf: Small resin-coated leaves trimmed from flowers during harvest.

Grown by Permalos Consulting

Grown by Permalos Consulting

Dynasty Seeds

Grown by Permalos Consulting

Dynasty Seeds

Grown by Permalos Consulting

Grown by Permalos Consulting

INDICA, SATIVA, RUDERALIS

Cannabis comes in three categories, each with its own distinct personality. Sativa and indica are most common.

Cannabis sativa is tall and lanky, with long, narrow, pointy leaves and fluffy, fruity flowers. When consumed, it delivers a bright, uplifting euphoria that many people appreciate for daytime use.

Cannabis indica is low and dense, with wide, rounded leaves and tighter structure. When consumed, it delivers a cozy, sedating, relaxed all-over body effect.

Cannabis ruderalis is less vigorous than indica and sativa, growing only about two feet tall, and is used mainly in crossbreeding for its ability to flower without changes in light cycles. Most people don't consume it because it doesn't contain much THC.

HEMP

Cannabis sativa L, or hemp, is a non-psychoactive cannabis subspecies used primarily for food and fiber. It provides valuable nutrients and other benefits to humans, but it won't get anyone high, no matter how much they consume. Industrial hemp is bred for fiber, food, and fuel rather than flowers, which is where THC resides, and hemp contains only about 0.25 percent of the psychoactive cannabinoid.

This earliest of textile fibers was sown in China 8,500 years ago and made its way through western Asia and Egypt to Europe. Farmers in the United States filled heavy demands for hemp to make sailcloth and cordage in the mid-nineteenth century, and it was an important domestic crop until the 1937 Marihuana Tax Act banned its production. (Ironically, in 1938 *Popular Mechanics* magazine touted hemp as "the new billion dollar crop" capable of being turned into more than 25,000 products.) Hemp fibers can be made into textiles, paper, concrete, insulation, and biodegradable plastic polymers. Hemp seeds are a high-protein food full of essential fatty acids, also used in beauty products.

Until recently, almost all hemp consumed in the United States has been cultivated in China, Romania, and Canada. As cannabis laws are reformed across the nation, many states are removing bans on hemp production. In 2014, Congress passed a federal farm bill agreement that put an end to the decades-long prohibition of hemp cultivation, and the first domestic hemp was harvested in Springfield, Illinois. Concentrated CBD hemp oil is now available in many states.

CANNABINOIDS

The cannabis plant contains active chemical compounds called cannabinoids, which are something of a miracle. In 1988, scientists discovered that the crystal-like hairs containing resin glands, or trichomes, on cannabis leaves and flowers contain active chemical compounds (nearly ninety have been isolated so far) that plug into cannabinoid receptors in the human brain. These plant-based versions of chemicals that our brains produce when under stress—a carbon copy of the cannabinoids in human breast milk—deliver powerful antioxidants and can shift neurological and physiological patterns.

Other plants such as cacao, black pepper, echinacea, and turmeric deliver cannabinoids, but none are as prolific and powerful as those in the cannabis plant. In 2003, the federal government was granted US Patent 6,630,507 for the use of cannabinoids as antioxidants and neuroprotectants. They're being studied as treatments for Alzheimer's disease, Parkinson's disease, PTSD, and stroke patients.

THC

The most famous—and nurtured—cannabinoid in cannabis is delta-9-terahydrocannabinol, or THC. THC triggers CB1 receptors, which are also mediated by anandamide, the first human cannabinoid discovered by Raphael Mechoulam in 1992. (*Ananda* means bliss in Sanskrit.) CB1 receptors determine how we see, smell, listen, and feel hunger, pleasure, and pain—which is why everything is beautiful, food tastes and smells amazing, and reality television can be enjoyable when people consume cannabis.

THC also activates CB2 receptors in the liver, heart, kidneys, blood vessels, endocrine glands, and lymph cells, making it a good overall tonic, but its psychoactive element has made it the darling of cannabis users. Breeders have met consumer demand with boutique *sinsemilla* boasting THC percentages in the high 20s and even into the 30s, though most cannabis today has less than 10 percent THC, according to the National Organization for the Reform of Marijuana Laws. The University of Mississippi's Marijuana Potency Project states that average THC content has increased from 3 to 4 percent in the 1990s to 13 percent today. Specifics aside, most cannabis has more THC today than it did a decade or two ago.

CBD

Cannabidiol (CBD) is an up-and-coming cannabinoid that's getting high-level attention because it delivers medical benefits without getting patients high. CBD doesn't bind to CB1 receptors, where psychoactive effects are triggered, and can actually mute THC's psychoactive effects by opposing its actions at CB1 receptors. The CBD cannabinoid stimulates receptors that mediate pain, inflammation, and body temperature and regulate oxygen, blood, and dopamine. CBD slows down serotonin receptor signals, giving it an antidepressant effect. It's being studied as a treatment for people with anxiety, sleep and eating disorders, pain, and nausea.

CBD was nearly bred out of most cannabis plants as growers sought more potently psychoactive cultivars over the past couple decades, and now researchers are scrambling to isolate the compound and study its medicinal effects. In 2013, a CNN documentary about Charlotte Figi—a young girl whose intractable seizures associated with Dravet syndrome were relieved after she ate oil made from a low-THC, high-CBD cultivar—spurred patients (and their parents) across the nation to seeking out CBDs. Breeders are meeting demand with cultivars containing up to 20 percent or more CBD content. Several states are considering or have passed legislation allowing patients to use CBD oil.

TERPENES

Cannabis gets its intense aroma and flavor (commonly referred to as "dank" or "loud") from more than 120 terpenes, pungent oils produced in the trichomes to seduce pollinators and shoo away predators and diseases. (All aromatic plants such as pine and citrus have terpenes, but cannabis has more than any other plant.) When cannabis flowers are dried and cured, oxidation converts terpenes into terpenoids, which interact with cannabinoids in the human body to modulate the effects of THC and regulate dopamine and serotonin.

As researchers discover that cannabis's full terpene profile is as important in determining its benefits and effects as THC content, both patients and growers are paying more attention to these volatile oils. Scientists are studying terpenes to treat pain, inflammation, depression, anxiety, addiction, epilepsy, cancer, and fungal and bacterial infections.

Cannabis Terpenes

Terpene	Aroma	Effects	Medical Benefits	Cultivars High in Terpene
Beta-Caryophyllene	Pepper, cloves	None discovered	Anti-inflammatory, gastro-protective, activates CB2 receptors	Super Silver Haze, Trainwreck
Borneol	Earthy, camphor	Pain relief	Analgesic, antiseptic, sleep aid	Haze strains
Eucalyptol	Spicy, mint	Calming, balancing	Antibacterial, anti-inflammatory, cough suppressant	Super Silver Haze
Limonene	Citrus	Relaxing, euphoric	Antifungal, antibacterial, mood enhancer	OG Kush, Super Lemon Haze
Linalool	Floral, sweet	Sedative, relieves anxiety	Anti-anxiety, anti-convulsant, antidepressant	Amnesia Haze
Myrcene	Musky, earthy	Sedating, relaxing	Antioxidant, anti-inflammatory	White Widow
Pinene	Pine	Clarity, counteracts some THC effects	Anti-inflammatory, expectorant	Super Silver Haze, Jack Herer, Trainwreck
Terpineol	Sweet, floral	Relaxing, sedative	Antibacterial, antiviral, immune system stimulant	Jack Herer

HOW IT GROWS

One of humankind's oldest agricultural crops, cannabis matures in about four or five months in most climates. It's as easy to grow (or as difficult, depending on your gardening skills) as tomatoes.

Like all plants (like all of us), cannabis responds best to a little nurture and good conditions: well-aerated, nutrient- and mineral-rich soil; clean water; and southern exposure with good sunlight. Cannabis adapts to less-than-ideal conditions, as growers forced into woods and alleys throughout prohibition can attest, but it likes the touch of a green thumb. Just like tomatoes and roses, cannabis can be pruned and trained for better yield, and it likes fortified, well-amended soil, a stake or cage to lean against, and a greenhouse for heat and privacy (still an issue, even where cannabis is legal).

The biggest difference between cannabis and most other plants in the garden is that it's dioecious, meaning each seed is male or female. Males produce less resin and can flower earlier so they can pollinate females and then, mission accomplished, slowly wither. They pummel the girls with pollen, given the chance, making the girls lackluster and seedy. For this reason, most gardeners yank the boys as soon as they show erect little flower balls (you can't make this up). The seedless, single girls produce more resin with higher concentrations of delta-9-tetrahydrocannabinol (THCP), the cannabinoid that gets people high, and become known as *sinsemilla*. (Cannabis plants grown from clones, or cuttings from mature plants, are all females, so this process isn't necessary.)

Staminate (Male) Flowers
Dynasty Seeds

PROCESSING CANNABIS

Cannabis growers have as many different techniques for processing the plant as the plant has cultivars. Every farmer swears by his or her own method, and they all cover common ground. Cannabis should be dried and cured so that it retains enough moisture to enjoy but is dry enough to prevent mold. Proper curing, which is dependent on the plant's genetics and environment, enhances and preserves the plant's aroma, flavor, and potency and removes chlorophyll. (Chlorophyll gives cannabis the strong "green" taste that turns many people off but also provides valuable nutrients when ingested.)

As a general rule, cannabis plants are ready to harvest when the trichomes (sticky resin glands on the flowers) turn cloudy white or light amber and the leaves start fading and take on autumn hues (a natural process called senescence). Plants can be harvested in stages, from the top down, so that less mature flowers on the lower part of the plant can have an extra week or so in the sun. Cannabis should be harvested in the morning because certain terpenes evaporate in heat as the day warms up.

Once the plants are harvested, the fan leaves are removed for juicing, cooking, composting, or mulching. (Once considered a waste product, these leaves are finally getting appreciation for their non-psychoactive health benefits.) The plants or individual branches are hung upside down on clotheslines or spread out on a screen to dry for four to ten days, depending on the climate and intended use.

For the smoothest flavor, cannabis should be dried as slowly as possible in a sixty- to seventy-degree room (moisture and warmth encourage mold) with good airflow that's not blowing directly on the plants. Fans, heaters, and dehumidifiers are sometimes necessary to maintain temperature and humidity. For small harvests, buckets of water or wet towels in the drying room can be enough to keep up the humidity.

When the stems are almost hard enough to snap off but the flowers are not yet crumbly, the plants are ready to trim and cure. Trimming is the process of snipping off the small sugar leaves surrounding the flowers, which can be saved and used for cooking and tinctures. Trimming carves out the flowers' nectar, where most of the sticky trichomes, rich with cannabinoids, reside.

Curing slowly allows the sugar in cannabis flowers to break down and draws moisture to the plant's surface, preventing mold growth. The most common curing method calls for placing the flowers—once they've stabilized at 58 to 63 percent relative humidity (depending on the plant's genetics and environment)—in an airtight jar and placing it in a cool, dark place for one to six months. Once a day for the first week, the jar is opened to check moisture levels and rotate the flowers. It's cracked open once a week or so after that until the moisture level is around 56 to 60 percent, optimal for long-term storage (relative, again, to genetics and environment). A Caliber III hygrometer, a handheld instrument that measures moisture content, can be placed inside the jar (see Resource Guide).

STORAGE

Good, old-fashioned Ball or Mason jars with airtight lids, proven since Grandma's been making pickles, are most people's vessel of choice for cannabis storage. Give jars a good wash and store cannabis away from heat, light, moisture, and airflow. Cannabis should keep for a year or more in a jar with a good seal.

Cannabis can also be stored in an airtight wooden box, and several companies market curing and storing boxes similar to humidors for cigars. The Cannador (see Resource Guide), a designer box that maintains ideal humidity for cannabis storage, sells for a couple hundred dollars.

SCISSOR HASH

There's no way around it. Trimming cannabis plants results in a coating of sticky, gummy trichomes on your scissors as well as your fingers or gloves. That's valuable stuff. You can make "scissor hash" by carefully rubbing the resin off your tools and your person and pressing it into balls or wafers for a concentrated little package of cannabinoids that's great for cooking.

Pura Vida/Grown by Permalos Consulting

Buyer's Guide

In the 1970s, the joke goes, there were two types of cannabis: good and bad. Cannabis was kind of like the scrawny organic produce at the bottom of the bins in hippie co-ops—not always all that palatable, but people took what they could get. Unless they grew their own cannabis, most people were happy when their dealer didn't short them and the cannabis was "good." A healthy dose of seeds and stems was included with every bag.

Today, patients with doctor's recommendations and adults in states where cannabis is legal can choose cannabis cultivars like they choose varietals of wine, bourbon, coffee, cheese, and chocolate. They can examine and buy (at no small price) artisanal *sinsemilla* to enhance their mood, help them sleep, and add the right spice to stew, choosing from dozens if not hundreds of cultivars with names like Afghan Kush, Blue Dream, Cheese, Girl Scout Cookies, and Pineapple Kush in every flavor from mint, chocolate, and musk to fruit, spice, and berries. They can select sativas for daytime use, indicas for sleep, and any number of sweet cultivars for making cake—and that's before they turn to the shelves full of bubble hash, wax, shatter, oils, edibles, drinks, capsules, tinctures, teas, lotions, and sexual lubricants (no lie). For help with all those choices, they can turn to a "budtender" or "cannabarista," something between an old-time neighborhood pharmacist and a really good waiter.

Hello, twenty-first century. For today's retail cannabis consumer, dispensaries and stores are like Whole Foods and farmers' markets in one, with inventory that no one would have dreamed possible twenty years ago and fresh product from local growers (guaranteed—cannabis can't cross state lines).

DISPENSARIES AND RETAIL STORES

Walking into a dispensary or retail store for the first time is celebratory for some, overwhelming for others. For longtime cannabis users, seeing jars full of manicured flowers, *for legal*

Dynasty Seeds

sale in a retail establishment, is surreal. For medical cannabis patients and others exploring cannabis for the first time (or the first time in a long time), seeing all those jars is confusing.

Whether you're visiting a retail store in a state where cannabis is legal or have access to a dispensary, the first time can be scary. How do you know where to buy, what to buy, and whether you're buying good quality organic cannabis? What should cannabis smell like when the budtender opens the jar and puts it under your nose? What should it look like if she hands you a magnifying glass to examine it?

Where to Buy

Like coffee shops and liquor stores, cannabis stores range from boutique to mega, with atmospheres from sketchy to spa-like. (Some dispensaries call themselves wellness centers and offer cannabis in addition to massage, acupuncture, and other natural therapies.) Customer service representatives (budtenders' proper industry name, though no one calls them that) vary in knowledge and presence as well. How each establishment grows, procures, processes, and handles cannabis makes a big difference in the quality of its products, especially when you're buying organic cannabis.

Do a little homework (at least check out the website) before you visit a cannabis dispensary. Find out how long they've been in business. Do they claim to sell organic cannabis? Are they marketing to people like you? Do you want to buy your food and medicine from an establishment that features a buxom "nurse" with a big green cannabis leaf on her chest in its advertisements? The beauty of a legal cannabis market is that no one has to buy cannabis from people they wouldn't normally associate with anymore, and you'll know right away whether you're in the right place.

The first thing you should notice when you enter a dispensary is the overwhelming smell of fresh cannabis. If you don't get hit with that fragrance as soon as you walk in the door, that's a flag. The clean fragrance of quality organic cannabis can't be contained, even in sealed glass jars.

Most dispensaries and retail stores offer cannabis in three quality levels. Sometimes they label or color code it that way, but pricing usually reflects where a cultivar stands. In general, price reflects quality—much like wine.

Don't buy anything if you feel like you're being hustled. A good budtender has tried much of the inventory and can offer sound advice on how different cultivars might deliver what you're looking for. A sketchy one will keep trying to sell you cannabis from the full jar on the top shelf, and he'll throw in a free joint.

Every state has different regulations about how (and whether) cannabis can be sold. Leafly.com and Weedmaps.com are excellent sources for finding out what's available near you.

How to Buy

Choosing quality cannabis isn't all that different from choosing quality tomatoes. With organic cannabis, it's all about fragrance and appearance—in that order. The same good sense that tells you not to buy a tomato that's mushy or smells musty will tell you when something's off about cannabis flowers. If cannabis smells like a piece of moldy bread, it might contain pathogens such as mold or fungus. If it smells like nothing, you won't get

ASK THE BUDTENDER

Many places market their cannabis as organic, but there's currently no widely accepted and agreed-upon set of standards when it comes to cannabis cultivation as there is for organic foods. Cannabis that's sprayed while in clone or during vegetation with harsh fungicides such as Eagle 20, a lawn chemical containing carcinogenic compounds, can still test clean for chemicals. If that doesn't sound tasty, ask your budtender the following questions:

- How was this cannabis grown?
- What makes you consider your cannabis organic?
- Were synthetic fungicides, insecticides, or pesticides used?
- Was it sprayed with organic and/or synthetic materials while in flower?
- Has it been tested, and what is the lab's accreditation?
- Was Integrated Pest Management employed?
- How was this cannabis dried and cured?

A good budtender will be able to answer all those questions. And once you've determined that you're dealing with someone you trust, always ask the following:

- What type of cannabis do you consume? Why?
- Do you consume organic cannabis exclusively?
- What would you buy and why?

the taste, aroma, and experience you're after. If it's dry and brittle, it's old or wasn't handled properly. Seeds? What is this, 1970?

Quality organic cannabis is a healthy green, with hints of purple, orange, red, and red-orange hairs. Look for flowers sparkling with trichomes, the frosting of crystal resin glands where cannabis's valuable cannabinoids reside. Trichome coverage can be a good indication of quality but not always the best indicator of quality genetics. The best way to find out is

South Fork Seeds

to follow your nose. The clean, sharp smell of aromatic terpenes should hit you as soon as the jar is cracked open. From there, aroma is a highly personal preference. Your nose will tell you when you've hit the aromatic profile you're after. Trust it.

Quality cannabis is dry, but not brittle, with dense flower formations. If you're able to touch it, it should feel sticky and crumble when you break it up. Flowers should snap off the stem easily without twisting or using scissors. Note that blue or purple color doesn't necessarily mean what it once did. As breeders figured out that purple always sells, more and more cultivars have taken on the hue. Some of these cultivars are purple because of their genetics, the natural aging process called senescence, or because of manipulations to environment, stress, and nutrient fluctuations.

In the end, the only way to know whether cannabis delivers the taste and effects you're after is to take it home and try it. Buy your top choices in smaller amounts the first couple times you visit a retail store and see how they work for you. Just don't get too attached to your favorites. Inventory isn't always consistent, even in the largest dispensaries and retail stores. A cultivar called Blue Dream at one dispensary could have a completely different genetic makeup from the Blue Dream at another.

DISPENSARY ETIQUETTE

Bring cash. At this point, most cannabis vendors can't get federal banking services or take credit cards because cannabis is still federally illegal. We anticipate that will change in time. Also know that you'll pay hefty taxes, so factor that in when you budget.

Get over it. Your first visit to a retail cannabis environment can be exhilarating. It's great to show your excitement and ask lots of questions (the budtenders are just as excited as you are about this history-making new marketplace), but don't go on and on. The budtender's heard it all, several times, and over-exuberance prevents you from objectively choosing quality cannabis. Try to be chill.

Don't breathe on the weed. When the budtender offers a jar to sniff, close your mouth and don't breathe into the jar. Someone's going to consume that cannabis.

Don't squeeze the weed. If a budtender pulls out a flower for you to examine and hands you the microscope, she intends for you to visually examine it and smell it. Touching it and squeezing the flower, as tempting as that may be, damages its resin glands.

Build a relationship with the budtender. A good budtender can make all the difference when you're learning about and choosing cultivars. Don't be afraid to talk with the budtender about your particular needs.

Leave your cell phone in your bag or car. Dispensaries are no place for Instagram moments. The same privacy rights that extend to patients at pharmacies and medical offices should apply.

Know that you'll be on camera. In most places, it's the law. Be aware if you're camera shy.

New products for home testing are emerging onto the market. Relatively inexpensive testing kits that allow you to analyze your cannabis for THC and CBD content are available from CBscientific. The MyDx Analyzer is a digital sensor that combines information about medically relevant cannabinoids and terpenes in a cannabis sample with user feedback to track how each cultivar works for each individual.

Regulation and testing protocols are being put into place, and the industry is evolving quickly. But without standardization and consistent testing, buying cannabis still has some of the crapshoot elements it had in the seventies. The good news? "Good" has reached a much higher level.

Buyer Beware

Problems and challenges associated with cannabis cultivation, particularly indoors, aren't always solved with consumers' best interests in mind. Plants with mold, pest, and fungal infestations can and do make their way from grow operations to retail stores. At worst, the plants could have traces of alfatoxins (a by-product of fungal growth and among the most carcinogenic substances known); heavy metals (arsenic, cadmium, lead, and mercury); and insecticides, pesticides, fungicides, and herbicides that haven't been deemed safe for human consumption (lawn chemicals).

In independent tests, KCBS Radio in San Francisco found that about half of the cannabis samples they procured were mislabeled for potency and had traces of mold and pesticides. Jeffrey Raber of The Werc Shop, an independent cannabis testing lab in Los Angeles, found pesticides on 10 percent of the samples his lab tested. "Right now, the general public is becoming aware of these issues within the cannabis industry and their potential health risks." Matt Davenport says.

If this doesn't sound tasty to you, ask to see cannabis under a microscope. Don't buy it if you see any of these signs that something went wrong during cultivation:

- Browning, yellowing leaves
- White spots on leaves (indicative of powdery mildew)
- Cobwebs (indicative of spider mites)
- Seed coats (pod-shaped tiny cups that once held a seed, indicative of hermaphroditism)
- "Nanners" (tiny banana-shaped pods in the flowers, indicative of poor genetics or stress)

CONCENTRATES

People have extracted and concentrated every possible drop from cannabis trichomes for centuries. As soon as early humans figured out that the cannabis plant's magic was in the frost on its inner leaves and flowers, they rubbed the flowers with their fingers (and eventually, a sieve) to separate the crystals and press them into wafers or blocks. This was the first *hashish,* and the sticky wafers traveled from Asia to every continent, inspiring poets, writers, and intelligentsia and infuriating powers-that-be.

Today, "concentrates" are an intimidating sector of the cannabis marketplace, including everything from simple oil extractions to things with exotic (and slightly scary) names like dabs, wax, and shatter. To make concentrates, producers extract the cannabinoid-rich resin glands from the plant matter, often using solvents. (As health advocates and consumers have expressed alarm about traces of those solvents, extractions made using ice water and dry-sifting screens rather than butane or propane are becoming more popular.) These highly concentrated extracts can have as much as 80 percent (or more) THC, and concentrates high in CBD are rapidly hitting the market. Some are more appropriate for smoking or vaporizing, and some are finding their way into the kitchen. Most of them are not cheap.

Hash: Compressed resin from mature female cannabis flowers, known as *hashish* or hash, has been around for centuries. Ethnobotanist Chris Kilham calls it "the cognac of ganja products." Quality hash is malleable and uniform in color. It imparts less herbal flavor when used in cooking because the plant material has been removed. For maximum effectiveness, always heat hash before consuming it. However, heating hash above 350 degrees Fahrenheit will degrade the THC.

Bubble/Ice Water Hash: One of the cleanest and safest extractions, bubble hash is made without solvents. To make it, cannabis plant material is gently blended with ice and water to separate resin glands, which are collected, dried, and cured.

Dry Sift (Kief): The simplest and most sustainable of all concentrates, kief is concentrated trichomes separated from the plant. Plant matter is sieved through a set of screens to obtain desired consistency. Kief can be pressed into rigid wafers, and the dry, crumbly powder can be ground and stirred into recipes.

Butane Hash Oil: Among the most potent concentrates available, BHO is used for vaporizing and cooking. A butane extraction pulls cannabinoids out of the plant, creating a crumbly dough-like mixture ("budder"), a honeycomb-like substance ("wax"), or a glassy, taffy-like substance ("shatter"). Acetone, alcohol, propane, CO_2, and hexane can also be used. BHO can contain trace contaminants of solvents if it's not made properly. Bubble hash is a better choice.

Tincture: Liquid concentrates extracted through alcohol were the primary means of cannabis delivery until the plant was outlawed in 1937. They capture all the cannabinoids and can also be made with vegetable glycerin. They're often sold as solutions to dissolve under the tongue and are even available as mouth sprays.

CERTIFICATIONS AND CONSUMER ADVOCACY

As states scramble to put regulations and testing protocols in place for the emerging cannabis industry, independent certification and consumer-advocacy programs are stepping in to fill the void.

The **Organic Cannabis Association** has developed rigorous organic standards and sustainable practices for the cannabis industry "to obviate practices from its criminal past." Cannabis consumers, the group states, "want and deserve to know what goes into their product just as they might want to know what is in their beer, wine, or spirits."

Products with a **Clean Green Certified** logo have been reviewed according to Organic Program Standards and other international standards for sustainability. The certification currently covers growing products such as nutrients and soils.

THE CHEFS' FAVORITE COOKING CULTIVARS

These bright culinary cultivars are our chefs' staples. Lack of standardization, however, means popular cultivars that have been constantly crossbred can vary drastically from state to state, grower to grower, and dispensary to dispensary. OG Kush from one grower might be completely different than OG Kush from another grower. The following are general guidelines.

AFGHAN KUSH (AK)

Indica
Lineage: Hindu Kush x Afghani
THC Content: High
Effects: Sedating, euphoric, body high, relaxing
Used to Treat: Insomnia, pain
Taste/Aroma: Sweet, piney, earthy
Appearance: Dense flowers, full of crystals
Grows: Indoors or outdoors

BLUE DREAM

Sativa-Dominant Hybrid
Lineage: Blueberry x Haze
THC Content: High
Effects: Glowy, cerebral with body high
Used to Treat: Pain, depression, nausea, anxiety
Taste/Aroma: Sweet, tangy, blueberries and cream
Appearance: Dense flowers, full of crystals, light hairs
Grows: Indoors or outdoors

BLUEBERRY

Indica-Dominant Hybrid
Lineage: Afghani x Thai x Purple Thai
THC Content: High
Effects: Euphoric, relaxing
Used to Treat: Pain, stress

Taste/Aroma: Sweet blueberries

Appearance: Conical lavender blue flowers

Grows: Indoors or outdoors

BRUCE BANNER

Sativa-Dominant Hybrid

Lineage: Strawberry Diesel x OG Kush

THC Content: High

Effects: Euphoric, cerebral, creative

Used to Treat: Anxiety, pain, ADD/ADHD, bipolar disorders

Taste/Aroma: Citrus, ginger and spice, earthy

Appearance: Dense, bright green buds, lots of crystals, purple leaves

Grows: Indoors

CHEESE

Indica-Dominant Hybrid

Lineage: Afghani x Mexican Acapulco Gold x Colombian Gold

THC Content: High

Effects: Heavy euphoria, body high

Used to Treat: Pain, anxiety, stress, insomnia

Taste/Aroma: Buttery cheddar with sweet and sour undertones

Appearance: Dense flowers, lots of crystals

Grows: Indoors or outdoors

COLOMBIAN GOLD

Sativa-Dominant Hybrid

Lineage: Colombian

THC Content: Medium

Effects: Uplifting, focused, cerebral, expansive

Used to Treat: Muscle tension, pain, depression, ADD/ADHD

Taste/Aroma: Sweet, floral, citrus, slightly diesel

Appearance: Fluffy gold-green flowers, lots of crystals

Grows: Indoors or outdoors

GIRL SCOUT COOKIES

Indica-Dominant Hybrid
Lineage: (OG Kush x Durban Poison x Cherry Kush) x OG Kush
THC Content: High
Effects: Euphoria, body high, hazy
Used to Treat: Pain, anxiety, insomnia, PTSD, anorexia, Parkinson's disease, MS
Taste/Aroma: Sweet chocolate mint
Appearance: Light green flowers with purple sugar leaves
Grows: Indoors or outdoors

GOLDEN GOAT

Sativa-Dominant Hybrid
Lineage: (Hawaiian x Romulan) x Island Sweet Skunk
THC Content: High
Effects: Cerebral, euphoric, creative
Used to Treat: Stress, anxiety, depression, pain
Taste/Aroma: Sweet, syrupy, tropical fruit punch
Appearance: Dense flowers with thin hairs and lots of crystals
Grows: Indoors

HARLEQUIN

Sativa-Dominant Hybrid, CBD-Dominant
Lineage: Colombian Gold x Thailand x Switzerland x Nepal
THC Content: Low
Effects: Very little psychoactive effect, relaxing
Used to Treat: Chronic pain, arthritis, anxiety
Taste/Aroma: Mango, pine, musk
Appearance: Dense flowers covered with orange-red hairs
Grows: Indoors

HEADBAND

Indica-Dominant Hybrid
Lineage: OG Kush x Sour Diesel
THC Content: High

Effects: Spacey euphoria, creative energy

Used to Treat: Nausea, eating disorders

Taste/Aroma: Piney, lemony, musky, some diesel taste

Appearance: Large light green flowers, dark leaves with lots of crystals

Grows: Indoors or outdoors

JACK HERER

Sativa-Dominant Hybrid

Lineage: Northern Lights x Shiva Skunk

THC Content: High

Effects: Blissful, creative, focus

Used to Treat: Stress, anxiety, pain, depression

Taste/Aroma: Sharp, spicy, pine

Appearance: Dense, large lime green flowers, long leaves, red hairs, lots of crystals

Grows: Indoors or outdoors

LAMB'S BREAD

Sativa

Lineage: Jamaican

THC Content: High

Effects: Uplifting, creative energy, focus, social

Used to Treat: Stress, anxiety ADD/ADHD, depression

Taste/Aroma: Woody, earthy, spicy

Appearance: Dense flowers, long hairs

Grows: Indoors or outdoors

LEMON KUSH

Indica-Dominant Hybrid

Lineage: Lemon G x Afghanistan Hindu Kush

THC Content: High

Effects: Uplifting, euphoric, creative

Used to Treat: Stress, anxiety, pain, anorexia

Taste/Aroma: Sweet-sour, lemon, herbal

Appearance: Light green flowers with lots of crystals

Grows: Indoors or outdoors

OG KUSH

Sativa-Dominant Hybrid

Lineage: Chemdawg varietal

THC Content: High

Effects: Euphoric, body high, trance-like

Used to Treat: Depression, stress, anxiety, PTSD, nausea, pain

Taste/Aroma: Woody vanilla, pine, some diesel

Appearance: Dense, resiny, lime green flowers

Grows: Indoors

PINEAPPLE EXPRESS

Sativa-Dominant Hybrid

Lineage: Trainwreck x Hawaiian

THC Content: Medium

Effects: Euphoric, happy, cerebral

Used to Treat: Stress, anxiety, depression, pain

Taste/Aroma: Pineapple, pine, mango

Appearance: Fluffy mustard yellow flowers

Grows: Indoors or outdoors

PINEAPPLE KUSH

Indica

Lineage: Pineapple x Master Kush

THC Content: Medium to High

Effects: Mellow, euphoric, relaxing

Used to Treat: Pain, anxiety, stress, nausea, ADD/ADHD

Taste: Pineapple, tropical with mint, vanilla undertones

Appearance: Light green flowers, lots of crystals

Grows: Indoors or outdoors

PURA VIDA

Sativa-Dominant Hybrid

Lineage: Hollywood Pure Kush x Appalachia

THC Content: Medium to High

Effects: Uplifting, cerebral, thought-provoking, stress-relieving
Used to Treat: Anxiety, depression, lethargy, loss of appetite
Taste/Aroma: Musky, woody, menthol "pine crème," floral, hints of floral and earth
Appearance: Dense, impressive trichome structure, frosty
Grows: Indoors or outdoors

SUPER LEMON HAZE

Sativa-Dominant Hybrid
Lineage: Super Silver Haze x Lemon Skunk
THC Content: High
Effects: Energetic, uplifting, creative
Used to Treat: Fatigue, anxiety, stress, depression, ADD/ADHD
Taste/Aroma: Lemony, sweet, tart
Appearance: Wispy flowers with dark hairs
Grows: Indoors or outdoors

SUPER SILVER HAZE

Sativa-Dominant Hybrid
Lineage: Haze x Northern Lights x Skunk
THC Content: Medium to High
Effects: Creative, physically soothing, body high, social
Used to Treat: Fatigue, mood disorders, nausea, migraines
Taste/Aroma: Sweet-tart, citrus, menthol
Appearance: Long, sticky flowers, lots of crystals
Grows: Indoors or outdoors

STRAWBERRY DIESEL

Sativa-Dominant Hybrid
Lineage: Strawberry Cough x NYC Diesel
THC Content: High
Effects: Relaxing, body high, clear
Used to Treat: Stress, anxiety, pain, depression, nausea
Taste/Aroma: Strawberry, pungent
Appearance: Light green flowers with orange hairs
Grows: Indoors

WHITE WIDOW

Indica-Dominant Hybrid

Lineage: Brazilian x South Indian

THC Content: High

Effects: Psychedelic, powerful

Used to Treat: Anxiety, PMS, pain, stress, depression

Taste/Aroma: Spicy, citrus, creamy vanilla

Appearance: Large, bright green flowers

Grows: Indoors

SOURCES:

http://en.seedfinder.eu/
www.wikileaf.com
www.leafly.com

Bruce Banner

CULTIVARS TO KNOW

Cultivated by master breeders and growers, these boutique-style cultivars are part of a unique new wave in the cannabis industry. They're also excellent in culinary gardens.

ALION

Pacific Northwest Roots

Sativa-Dominant Hybrid

Lineage: Blue Dream (Snoops) x AlienKush (F2)

THC Content: Extremely high

Effects: Euphoric, mood lifting, stimulates creativity, appetite and energy

Used to Treat: PTSD, depression, anxiety, hunger

Taste/Aroma: Blueberries, kush and haze undertones

Appearance: Large, crystal-laden buds with purple hues and frost

Grows: Indoors, outdoors

AMBULANCE

303 Seeds/Grown by Kabdank

Indica/Sativa Hybrid

Lineage: Bio-Diesel #2 x Z7

THC Content: Medium-High

Effects: Blended THC/CBD content with a range of relaxing mental and body effects

Used to Treat: Epilepsy, Alzheimer's, bipolar disorder, PTSD, chronic pain, nerve damage, ocular function, appetite issues

Taste/Aroma: Sweet berries, citrus overtones

Appearance: Beautiful silver buds with color-tinted trichomes

Grows: Indoors, outdoors (60–70 days)

BIODIESEL

Indica/Sativa Hybrid

Lineage: (SensiStar x Sour Diesel) x High Country Diesel

THC Content: Very High

Effects: Smashes pain and tension, relaxation, uplifting, appetite-inducing

303 Seeds/Grown by Kabdank

Used to Treat: Sleep disorders, PTSD, chronic pain, nerve damage, ocular function, appetite issues

Taste/Aroma: Pungent, sharp sour citrus/limonene

Appearance: Frosted red-haired monsters that turn purple and black in cooler temperatures

Grows: Indoors, outdoors

BLACK AFGOJI

Rising Moon Seeds

Indica-Dominant Hybrid

Lineage: Black Afghani x Goji OG

THC Content: Generously high

Effect: Calming, meditative, euphoric

Used to Treat: Anxiety, nausea, relaxation, pain, appetite

Taste/Aroma: Smoky wine, mint, dark earth, soft lavender, grapes, pastry

Appearance: Dense lime green/white flowers with hints of purple and blue

Grows: Indoors, outdoors

BLACK LIME RESERVE

Aficionado Seeds/Grown by Graham McNamee

Indica-Dominant Hybrid

Lineage: Black Lime x Chemdawg Special Reserve

THC Content: High

Effects: Strong, complex effects on both body and mind

Used to Treat: Depression, appetite loss, sleep disorders

Taste/Aroma: Kaffir lime, citrus, galangal ginger, lemongrass, mojitos

Appearance: Narrow flowers, large bracts and large trichomes, light green, tan to orange pistils

Grows: Indoors, outdoors

BLUE LIME PIE

Indica/Sativa Hybrid

Lineage: Key Lime Pie Clone x Blue Power

THC Content: High

Effects: Uplifting, thought-provoking experience without the crash

Used to Treat: Depression, anxiety, PTSD

Taste/Aroma: Lime, berry, smooth kush

Appearance: Dense, bulbous spears, oozing resin and trichomes

Grows: Indoors, outdoors, greenhouse

Sin City Seeds

BLUNIVERSE

Indica-Sativa Hybrid

Lineage: Blue Magoo x Ms. Universe # 10

THC Content: Extremely high

Effects: Strong heady high followed by sedating relaxation

Used to Treat: Anxiety, sleep disorders

Taste/Aroma: Berries, fruity and floral haze undertones, caramel, sandalwood, vanilla

Appearance: Copious resin, colorful blue/purple hues

Grows: Indoors, outdoors, greenhouse

Dynasty Seeds

HELLHOUND

Indica-Dominant Hybrid

Lineage: Stardawg x Pestilence (Abusive OG x West Coast Dog/OGers)

THC Content: High

Effects: Nice strong high, relaxing, sedating, euphoric, body high

Used to Treat: Insomnia, pain/nerve pain and MS

Taste/Aroma: Sour fermented fruit, funky grapes, pungent earth

Appearance: Dense colorful flowers, extremely frosty and fragrant

Grows: Indoors, outdoors, greenhouse

Illuminati Seeds

KOFFEE

Indica-Dominant Hybrid

Lineage: AlienOG x AlienKush (F2)

THC Content: Extremely high

Effects: Sedating, sleep-inducing, hunger-inducing, body high, relaxing

Used to Treat: Pain, insomnia, PTSD

Taste/Aroma: Coffee, scotch, caramel, mint, sweet spice, earth

Appearance: Large dense flowers with a silver hue, purple fan leaves

Grows: Indoors, outdoors, greenhouse

Pacific Northwest Roots

LAVENDER

Indica-Dominant Hybrid

Lineage: Super Skunk x Big Skunk Korean x Afghani Hawaiian

THC Content: Medium-high

Effects: Relaxing, body high, euphoric, sedating

Used to Treat: Chronic pain, insomnia

Taste/Aroma: Sweet, mixed berry, floral

Appearance: Dense lavender-colored flowers covered with trichomes

Grows: Indoors, outdoors, greenhouse

Josh Williams Photography for Green Life Productions with Permalos Consulting

LONG VALLEY ROYAL KUSH

Indica/Sativa Hybrid

Lineage: Sour Diesel x Garberville Purple Kush x Highland Afghani

THC Content: High

Effects: Sedative body high offset by an intense cerebral sensation

Used to Treat: Pain, depression, anxiety

Taste/Aroma: Sour candy, lemon balm with deep layers of chardonnay, cardamom and crushed lavender

Appearance: Tight and robust bud set with large calyxes draped in white sheets of snow

Grows: Indoors, outdoors

Aficionado Seeds

MENDO BREATH

Indica/Sativa Hybrid

Lineage: OGKB x Mendo Montage

THC Content: Extremely high

Effects: Trance-inducing, vision-inducing

Used to Treat: Calcified pineal gland, imbalance, inflammation

Taste/Aroma: Blueberry pic

Appearance: Crystal spears of silver, blue and purple

Grows: Indoors, outdoors

Gage Green Group/Grown by Norcalicmag

MR. MAJESTIC

Indica/Sativa Hybrid

Lineage: Purple Trainwreck x Chemdawg OG

THC Content: High

Effects: Creative buzz with both head and body expansion

Used to Treat: Hard-headedness, anxiety, stress

Taste/Aroma: Lavendar, kush, fuel-drizzled flowers

Appearance: Rock-hard crystal balls

Grows: Indoors, outdoors

Gage Green Group/Grown by GStash

9LB HAMMER (TGA)

Indica-Dominant Hybrid

Lineage: Gooberry x Hells OG x Jack the Ripper

THC Content: High

Effects: Full body high, relaxing, sedating

Used to Treat: Insomnia, pain, stress

Taste/Aroma: Grape, sweet with earthy, piney undertones

Appearance: Dense flowers, large heavily frosted calyxes, beautiful autumn colors

Grows: Indoors, outdoors, greenhouse

Josh Williams Photography for Green Life Productions with Permalos Consulting

OFF GRID KUSH

Indica/Sativa Hybrid

Lineage: Chem 4 x Goji OG

THC Content: High

Effects: Mentally stimulating, strong head high

Used to Treat: Headaches, appetite stimulant, ADHD

Rising Moon Seeds

Taste/Aroma: Fermented fruit, astringent earth, guava with hints of leather and coffee

Appearance: Thick, stout greasy flowers with a high flower-to-leaf ratio

Grows: Indoors, outdoors

OG KUSH IX

Indica/Sativa Hybrid

Lineage: OG Kush x OG Kush Incross (IX)

THC Content: Very high

Effects: Very strong, functional high

Used to Treat: Pain, appetite, insomnia

Taste/Aroma: Lemon overtones with pine and earth

Cannarado Genetics

Appearance: Smaller, very dense flowers coated in trichomes

Grows: Indoors, outdoors

PESTILENCE

Sativa/Indica Hybrid

Lineage: Abusive OG x West Coast Dog/OGers

THC Content: High

Effects: Very strong, felt in head first and then in the body, great for relaxing

Used to Treat: Insomnia, pain/nerve pain, MS

Illuminati Seeds

Taste/Aroma: Earthy with slight lemon

Appearance: Dense flowers, full of crystals

Grows: Indoors, outdoors, greenhouse

PLATINUM HUCKLEBERRY COOKIES

Dynasty Seeds

Indica-Dominant Hybrid

Lineage: Platinum Girl Scout Cookies x Oregon Huckleberry

THC Content: Extremely high

Effects: Intense euphoric high followed by sedating body buzz

Used to Treat: Depression, stress, PTSD

Taste/Aroma: Caramel, haze, spices, fruit, pepper

Appearance: Spears coated in large amount of resin

Grows: Indoors, outdoors, greenhouse

PURPLE PUNCH

Supernova Gardens/Grown by Budologist420

Indica-Dominant Hybrid

Lineage: Larry OG x GDP

THC Content: Medium

Effects: Relaxing, body high, appetite-stimulating, euphoric

Used to Treat: Insomnia, depression, anxiety, effects of chemo/radiation

Taste/Aroma: Sweet, grape, blueberries, Fruity Pebbles

Appearance: Large, round, dense flowers with a hint of purple, sugar-coated with frost

Grows: Indoors, outdoors

SIN MINT COOKIES

Sin City Seeds

Indica/Sativa Hybrid

Lineage: GSC Forum Cut x Blue Power

THC Content: Very High

Effects: Energetic, mental and body high with a heavy after-effect

Used to Treat: Inflammation, sleep disorders, stress

Taste/Aroma: Cookies, sweet, rich, acrid, floral, botanical, acidic, pungent

Appearance: Solid, dense, globular spears

Grows: Indoors, outdoors

SIRIUS

Indica/Sativa Hybrid

Lineage: Stardawg (Chemdawg 4 x Tres Dawg) x Chemdawg 4 B3

THC Content: Extremly high

Effects: A long-lasting journey that starts with an invigorating punch followed by a numbing body high

South Fork Seeds/Grown by Elite Cannabis

Used to Treat: Antiemetic, pain relief

Smell/Aroma: Sour, pine, lemon

Appearance: Bulky, trichome-encrusted flowers with unique metallic sheen

Grows: Indoors, outdoors

WOOKIES

Sativa/Indica Hybrid

Lineage: (Durban x OG Kush) x White Kush

THC Content: High

Effects: Initial cerebral rush followed by functional body high

Cannarado Genetics

Used to Treat: Insomnia, appetite, MS, arthritis, general pain

Taste/Aroma: Creamy kush with undertones of fresh-baked cookies, earthy

Appearance: Many mid-sized ultra dense flowers heavily coated in short trichomes

Grows: Indoors, outdoors

RAW

When the first humans were rooting around for sustenance, ethnobotanist and Harvard educator Richard Evans Schultes writes, the sticky tops of raw cannabis plants were likely among the seeds, nuts, and berries they explored. The euphoria that resulted from eating those flowers, Schultes believes, may have spawned religion. Hindus believe that raw cannabis leaves were Lord Shiva's favorite food.

Raw cannabis, part of the human diet since eating began, is a digestible complete protein with essential amino acids and omega fatty acids and the plant kingdom's largest source of cannabinoids (see page 38). Technically, it's a vegetable. Yet it's been largely ignored since humans discovered that heating cannabis flowers or otherwise extracting their resins heightens their psychoactive effects.

Unless you grow your own cannabis or have a friend who does, fresh leaves and flowers aren't easy to find. Most growers dry cannabis flowers to maximize the resin's psychoactive effects (and prepare them for market) and compost or discard the fan leaves and stalks at harvest. This is a tremendous waste. The plant has much more to offer than tiny crystal glands for extraction.

Heating cannabis to convert the carboxylic acid THC-A into psychoactive delta-9 THC changes the plant's chemical composition, stripping out cannabinoids—including a healthy dose of antioxidant and anti-inflammatory CBDs—and terpenes, which are being studied to treat a number of conditions, including epilepsy and cancer. Dr. William Courtney, a Mendocino County physician, recently made headlines with his recommendation that patients eat raw cannabis flowers or juice raw cannabis fan leaves every day to maximize the herb's therapeutic impact while minimizing psychoactive effects. Courtney's domestic partner, Kirsten Peskuski, has been in remission from lupus, interstitial cystitis, and rheumatoid arthritis since she began the regimen of fifteen leaves and two large flowers a day, which requires having forty cannabis plants in cultivation. (Doctors in Colorado and California are writing recommendations that allow juicers to grow forty or more plants.)

In "Cannabis as a Unique Functional Food," Courtney states that heating THC reduces the total antioxidant dose it delivers to one-fiftieth of what it was when the plant was raw. He became a champion for raw cannabis after reading that CBDs could regulate communication between human cells and immune systems and reduce inflammation. In addition to CBD's benefits, the terpenes in raw cannabis boost mood and energy levels, Courtney posits, but THC-A won't alter people's minds. (A good number of Courtney's patients aren't interested in getting high.)

It's true that consuming raw fan leaves, which have trace amounts of THC-A, won't get most people high. But every person's sensitivity to THC-A is different. When they eat raw cannabis flowers, some people feel the same euphoria that early hunters and gatherers experienced. Whether THC-A must be "decarboxylated" through heat or extraction to produce psychoactive effects (see page 78) is a hotly debated—and deeply personal—subject.

As is always the case with cannabis, the only way to find out how eating raw flowers affects you is to try it. Start by blending the smallest flower you can find into juice or a smoothie. You should know in about an hour.

LEAVES AND FLOWERS

Juicing is the most popular form of consuming raw cannabis leaves and flowers (see page 149), but chefs and home cooks with access to the plant are finding creative ways to incorporate it into cuisine. When Andie Leon and Scott Durrah have raw cannabis leaves, they throw them into salads. Scott says the fresh leaves add crisp flavor, like cilantro, in addition to overall health benefits. Andie believes the raw plant is the ultimate superfood. Mike DeLao juices fresh-picked flowers along with other healing fruits, herbs, and vegetables every morning.

Raw cannabis is an acquired taste. The cannabis flowers taste like a gooey, grassy mouthful of pine and dirt. They're best integrated into juice or smoothies. Cannabis leaves taste bitter to most people, so many cooks snip them or roll them and slice them into smaller pieces (*chiffonade*) to mix them with other ingredients. You can use raw leaves the same way you would use any green or leafy green herb, tossed into salads or sprinkled on top of soups and fish. They can also be included in *beurre blanc*, *chimichurri* sauce, pesto, and *tabbouleh*.

PREPARATION AND SAFETY

—Use only organic leaves and flowers, grown without bottled nutrients, if possible. Others could have trace amounts of chemicals, fungicides, and pesticides used during cultivation.

—Use flowers and leaves from plants in early flower stage.

—Thoroughly wash flowers and leaves in water. Soak leaves for up to five minutes to soften and remove dirt.

—Remove all stem material, which has tiny stalactites that can irritate the mouth, throat, and stomach.

—If your immune system is compromised, don't eat raw cannabis. The risk of pathogens is small but present.

SEEDS

In this age of *sinsemilla*, consumers don't see a lot of cannabis seeds. Most growers toss them if they're not saving them for the next harvest or the market. That's too bad; the little balls have juice.

Cannabis seeds, rich in omega-3 and omega-6 fatty acids and healthy protein, have been an essential food for humans throughout history. Indians have mixed cannabis seeds with amaranth, rice, and wheat for generations. Crushed cannabis seeds sustained people in Europe during World War II and in China during the 1960 famines, according to *Cannabis: A History* by Martin Booth.

Cannabis seeds have extremely low THC content and taste creamy and nutty, without the bitterness of the plant material. They can be shelled and eaten like sunflower seeds, tossed into salads and smoothies, and sprinkled over yogurt. Ground into a powder, they can be mixed with oil and substituted for hemp powder in recipes.

To shell cannabis seeds, place in a single layer on a table and place a board on top. Tap up and down the length of the board with a wooden mallet to rupture seeds, then pour the seeds into a bowl of water and stir vigorously. Use a strainer to skim off the shells as they rise to the top. Pour the water through a colander and pick out any shells that remain.

Pure Sunshine/Cultivated by Permalos Consulting

Raw Food

Raw foodists believe that heating food above 112 degrees Fahrenheit cooks out valuable living enzymes, including oxygenating and blood-stimulating chlorophyll. For that reason, most raw foodists' diets consist of 75 to 100 percent uncooked food. Considered a fringe culinary movement—and hotly debated among nutritionists, dietitians, academics, and foodies—the idea is hardly new.

Pythagoras, Hippocrates's teacher, told people to eat only raw vegetables. Pelegasians in ancient Greece (with average lifespans of two hundred years) primarily dined on raw fruits, vegetables, nuts, and seeds. The first raw food restaurant opened in the United States in 1917, and in the 1940s celebrities and desperately ill patients flocked to a wellness center in Mexico run by Dr. Edmond Szekely, whose "living food" philosophy was inspired by the eating habits of the Essenes at the beginning of the first century. In 1994, Raw restaurant opened in Los Angeles, and A-list celebrities' passionate sound bites about the benefits of eating raw sparked interest among the masses. Raw, since closed, spawned haute raw cuisine followers from coast to coast.

Dynasty Seeds

INFUSIONS AND EXTRACTIONS

Infusions are the heart and soul, the building blocks, of great cannabis food. Every chef has her or his method, distilled from years of trial-and-error. Extracting and activating the cannabis plant's valuable cannabinoids, including THC and CBD, is something of an art, but scientific principles apply.

The science behind edible extractions is simple. Fat-soluble THC-A and CBD-A molecules bind with fats (oils, butter, milk, honey) and alcohols when heated. Fat extracts the cannabinoids, and heat converts THC-A and CBD-A into THC and CBD, delivering enhanced goodies once concentrated in the plant's trichomes. "The foundation of all methods of extraction," Chris Kilham says, "is to get the goodies out of the cellulose walls or off the material and leave the skeletal cellulose behind."

The art of infusions is a bit messier, as art tends to be. Everyone has his or her own way of doing them. No way is "right" or "wrong" as long as you follow some basic guidelines. You can use a crockpot, a hot plate, a pan on the stove, or the oven. You can fast-infuse it, as Chris Kilham does (see page 103), or you can let it simmer for days (as long as you watch it carefully and don't let it burn). As is always the case with cannabis (and a beautiful thing), the only way to find the infusion that works best for you is to try a few.

To make edible extractions, cannabis is heated gently in a fat or alcohol to extract the fat-soluble cannabinoids. (We focused on infusions made using alcohol, butter, oil, milk, and honey—which is not technically a fat but a good agent for suspension of cannabinoids—because they're the ones our chefs use.) Methods of doing this range from primitive to high tech. Leslie Cerier stuffs jars full of plant material and oil and sets them in a window to let sunlight do the work (see page 99). Joey Galeano uses a MagicalButter machine that extracts, stirs, and maintains temperature balance and gives him extractions in an hour (see Resource Guide). They both report euphoric results.

Most chefs are somewhere in between, following roughly the same guidelines: cook slow and low, giving the cannabinoids and terpenes time to infuse while never letting the temperature get high enough to evaporate the cannabinoids and terpenes (about 180 to 220 degrees Fahrenheit). Scott Durrah gently simmers cannabis flowers in butter for two or three days over very low heat to extract cannabinoids as well as flavor, and Andie Leon lets flowers or trim infuse into coconut oil in a very low oven for eight to ten hours. Donna Shields puts cannabis and butter or oil in a heatproof glass vessel and sets it in a crockpot half full of water on low heat for six to eight hours. (This modulates the temperature, as some crockpots get too hot even on their lowest settings and can burn the infusion.)

Herb Seidel uses hash for personal infusions (see below) but teaches beginners a method that calls for simmering cannabis in water, which has a lower boiling point than butter or oil, to prevent burning (see page 80). Herb's goal is to produce a cannabis-infused product that's as close to the original as possible by slowly pulling out cannabinoids without too much heat. "If butter loses its viscosity in the extraction process, it won't work in cooking," Herb says. "Cookies will flatten out and won't rise, and you can't make hollandaise sauce with it. You want to be able to use your butter and oils the same way you did before any infusion was made."

KITCHEN CONFIDENTIAL

Heating cannabis, whether in a crockpot, on the stove, or in the oven, fills your kitchen and much of your house (depending on its size) with the rich aroma of a slow-roasting plant releasing aromatic essential oils. As long as you're not burning the infusion, cannabis extractions envelop the kitchen in the pleasant omnipresence of a roasting turkey (you smell nothing else, but why would you want to?).

The aroma *will* prompt anyone who stops by to ask what you're making. Fans and good ventilation help, but there's no hiding the smell of cooking cannabis. The aroma will make its way into the hallway if you live in an apartment. If privacy or neighbors are a concern, plan accordingly.

FLAVOR

Infusing oil and butter with cannabis gives it the acrid, herbal taste that's best—and really, only—described as "green." No culinary adjectives exist for the taste of cannabis; "Earthy" is the overused term because we don't yet have the language to describe the plant's depth.

Until fairly recently, most cannabis chefs sought to cover up the cannabis taste with other strong flavors so that diners could medicate without tasting the medicine. That's an art in itself and, again, a highly personal choice. (We included a few recipes that completely mask the cannabis taste for that reason.) But as the cannabis market opens up, giving chefs an almost unlimited palette of cannabis "flavors" to work with, cannabis is being treated as an important seasoning, right up there with oregano, basil, and tarragon. Chefs are playing with cannabis flavors the way painters play with color and musicians play with notes.

Joey Galeano puts nutty-tasting cannabis cultivars (try Chocolate Chunk or White Kush) into confections and integrates more savory cultivars (Sage or Cheese) into entrées and dishes. The cannabis in Joey's infusions adds subtle flavor much as his grandmother's basil-infused olive oil did. "It's a beautiful accent," Joey says.

Rowan Lehrman loves the taste of the plant. She'd been frustrated with cannabis cuisine until recently because sugar-laden sweets designed to hide the cannabis flavor didn't appeal to her. Masking the flavor, Rowan believes, encourages over-consumption. When that brownie tastes so good (and brownies *do*), it's easy to forget that it's also getting you high. Keeping a little "green" flavor, as well as color, Catja Redfern says, "keeps it real."

Most chefs who cook with cannabis appreciate the plant's place in their repertoire, a healing herb with a strong taste profile not unlike turmeric or garlic (with a psychoactive twist). For Scott Durrah, cooking with cannabis is like mixing a martini with quality spirits. "You want to taste the gin or vodka," Scott says. "It's the same with cannabis, and that's the difference between cooking with cannabis and being a chef with cannabis. You get that flavor."

FLOWERS AND SUGAR LEAVES

Extracting cannabinoids from flowers and the tiny "sugar leaves" that are clipped off when flowers are manicured (also known as "trim") is the most common method of making infusions. Flowers have more trichome coverage and make a more potent infusion with more consistent results than trim. Flowers also impart a stronger herbal flavor. Sugar leaves taste bitter because they have more chlorophyll.

Use dried flowers and sugar leaves for infusions. For most methods, the flowers and leaves must be finely ground. This can be done using a coffee grinder, a mortar and pestle, or a fine mesh screen. Place the screen over a tray and rub the flowers and leaves on the screen with your hands (wear gloves; it will be sticky) to grind them into a powder.

WASTE NOT, WANT NOT

If you use a vaporizer, you've probably thrown out a lot of valuable cannabinoids. The science isn't clear, but consensus says that vaporizing cannabis doesn't burn off all the THC and other cannabinoids. Anywhere from 10 percent to 50 percent of the active components remain in the cannabis, which can be used again to make butter or oil. (Joey Galeano blends it into meatballs.) Because some cannabinoids burn off during vaporizing, "already been vaped" (ABV) makes less potent extractions. In general, use about forty grams of ABV for every two sticks of butter or eight and a half ounces of oil.

DECARBOXYLATION

De-*what?* Decarboxylation is the process of heating cannabis to activate THC and CBD. Decarboxylation has been a subject of hot debates since US government researchers discovered in 1970 that heating cannabis to about 200 degrees Fahrenheit breaks off THC-A's and CBD-A's carboxyl radicals and increases THC and CBD percentage, making cannabis far more potent.

Some chefs believe decarboxylation is always necessary when cooking with cannabis and making tinctures. Some skip the step altogether, seeing it as a waste of time that could potentially vaporize valuable compounds. (Little or no vaporization of cannabinoids and terpenes takes place if the temperature remains below 246 degrees Fahrenheit.) Most chefs don't bother to decarboxylate cannabis before making oil and butter infusions because that extraction process sufficiently heats the cannabis to convert THA-A into THC.

To decarb or not to decarb is, again, a highly personal preference. Joey Galeano always decarbs cannabis before he makes oils, butters, or tinctures because, he says, it "just seems to do the trick." Joey enjoys a good high and also appreciates that CBD, which is also released in the process, helps him sleep. To activate CBD, Joey sets the oven slightly higher and lets the cannabis heat for an extra fifteen minutes. Joey's simple process of heating flowers in an oven bag follows.

Joey Galeano's Decarboxylation Process

You will need:

- oven bag

- oven-safe dish

- whole cannabis flowers and/or sugar trim leaves

Preheat oven. To activate THC, set oven to 250°F. To activate CBD, set oven to 275°F.

Place cannabis in oven bag and push out all the air. Tie a knot to seal the bag.

Put bag into an oven-safe dish and place in middle of preheated oven.

To activate THC at 250°F, heat for 30 minutes. To activate CBD at 275°F, heat for 45 minutes.

Remove from oven and let cool completely. You can put the bag in the freezer to speed up the process.

OIL AND BUTTER EXTRACTIONS

Every chef has a slightly different method of infusing oil and butter, but most follow the same general guidelines. You can use anywhere from a quarter to an ounce of trim or flowers per quarter pound of butter or quarter-cup of oil—and again, this ratio is highly personal. The cannabis-to-fat ratio directly affects the infusion's potency, which also largely depends on the quality, age, and condition of the cannabis you use. Infusions will likely differ from batch to batch unless you can get the cannabis tested.

The key to oil and butter infusions is to cook them low and slow, optimally at around 200 degrees Fahrenheit. Temperatures above 350 degrees Fahrenheit cause volatile oils and terpenes to evaporate, and the fats will burn. Keep a good eye on the butter or oil as it simmers, stir occasionally, and use a candy thermometer if you're worried about it getting too hot. When he makes his 20-Minute Cannabis Olive Oil (see page 103), Chris Kilham allows only the slightest bubbling simmer and stirs for the entire time the oil is on the stove. "It's no different than cooking any food," says Scott Durrah. "If it's burned, it's burned. But that's an expensive mistake because you've just burned an ounce of cannabis."

For this reason, many chefs introduce water, which has a lower boiling point than butter or oil (212 degrees Fahrenheit), into the process. (See Herb Seidel's Beginner's Oil on page 100.) Water moderates the temperature, preventing the fat and cannabis from burning, and also absorbs chlorophyll, which contributes to the "green" smell and taste of cannabis. For some, that's an improvement. For those who want chlorophyll's blood-oxygenating effects, that's a downside.

Whatever method you use, your oil or butter will be green if you infuse it with flowers and sugar leaves. Depending on the raw materials you use, the finished product will range from lime green to forest green, almost brown.

The chefs' recipes for oil, butter, milk, honey, and alcohol extractions begin on page 99.

HASH INFUSIONS

Hash, concentrated resin trichomes, can be used instead of plant material in most infusions and has some advantages. One is that hash can be melted directly into oil or butter, eliminating the need to strain out cannabis particles and deal with messy cheesecloth. The process also removes the tiny hairs on the plant (sharper than they look), which can be difficult for people with intestinal tract problems to digest. Using hash instead of plant material also eliminates the green hue and much of the herbal flavor.

Because it's concentrated, hash is more potent than flowers and sugar leaves. Two to three

Dry sift by Permalos Consulting

grams of hash in a stick of butter or four ounces of oil makes a mild infusion, and three to five grams is generally the standard—but it all depends on the potency of the cannabis.

Hash can be purchased in dispensaries and retail stores, but not all hash is created equal (see page 52). Hash that has been extracted improperly with butane could add butane to your food. For the healthiest and safest results, look for bubble hash or dry sift.

You can make your own ice water hash—though we don't recommend doing so without doing your homework or finding a good teacher. (See Resource Guide for reliable sources on the art of extracting.) No matter what you hear or read, do not attempt to make hash with butane. It's dangerous and potentially unhealthy, and several municipalities in states where cannabis is legal are outlawing the practice.

TINCTURES

Tinctures, extracts made using alcohol or a sugar alcohol such as glycerin, were the primary means of delivering cannabis in over-the-counter medicines before prohibition in 1937. Alcohol extracts and preserves the plant's resins and soluble compounds, including THC and CBD.

When making tinctures, chefs use anywhere from one gram to six grams of dried cannabis per fluid ounce of alcohol. Potency is a personal preference, and the amount of cannabis you use directly affects it. Finding what's right for you requires experimentation. Start with one gram and increase by a gram each time you make a tincture until you find your level.

The chefs use a range of quality spirits, from gin and vodka to Chartreuse and Everclear. The liquor should be at least 100 proof (50 percent alcohol) for maximum efficiency. The alcohol softens and separates the cannabis in a process called maceration that can take from six hours to ten days. Heating the infusion hastens the process and increases potency.

Tinctures come on much faster than fat-based infusions but generally don't last as long. Most people start to feel the effects after about fifteen minutes, but always wait at least an hour before ingesting more. Tinctures are powerful medicine, and the concentrated THC can cause panic and anxiety. Go slow.

Recipes for alcohol and glycerin tinctures begin on page 111.

DOSING

"The enlivening, expansive, joy-producing effects of cannabis result from high-quality material used judiciously and moderately. This, as with the other psychedelicacies, is key. Moderation, not habituation, leads to a maximally satisfying experience. If you resort to cannabis first thing in the morning and throughout the day, then the use of cannabis becomes a dulling habit, which in time produces lethargy and forgetfulness. But used sparingly, occasionally, and in happy circumstances, cannabis increases pleasure and overall *joie de vivre*."

—Chris Kilham, *The Ganja Road*

In the summer of 2014, just after Colorado opened the adult-use cannabis market, *New York Times* columnist Maureen Dowd visited the state and tried a cannabis-infused chocolate bar. The people who hosted Dowd on a bus tour of Denver's cannabis scene claim that they told Dowd that Colorado's recommended dose of THC is 10 milligrams and that each little square of the chocolate bar she bought at a retail dispensary was one dose. But alone with only a bottle of chardonnay in a Denver hotel room, Dowd got impatient when the little square didn't affect her and ate another square.

Know anyone who's eaten a whole Ex-Lax bar? This story ends that way, but the explosion took place in her head. While Dowd was waiting for the cannabis to come on, she drank some chardonnay. Her resulting freak-out, chronicled in the *Times*, is cannabis legend. Eating too much cannabis food and experiencing the heart-pounding anxiety, paranoia, and—seriously, terror—that results is now known as "overdowding."

Riding the Internet sensation that her "Dowd and out" column sparked, Dowd sought advice on what went wrong for another column from a reliable source (and legend), Willie Nelson—whom she deemed her cannabis *sensei*. Nelson told Dowd about a similar experience with cannabis-laced cookies that left him "laying there, and it felt like the flesh was falling off my bones."

Well, that doesn't sound pleasant. And it's not. Eating too much cannabis sends your heart rate soaring, makes you dizzy, makes you feel like you can't breathe (you can), dries out your mouth, and slows your reactions. Those are the physical symptoms. Your head spins into paranoia and anxiety, even a full-on psychedelic "trip" that could last for up to twelve hours. You lose sense of time, can't remember anything (including where you are), and you think you're going to die. People don't die from cannabis overdoses because cannabis isn't toxic to human cells and organs, but every year (in increasing numbers as cannabis edibles dominate the legal retail market) countless souls visit emergency rooms thinking it's happening.

Overdosing on cannabis food is alarming. The effects range from mush brain (do not eat cannabis edibles before events where you might meet important people) to near catatonia. Your mind becomes a wooden rollercoaster—slow, creaky, with deep twists and plunges. Cannabis food overdose makes you ridiculous in social situations, though in a much kinder way than downing too many martinis. (*Scientific Reports* states, in fact, that cannabis may be as much as 114 times safer than alcohol.) You'll have a head full of cobwebs the next day, but you won't have to worry about what you said or did. You said, "Can I just lie down on the couch?" And that's pretty much what you did.

SIDE EFFECTS

Consuming cannabis, in any form, can cause the following side effects.

- Increased heart rate and blood pressure
- Dry mouth
- Red eyes, dilated pupils
- Loss of motor coordination
- Slower reaction times
- Sensory distortion
- Short-term memory problems
- Impaired mental functioning

EATING IS NOT SMOKING

Eating cannabis presents some obvious benefits over smoking—it's less irritating to lungs and the effects last longer—and it is an entirely different animal. Whether you've been a wake-and-baker for decades or are trying cannabis for the first time at your doctor's advice, *you* are a *noob* the first time you eat cannabis food.

All too often, frequent cannabis smokers or vapers think they have the tolerance to handle more cannabis food than they should. Tolerance to smoked cannabis doesn't translate to cannabis food. The THC delivery process is entirely different.

When cannabis is smoked or vaped, delta-9 THC enters the bloodstream through the lungs within fifteen minutes. When it's eaten, the stomach and intestines break it down with acid and enzymes before sending it through the liver, and that's where everything changes. The liver converts delta-9 THC into 11-hydroxy-THC, which crosses the blood-brain barrier more rapidly, causing more psychoactive effects and a very different "high" than smokers experience. This process takes much longer to deliver psychoactive effects to the brain, especially when cannabis is infused into rich, dense food like Maureen Dowd's chocolate bar. 11-hydroxy-THC delivers an overall body high that is quite different than delta THC-9 (we don't know why), with much longer-lasting effects.

It's almost impossible to compare eating cannabis to smoking it, but the easy equation is that you must eat much less cannabis than you would smoke to feel the effects. (Hash is up to three times more potent when it's eaten.) When Scott Durrah roughly translates two teaspoons of his cannabis-infused extra-virgin olive oil into smoker lingo, it equals about three and a half to four joints (about one and a half to two grams of cannabis). Joey Galeano says that eating a gram of cannabis is like smoking five grams. And unlike smoking cannabis, he says, "when you eat it, you just keep going further down the rabbit hole."

> **FULL BELLY**
>
> To avoid getting overly intoxicated, enjoy cannabis food when other good food is already in your belly. Consuming cannabis on an empty stomach exacerbates the intoxicating effects. Once cannabis food is in your system, adding more food (particularly fats and proteins) can push even more THC into your bloodstream.

WAIT

How food is prepared, the type of infusion, the food it's combined with, and how much you've already eaten all affect how long it takes for cannabis to hit your system. Fatty, protein-rich foods intensify the effects, sugar creates a faster high that dissipates more quickly, and alcohol can compound the effects and create paranoia. Combine that with each individual's metabolism, body size and mass, personal biochemistry, age, and tolerance, and you have a complicated set of variables that make it impossible to know how and when the effects of cannabis food will hit each diner.

Everyone else at the dinner table could be giggling and settling more happily into their chairs while you feel nothing. Two hours could go by. The temptation to grab one more bite, especially when the cannabis food is divine, can be fierce. The consequences (over-dowding) can be embarrassing at best, tragic at worst—and last for hours, even into the next day.

When delivered through food, cannabis can take two hours or more to dial in. If it finally does, and you added a few more nibbles to the equation, the whammy triples. Especially if you're new to cannabis food, eat a small amount and don't have seconds. If nothing happens, you enjoyed delicious food and it's not the end of the world. Eat a little more next time.

NOT CREATED EQUAL

Unless you've already tried a cannabis dish or have your cannabis tested for THC content (and even then, there are factors beyond your control), you can't predict how it will affect you—no matter what your tolerance. An ounce of Golden Goat from one grower can have wildly different potency than an ounce of the same cultivar from another. Potency, affected by environmental factors, growing conditions, and genetics, varies even in a cultivar with the exact same genetics as another one grown at a different time by the same grower.

Consider any food made with cannabis that hasn't been independently tested to be potent—and eat it that way. Test cannabis food in small amounts on yourself and only yourself. Never rely on someone else's opinion.

START LOW, GO SLOW

It can be difficult, especially when you're surrounded by the smell of warm scones straight from the oven, but the only way to avoid over-intoxication is to start with a sample portion of cannabis food and wait two hours or more to see what happens. When Andie Leon serves her cake or brownies to novice cannabis eaters, she suggests starting with pieces roughly the size of their thumb pads. Joey Galeano recommends approaching cannabis food as you would 100-proof (or more) alcohol. "Start out sipping," he says. "If you chug a bottle of tequila, you'll have a horrible day. The same thing applies."

Scott Durrah starts people out on cannabis food with condiments, tiny bowls of soup, or small appetizers. "There's no way anyone can eat an entire meal," he says. "You can't do it. You would be comatose." Offering cannabis in food that can be added to other dishes as needed allows everyone to be responsible for his or her own destiny at the dinner table—and that's key. Make non-infused versions to offer guests so they're not overly tempted by the sight and smell of food they shouldn't eat.

> "Remember the guidelines of set and setting. Set is your state of mind. If you're in a reasonably balanced mental condition, then that may be a good time to use cannabis. If you're feeling out of sorts, paranoid or on edge, it is probably an excellent time to abstain. And don't rely on it to help you beat depression, or cure your problems. It won't. Setting is your environment. Pick a nice place to relax, listen to music, or do something fun and non-dangerous. Enjoy the experience. Cannabis offers a delightful reverie when used properly."
>
> —Chris Kilham, *Ganja Road*

There is no going back once you've eaten too much cannabis food. If you experience that once, you're not likely to do it again. Why put yourself through it at all?

FINDING YOUR DOSE

Cannabis was disappearing from the pharmacopeia, even before it was outlawed, because herbal medicine is difficult to standardize. A tablespoon of cannabis butter (generally considered one dose) can vary wildly in potency from another tablespoon. With so many variables, "dosing" with cannabis food is a messy, inexact science. It's actually more of an art.

When he makes a new batch of oil or butter, Chris Kilham performs what ethnobotanists wryly refer to as a "bio-assay" (a biological assessment to gauge a substance's effects) on himself before he cooks with it. He follows some general guidelines for the amount of cannabis he uses per serving—generally a third of a gram or less for quality flowers and a sixth of a gram for hash (any more, he says, induces panic in too many people)—but every batch translates that differently and every person's sensitivity is different. THC counts in cannabis infusions will run the scales, even when the exact same recipe is followed with precision. Without independent testing, an individual "bio-assay" is the only way to know how cannabis food affects you.

Keep a journal of infusions and recipes that you've tested. Write down the date, time, cultivar, and where you purchased or grew and harvested it, how much you consumed, and how it affected you. Over time you'll start to see patterns and understand how different cultivars and infusions affect you—and also how vastly different every batch can be.

CALCULATING DOSAGE

THC and CBD content are measured in milligrams. Because THC content in cannabis varies so wildly, making accurate calculations about how many milligrams a recipe contains is impossible without independent testing. We based our THC calculations on cannabis with 10 percent THC content, the grudgingly accepted industry standard in the absence of standardization. Calculating rough THC content based on this average can be helpful when comparing recipes but will not be a foolproof indication of how potent a dish will be.

The calculation reads something like income tax instructions. It goes like this: A gram of dried cannabis weighs 1,000 milligrams. Ten percent of 1,000 is 100 milligrams, meaning that a gram of cannabis has at least 100 milligrams of THC. You can calculate the THC content of an infusion by dividing the total number of milligrams in the recipe (based on 100 milligrams per gram) by the number of cups it yields. You can then calculate the percentage of THC in recipes by multiplying the number of cups of butter or oil in the recipe by how much THC was in that infusion (based on previous calculations). That's the THC content for the entire dish. Divide by number of servings to get dosage per serving.

RECOMMENDED DOSES

The Colorado Marijuana Enforcement Division's standard dose per serving is ten milligrams, which most people compare to having one beer, glass of wine, or cocktail.

That number's still too high for the Council on Responsible Cannabis Regulation, which suggests in its First Time 5 campaign that new cannabis consumers eat just five milligrams. "For some people, ten milligrams of THC is a comfortable amount; for others, especially novice users, it can be a bit too much," the campaign states. "If you are the type of person for whom over-intoxication is discomforting, why take that chance?"

SET AND SETTING

Inviting friends for a cannabis-focused evening is a new luxury in states where prohibition has ended—and a whole new way of entertaining. Unlike alcohol, which dulls senses and lowers inhibitions, cannabis heightens people's sensitivity to everything from the song in the background to the *interesting* painting in the hallway that they'd never noticed before. No one knows this better than Jane West, whose Denver catering company, Edible Events, produces artful cannabis-focused parties designed to soothe and stimulate all five senses.

"It may sound funny, but I get a lot of inspiration from children's birthday parties," Jane says. "And that really makes sense because people become more lighthearted, inquisitive, open-minded—childlike—when they use cannabis."

Jane, a pioneering cannabis advocate who founded the organization Women Grow, graciously shared her platform for creating sensual, soulful cannabis events.

- **Give people fun things to do (that don't involve having a drink in their hands).** Set out art and origami books, sketchpads, books of brain teasers and adult puzzles; quick, repeatable games such as Connect Four; and even a basket full of kids' instruments to satisfy brains looking for stimulation.

- **Bathe, don't blast, guests in light.** People's pupils will dilate, and colors will become more bold. Keep lighting soft, indirect, and cozy. Change it throughout the night: brighter for dinner and seductive during dessert. (This matters in the bathroom, too—and a basket of single-use Visine eye drops next to the sink is one of Jane's brilliant touches.)

- **Make playlists.** People will get lost in songs, and music will set the event's tempo. Make three ninety-minute play lists (for cocktail hour, dinner, and after-dinner) with songs that provide down-tempo, steady background beats.

- **Tickle their noses.** Warm the room's olfactory ambience with natural candles scented with almond or eucalyptus, faintly mirroring the fragrance from the volatile oils in cannabis food.

- **Get cozy.** Encourage people to relax with floor pillows, blankets, and poufs. Shift the furniture and open up a space for people to lounge and wind down after dinner.

- **Serve cannabis food as early in the evening as possible because it takes a while to set in.** Passing cannabis-infused dressings and sauces rather than dosing every plate yourself allows guests to control their own destinies. (Jane says that Japanese soup spoons usually provide perfect doses.)

- **Let guests help make dinner.** "Too many cannabis cooking classes focus too much on cannabis—you can't eat that much cannabis!" Jane says. "But guests love to be involved in making their dinner and controlling how much cannabis they consume."

- **Keep the focus away from alcohol.** Jane likes to serve one *digestif* after dinner and keep cocktails on the back burner for the rest of the event. She makes sure to offer plenty of cider, tea, coffee, and herbal sparkling waters instead.

- **Keep track of the evening.** Consuming cannabis alters your sense of time. Be prepared with notecards about what needs to happen throughout the night.

WHEN YOU EAT TOO MUCH

Breathe. Five counts in, five counts out through the nose. That's all you need to think about.

Remember, nobody has died. Cannabis is not toxic to your systems. It provokes uncomfortable physical reactions, but the terror truly is all in your head. As deadly as it feels, the situation is, fortunately, temporary.

Lay down. Lay on your side, not your back. Lying on your back lowers your blood pressure and might make you nauseous.

Close your eyes. Eliminate visual chaos and focus on breathing.

Drink juice. Fruit juice or Emergen-C will raise your blood sugar, which may help you feel more stable.

Get some CBD. CBD regulates THC's psychoactive effects. A drop or two of a high-CBD, low-THC tincture under the tongue could balance out the THC explosion.

Eat an orange. Citrus fruit is high in the terpene limonene, which can help mitigate strong THC effects. Persians prescribed it as an antidote to cannabis over-intoxication in the tenth century.

Get help. Let people know you've had a bad reaction and ask them to watch you. If you feel your case is extreme, ask someone to drive you to the emergency room or call 911. Do not drive yourself anywhere. Public transportation is pretty much out of the question as well.

SAFETY

Federal law states that cannabis is illegal. The feds can take away benefits such as public housing assistance and college financial aid if they find out you're consuming it. Public and private employers can fire you. As long as cannabis is illegal under federal laws, you are taking a risk, no matter where you live or visit. Only you can decide whether that risk is acceptable.

Even in states where it's legal, cannabis is a controlled substance. It should be treated with the same respect and care that you would give to alcohol or prescription medications. Store it where children can't reach it, and consider locking it up as you would a liquor cabinet if you have either young children or teenagers.

Never eat cannabis and drive. Just as with alcohol and prescription medication, driving while under the influence of cannabis is dangerous and illegal. Colorado and Washington have set legal limits for how much cannabis can be in a driver's blood, and they are enforcing them. Cannabis can remain active in your system for up to five hours. After you've eaten cannabis food, don't get behind the wheel for the rest of the day.

Always label storage containers clearly. Do not unwittingly dose Grandma, the babysitter, or even yourself. Label containers with large, unmistakable messages that make it crystal clear the food inside contains cannabis.

Keep cannabis food away from pets. They can't handle it, and the vet bill for treating over-intoxicated animals is not cheap. Cannabis food can be lethal to animals. Do not feed it to them and clean up immediately if it falls on the floor.

Dispose of food properly. Don't throw leftovers into the garbage, where a pet or child could dig them out.

Women who are pregnant or nursing should not consume cannabis. Period.

Consult your doctor before you begin using cannabis. Cannabis can increase your risk of heart attack, damage your immune system, and reduce sperm count and quality. It could make some health conditions worse. Talk with your doctor about what the risk is for you.

TOOLS

You likely have almost everything you need to make cannabis food in your kitchen. The tools listed here are the chefs' staples.

If you're worried about cross-contamination with other food or have people in your household who are very sensitive to cannabis, keep a separate supply of saucepans, spoons, and other tools to use solely for cannabis cooking.

Coffee Grinder

Many chefs recommend electric spice or coffee grinders for grinding cannabis. You'll want a grinder dedicated to cannabis cooking because the process leaves the grinder a sticky mess that can be difficult to clean completely. (Isopropyl alcohol, available at the grocery or pharmacy, will do the trick.) Coffee grinders are available in a range of prices and classes. You don't need a fancy one to grind cannabis.

Vitamix or Blender

If you're fortunate enough to own a Vitamix, the machine grinds cannabis (and everything else) with ease.

Mortar and Pestle

People have been crushing herbs in a mortar (bowl) using a pestle (a club-shaped tool) for centuries. It's a time-honored, meditative way to crush smaller amounts of cannabis. Use a ceramic or polished stone mortar and pestle for the finest cannabis grind. Rough stone can infuse fine particles into cannabis as it's being ground. Wood mortar and pestles are durable but porous and absorb the plant's aroma and flavor over time.

Fine Mesh Strainer

You'll need to strain cannabis infusions through a fine mesh strainer lined with cheesecloth. An inexpensive hand-held strainer is fine, but look for one with very fine mesh for best results.

Cheesecloth

Cheesecloth is a cotton gauze cloth with many uses that can be found in the supermarket cooking supplies section. (Instead of using cheesecloth for straining, Catjia Redfern uses a flour sack or hemp cloth, which can be washed and reused.)

Candy Thermometer

The little thermometers used to measure the temperature of sugar solutions as they cook are critical for gauging whether your infusions are getting too hot. You can do without one, but they cost only a couple of bucks—a tiny investment to prevent burning fine cannabis.

Dutch Oven

Dutch ovens, heavy cooking pots made of cast iron, ceramic, or clay with tightly fitting lids, are well suited for the long, slow cooking that cannabis infusions require.

Crockpot

You can buy an electric slow cooker in a grocery store or even a flea market, but when you're cooking with cannabis, it's worth knowing that not all crockpots are equal. Shop for one with settings below 180 degrees and read reviews about your choices. Some crockpots run hotter than their settings suggest and they can boil your butter. When you're making cannabis infusions, that's an expensive mistake.

Ball or Mason Jars

Heavy glass jars with two-piece lids that seal onto the jar are most people's preferred storage vessel for both cannabis and cannabis infusions. Lids on these jars seal effectively only once and shouldn't be reused.

Labels

Always label cannabis and cannabis food clearly and alarmingly on permanent adhesive labels stuck to the jar or container. Include cultivar used and date the product was made.

Ice Cube Trays

These aren't a necessity, but they're a great way to preserve cannabis sauces, pesto, and other goodies in small portions in the freezer.

> ## MAGICAL
>
> This MagicalButter machine is a luxury. The micro-processing machine grinds, heats, extracts, and stirs herbal infusions, ensuring even heating and consistent results in an hour, making them blissfully easy (see Resource Guide).

FOR COCKTAILS

Cannabis cocktails don't require any special tools, but cocktails do require these common bar items.

Cocktail Shaker

A stainless steel vessel with a lid used to shake cocktails with ice for quicker cooling.

Cocktail Strainer

This round, flat strainer with a handle fits over a cocktail glass to catch ice cubes or other particles when the cocktail is poured from the shaker.

Mixing Glass

These come in all sorts of fancy designs, with prices that reflect them. You can invest in one or use a heavy, durable glass.

Swizzle Sticks

The small sticks used to hold fruit garnishes or stir drinks are easy to find online, in specialty retail stores, and even flea markets. Avoid sticking plastic into your cocktail if you can. Glass, bamboo, and raw sugar cane are healthier and more fun.

Recipes

The six-leaf potency scale for these recipes is based on rough THC percentage and is for comparison purposes only. The cannabinoid and terpene content of the cannabis you use is the most important indicator of how a recipe will affect you.

OILS

Infused oils are the basic building blocks
of cannabis cooking. Once you've found
the method—or methods—that work
for you, you can stock oils with varying flavors and potencies. Extra-virgin
organic olive oil and unrefined organic
coconut oil are the chefs' first choices
when making cannabis infusions.

Harvest Time Oil de Mary Jane Leaf

Leslie Cerier

At harvest time, when cannabis is abundant, Leslie Cerier stuffs jars with fan leaves, sugar leaves, and buds (sometimes spicing it up with fresh chilies, basil, cilantro, or oregano), covers the plant material with extra-virgin olive oil, and lets nature do its work. She ripens her oils in direct sunlight (the infusion happens more slowly in diffused sunlight) for a couple weeks and stores one in her kitchen cabinet and the rest in her basement cellar. Throughout the year, long past harvest, Leslie can pull out cannabis oil to sauté eggplant, stir-fry whatever her garden's providing, or garnish stews. (She's been known to eat a tiny spoonful, outside of any recipe, when she's in the mood for a straight shot of herbal yum.) Oil made from fan leaves will have much less THC than oil made from sugar leaves, and oil made from flowers will be strong. With an abundance of whole plant at your fingertips and good storage space, you can create a line of oils ranging in potency to use throughout the year. Because the cannabis is not heated to extract THC, this is a relatively mild infusion for most people.

Makes about 1 cup

THC per serving: ✿ ✿ ✿ ✿ ✿

2 cups fresh cannabis fan leaf, sugar leaf, or flower, coarsely chopped
1¼ cups extra-virgin olive oil
fine mesh strainer
cheesecloth
airtight glass jar

Wash and thoroughly dry cannabis. Loosely pack cannabis in a clean, dry pint jar, leaving about 1" of space at the top. (Moisture on the plant material or in the jar can cause mold to grow.)

Add enough oil to cover (still leaving 1" of space).

Using a butter knife, gently press down on the herbs to eliminate any air pockets.

Put cap on jar and a label that includes contents, date prepared, and approximate date oil will be ready (2–6 weeks from preparation date).

Place jar on a small plate and set on a windowsill.

After 2 weeks, taste oil. To make it stronger, let it continue to steep. From now until it's at the level you want it to be, check it once a week.

When oil is ready, line a fine mesh strainer with cheesecloth and place over a bowl, wide-mouth jar, or measuring cup. Twist herbs with cheesecloth, squeezing out every last drop of oil. Compost cannabis solids.

Transfer oil to a clean clear or dark bottle or jar with a lid or cork. Label with the type of oil and date. Store in a cool, dry place for up to a year.

Beginner's Oil

Herb Seidel

Herb Seidel wants to make it easy for novices to infuse oil without any danger of scorching it or turning it into sludge. Herb's process of simmering a half ounce of ground cannabis flowers in water and letting the infusion cool to room temperature a couple of times, then adding oil and simmering for fifteen minutes before straining and freezing, cold-extracts the THC oil from the water. The process is time-consuming but eliminates the possibility of error, and that's a beautiful thing. The oil binds with fat-soluble THC during the simmering process and separates from the water, which goes murky from taking on water-soluble chlorophyll and other terpenes, when it's frozen. Herb separates the frozen water from the frozen oil with a sharp knife, discards the water, and ends up with mild-tasting oil with a hint of cannabis flavor that won't overpower whatever recipe you're making. You can use this method with any type of oil, including coconut, extra-virgin olive, grapeseed, sunflower, and canola.

Makes about 1 cup

THC per serving: 🌿

½ ounce cured cannabis flowers or
    trim, finely ground
2 cups water
1 cup olive, grapeseed, vegetable, sun-
    flower, or canola oil
fine mesh strainer
cheesecloth
airtight glass jar

Combine cannabis and water in a saucepan and bring to simmer. Let simmer for about an hour and a half. Don't let it boil. If water boils off, add enough to keep level at about 2 cups.

Remove cannabis and water mixture from stove and let sit at room temperature for about 2 hours.

Return to stove and let simmer over very low heat for about an hour and a half.

Stir and check water level. If moisture has evaporated, add enough water to make about 2 cups.

Remove from burner and let sit at room temperature for about 2 hours.

Add oil to saucepan and stir. Return to low flame and simmer for about 1 hour and 15 minutes.

Stir. Turn off flame. Let oil and water sit at room temperature for about an hour.

Line a fine mesh strainer with cheesecloth and place over a bowl, wide-mouth jar, or measuring cup. Twist cannabis with cheesecloth, squeezing out every last drop of oil. Compost cannabis solids.

Pour mixture into freezer-proof container and place in freezer overnight.

The next day, invert container and let frozen oil and water slide out. Water and oil will have separated. Use a sharp knife to separate oil from water. Discard water.

Return oil to container, label, and store in freezer or refrigerator. To use, bring to room temperature.

Cannabis-Infused Coconut or Olive Oil

Andie Leon

Andie Leon enjoys the simple physical effort of using a potato masher to press sugar leaves into water and oil for this low-tech, low-stress method of infusing oil. "When you put your energy into that mashing, you enhance the oil with your energy," she says. Andie's method of simmering the cannabis in water softens the plant material, making it easier to strain later, and pulls out chlorophyll, which can mess with the oil's flavor and color. Andie uses cannabis flowers for stronger oil and sugar leaves for milder fare. She always infuses with her favorite cultivars, Sour Diesel and Kryptonite, when she can find them grown organically, but it's more important to her that the cannabis be organic. Just as she chooses only the freshest, healthiest foods for her restaurant, Andie uses only the best organic cannabis when she cooks for herself, friends, and catering clients. Make no mistake; *this oil is potent even when you make it with trim rather than flowers. A little goes a long way.*

Makes about 5 cups

THC per serving: 🌿 🌿 🌿 🌿

1½ cups spring water

8–10 ounces organic cannabis trim, finely ground

5 cups organic coconut, grapeseed, or extra-virgin olive oil

fine mesh strainer

cheesecloth

airtight glass jar

In a large pot, combine cannabis and water.

Over very low heat, press down on cannabis with a potato masher to extract a dark brown liquid. Simmer until water evaporates, about 5 minutes maximum.

Add oil and simmer at very low temperature for 4–5 hours.

Line a fine mesh strainer with cheesecloth and place over a bowl, wide-mouth jar, or measuring cup. Twist cannabis with cheesecloth, squeezing out every last drop of oil. Compost cannabis solids.

Transfer oil to a clean clear or dark bottle or jar with a lid or cork. Label with the type of oil and date. Store in a cool, dry place for up to a year.

Cannabis, Hemp, and Coconut Oil

Mike DeLao

Mike DeLao adds nutty hempseed oil to his coconut oil extractions because it's easily digestible, is full of essential amino acids and essential fatty acids, and has antioxidant and anti-inflammatory properties. Mike often eats a teaspoon of this oil straight or blends it into smoothies. Because hemp oil has a low smoke point, it could burn if left to simmer for hours. Mike stirs in the hemp oil after he's infused two cups of coconut oil with an ounce of fresh cannabis flowers and an ounce of cannabis sugar leaf trim in the crockpot for eight hours. (You could use two ounces of flowers for more potent oil or two ounces of trim for less potency.) Mike makes this infusion in a crockpot on low setting. Every crockpot is different, so watch the infusion carefully. You can use a candy thermometer to make sure it doesn't get hotter than 200 degrees Fahrenheit.

Makes about 3 ½ cups

THC per serving: 🌿

1 ounce cannabis flowers, finely ground

1 ounce cannabis sugar leaf trim, finely ground

2 cups coconut oil

12 ounces organic cold-pressed hemp oil

crockpot

fine mesh strainer

cheesecloth

airtight jar

Place coconut oil and cannabis in crockpot. As coconut oil warms and melts, stir cannabis into oil with a wooden spoon. Set crockpot on low.

Simmer for 8 hours, stirring occasionally.

Place cheesecloth inside strainer and pour coconut oil through while still warm to catch cannabis solids. Squeeze every last bit of oil out of cheesecloth and compost cannabis solids.

While coconut oil is still warm, pour in hemp oil and stir well with wooden spoon to combine.

Pour into labeled airtight jar and store in refrigerator for up to 6 months.

20-Minute Cannabis Olive Oil

Chris Kilham

Chris Kilham's immediate-gratification infused olive oil is a no-mess way to extract full benefits from the plant in less than an hour. When he's in a hurry, Chris grinds cannabis for this recipe in a coffee grinder, but it makes a mess of the machine. If he has the time, Chris prefers the simple meditation of laying out cannabis on a cutting board and chopping for hours until it's micro-pulverized. (Hand chopping is a luxury that adds substantially to prep time.) To make his oil, Chris stirs together a quarter ounce of ground, cured cannabis flowers and a quarter cup of extra-virgin olive oil for about twenty minutes and strains it. That's it. This easy, versatile staple can be stirred into pasta sauce, brushed on bruschetta, and used in many recipes that call for extra-virgin olive oil.

Makes about ¼ cup

THC per serving: 🌿 🌿 🌿

¼ ounce cured cannabis flowers, finely ground
¼ cup organic extra-virgin olive oil
coffee grinder
fine mesh strainer
cheesecloth

Place cannabis into a coffee grinder and grind until powdered. The cannabis will stick to the insides of the grinder, so scrape it out thoroughly. (Be careful about licking the spoon; that's some potent goo.)

Place oil into a 6" diameter shallow frying pan or saucepan. Using a wooden spoon, continuously stir cannabis into oil over very low simmer for 10–20 minutes.

Remove from heat and let cool.

Line a fine mesh strainer with cheesecloth and place over a bowl, wide-mouth jar, or measuring cup. Twist cannabis with cheesecloth, squeezing out every last drop of oil. Compost cannabis solids.

Use oil immediately or transfer oil to a clean clear or dark bottle or jar with a lid or cork. Label with the type of oil and date. Store in a cool, dry place for up to a year.

Solventless Hash and Coconut Oil

Matt Davenport

Many chefs prefer using bubble hash, extracted resin from mature cannabis flowers, for infusions because it melts easily and smoothly into oil and butter. Hash tastes less herbal because the green plant material has been removed. Matt Davenport, founder of Permalos Consulting and a regenerative cannabis grower, perfected this method of making hash oil by heating five to ten grams of finely ground bubble hash or dry sift with a cup of coconut oil and water in a crockpot or double boiler for six to seven hours. The water prevents the hash from burning too quickly. Because all crockpots are not created equal, use a candy thermometer to ensure that the oil remains between 180°F and 210°F to preserve terpenes and cannabinoids. You can choose to decarboxylate the hash before you make the infusion to make it more potent. If you do, reduce the cooking time to two or three hours. Matt suggests dribbling just enough coconut oil over the hash to cover it during decarboxylation, which will prevent scorching. Hash is potent—THC content for food-grade (half melt) bubble hash can range from 30 percent to 60 percent—and so is this oil. Start low and go slow when experimenting with this one.

Makes 1 cup

THC per serving: 🌿 🌿

5–10 grams bubble hash and/or dry sift, finely ground
1 cup organic, unrefined coconut oil, melted
2–3 cups purified water
crockpot or double boiler
candy thermometer
fine mesh strainer
cheesecloth
Mason or Ball jar

Crumble dry hash with your hands until finely ground.

If you choose to decarboxylate hash (see page 78), heat hash in oven at 200°F to 220°F for about 30–40 minutes. The material will turn a bit darker and release a slight aroma, much milder than the aroma of roasting flowers.

Melt coconut oil in crockpot or double boiler.

Stir in bubble hash and/or dry sift. Continue stirring as hash melts into oil.

Add 2–3 cups of water. You can add more water as it evaporates during heating.

Set temperature on crockpot or double boiler. Use a candy thermometer to ensure that the temperature remains between 180°F – 210°F and cook for 2–3 hours for decarboxylated hash or 6–7 hours for hash that wasn't decarboxylated. Stir occasionally.

Let cool to room temperature. The oil and water will separate, leaving oil on top. To remove water from bottom, poke a hole in oil layer and pour water out.

Line strainer with cheesecloth and pour oil through strainer into a bowl. Cautiously squeeze cheesecloth and compost hash. Pour oil into labeled jars and store in refrigerator for up to 6 months.

BUTTERS

If you can master the art of cannabis-infused butter (and these recipes make it easy), you can master cannabis cooking. Cannabis-infused butter can be refrigerated for up to two months and keeps in the freezer for up to six months, so you can make these recipes into small batches and pull out butter as needed.

Beginner's Butter

Herb Seidel

Herb Seidel's mission is to make it easy for everyone to enjoy making cannabis butter without fear. His method, tailor-made for beginners, calls for simmering a half ounce of cannabis in water for an hour, letting it cool to room temperature, then simmering it again for another hour. Herb strains out the cannabis and puts the butter in the refrigerator overnight to let the water and fat solids separate, then he simply removes the butter and discards the water the next day. Herb's method won't overcook the butter, so its structure remains relatively intact. Unlike butters that have been broken down in a long heating process, this butter performs in recipes just like the butter you've always known. Herb's technique stretches out over two days, but he says it's worth taking the time to do it right—especially if you're just learning how.

Makes about 2 cups

THC per serving: 🌿

2 cups water
½ ounce cannabis, finely ground
½ pound butter
fine mesh strainer
cheesecloth
airtight containers

Combine cannabis and water in a saucepan and bring to a boil. Simmer for 1 hour. If moisture reduces, add enough water to make 2 cups.

Remove from heat, cover, and let cool to room temperature (about 2 hours).

Return to stove, add butter to pan, and simmer for about 1 hour.

Cover and refrigerate overnight.

The next morning, place saucepan over low heat and bring to simmer. Stir. Remove from flame, cover, and let cool to room temperature.

Line a fine mesh strainer with cheesecloth and place over a bowl, wide-mouth jar, or measuring cup. Pour butter through strainer to strain out cannabis. Twist cannabis with cheesecloth, squeezing out every last drop of oil. Compost cannabis solids.

Transfer butter into airtight container. Refrigerate overnight. Butter will separate from water.

The next morning, run a knife around edges of container to loosen butter. Use knife to remove butter that has separated from water in bottom of container.

Line a fine mesh strainer with cheesecloth and strain remaining butter.

Place butter in airtight containers, label, and store in the refrigerator for up to 2 months or the freezer for up to 6 months.

Simple Cannabis Butter

Rowan Lehrman

Rowan Lehrman makes cannabis butter like she makes chicken stock. She simmers an eighth of an ounce of cannabis with a pound of butter and two cups of water for about two hours, strains it, refrigerates it overnight, and skims off a layer of solidified butter drenched in fat-soluble THC in the morning. The process is just like making chicken stock, but the chicken fat (a by-product for making *schmaltz*) isn't nearly as valuable as the cannabis butter that Rowan ends up with. (Rowan throws out the liquid, which looks and smells like it's spent time inside a bong.) She keeps this butter in a labeled airtight container in the refrigerator to enjoy on toast with honey from her bees and uses it all the time when she's infusing food.

Makes about 2 cups

THC per serving: ☙

⅛ ounce cured, well-trimmed canna-
    bis flowers or trim, finely ground
1 pound (2 cups) butter
2 cups water
strainer
cheesecloth
airtight container

Combine cannabis, water, and butter in a lidded saucepan. Stir gently with a wooden spoon over medium-low heat until water just begins to simmer.

Lower heat and place lid on pan, leaving a slight crack. Simmer for about 2 hours.

Place cheesecloth inside strainer and place over a bowl. Pour liquid butter through strainer into bowl. Squeeze cheesecloth to release all liquid. Compost ground cannabis.

Return butter to pan, place lid on tightly, and refrigerate overnight.

Store in labeled, airtight container in refrigerator for up to 2 months or freezer for up to 6 months.

Cannabis Ghee

Catjia (Catherine) Redfern

In Ayurveda, ghee is considered a *satvic* food, promoting positivity, growth, and consciousness expansion. Catjia Redfern's version, infused with cannabis, packs a euphoric double punch. Ghee, a fat used in traditional Indian cooking, is similar to clarified butter but is cooked longer so the sugars caramelize, giving it a distinctly nutty flavor. Because the milk solids are simmered out, ghee is preferable for people with lactose intolerances, and it's high in vitamins A, D, E, and K as well as fatty acids that can reduce inflammation, improve digestion, and boost energy. Indians used ghee to treat burns and swelling; it reduces inflammation when rubbed on skin. To make her infused version, Catjia simmers a pound of cultured butter for about a half hour, then strains it to remove the milk solids. (Catjia prefers European-style cultured butter, which is churned longer to decrease the moisture content and increase the butterfat content for better performance in cooking and baking.) She stirs in a half cup of finely ground cannabis flower or trim and lets the ghee infuse in a low oven. This ghee does not have to be refrigerated and keeps for up to a month and a half in a cool cupboard or at room temperature.

Makes about 2 cups

THC per serving: 🌿

1 pound (2 cups) unsalted organic
    butter (cultured is best)
½ cup cured cannabis flowers or trim,
    finely ground
fine mesh strainer
cheesecloth
Dutch oven
Glass jars or containers

Put butter in a Dutch oven or ceramic pot with a lid over low heat, keeping it below a simmer.

When butter starts to foam, reduce heat and leave uncovered for 15–30 minutes. Do not move. As water vaporizes, you will hear tiny pops and the butter will turn a clear golden color.

Let ghee cool.

Preheat oven to lowest setting (170–180°F).

Line a fine mesh strainer with cheesecloth, flour sack, or hemp cloth and place over a bowl. Pour butter through to remove milk solids. Discard them.

Return butter to Dutch oven or ceramic pot, stir in cannabis, and cover with lid.

Heat in oven for 2–3 hours.

Remove from oven and let cool.

Line fine mesh strainer with cloth and strain again, squeezing out as much oil as possible.

When ghee is completely cool, pour into glass jars or containers and cover tightly.

Label jars and store in a dry place out of sunlight for up to 6 weeks.

Sweet Bonzo Butter

Chris Kilham

In 1983, Chris Kilham made his first cannabis-infused butter as a way to get extremely high. Over the years, as he came to understand the plant's healing qualities, his intentions and techniques have evolved. His butter has become more delicious and nutritious, boosting cannabis's health benefits with the antibacterial and anti-inflammatory properties of honey. To make his butter, Chris simmers a third of an ounce of cannabis with a stick of butter over low heat for about twenty minutes, strains it, whisks in honey, and lets it solidify. Chris prefers to use a sativa for this staple, which he shares with many friends. It's lovely as a dab on toast or a dollop in a smoothie, and it works well in many recipes.

Makes about 1 cup

THC per serving: 🌿

⅓ ounce cannabis flowers
1 stick butter (1 cup)
½ cup organic honey
1 dash vanilla extract
coffee grinder

Place cannabis into a coffee grinder and grind until powdered. The cannabis will stick to the insides of the grinder. Scrape it out thoroughly; you don't want to waste that.

Place butter in a 6", shallow frying pan or saucepan. Melt butter slowly over low heat.

Slowly add ground cannabis to butter. Stir constantly with a wooden spoon while butter simmers at very low heat for 10–20 minutes.

Pour butter and cannabis mixture into a small bowl. Let cool until butter starts to solidify, about 20 minutes in the refrigerator.

Whisk in honey.

Let cool for about an hour and whisk again, ensuring butter and honey are fully blended.

Transfer to a jar, label, and store in refrigerator for up to 2 months or freezer for up to 6 months.

ALCOHOL TINCTURES

Cannabis retains its medicinal value much longer in alcohol tinctures than in other media—and alcohol tinctures last for years—a wonderful thing because a little goes a long way. Use the highest proof alcohol you can find for the most optimal extractions and go for higher-quality bottles. You don't have to use top-shelf liquor, but if you're investing the time and effort to infuse it with gourmet cannabis, why wouldn't you? Even the cannabis can't make gin and vodka from plastic bottles taste any less like rubbing alcohol.

Shaman's Tincture

Andie Leon

Andie Leon's shaman in Ecuador uses this tincture for healing rituals and often adds rosemary, cinnamon, and other medicinal plant roots to the infusion. Andie's method calls for decarboxylating an ounce of cannabis flowers for forty-five minutes in a low oven (see decarboxylation instructions on page 79), grinding them with a mortar and pestle, and letting them soak in spring water overnight. The next day, Andie combines the cannabis and water with vodka or tequila in an airtight jar and puts it in a cool, dark place to infuse for ten to twelve days. Andie shakes the tincture every day as it macerates, a daily ritual that reminds her to give thanks for the cannabis plant's many gifts.

Makes about 2 cups

THC per serving: 🌿

1 ounce cured organic cannabis
    flowers, finely ground
1 cup spring water
1 cup high-quality vodka or tequila
    (100 proof)
mortar and pestle
fine mesh strainer
cheesecloth
airtight glass jar or bottle

Preheat oven to 200°F.

Place cannabis in single layer on baking sheet and bake for 45 minutes.

Remove from oven and let cool slightly. Use a mortar and pestle to grind cannabis to powder. Put in a bowl and cover with spring water. Let soak overnight.

The next day, pour water and cannabis along with vodka or tequila into a large Mason jar. Make sure liquid completely covers cannabis. Seal with a tight-fitting lid.

Store in a cool, dark place for 10–12 days. Shake daily.

After 12 days, line a fine mesh strainer with cheesecloth and place over a bowl, wide-mouth jar, or measuring cup. Pour tincture through strainer to strain out cannabis. Twist cannabis with cheesecloth, squeezing out every last drop. Compost cannabis solids.

Pour into clean jar and seal tightly. Label and store in a cool, dark place.

Gin or Vodka Infusion

Catjia Redfern

Catjia Redfern decarboxylates cannabis in a low oven for forty-five minutes, grinds it, and shakes it up in an airtight Ball or Mason jar with a fifth of vodka or gin to get this infusion started. She stores this potion in a cupboard near the front of her pantry and shakes it every day for four days, then places the jar in a pot of hot water for thirty minutes to hasten the extraction process. Alcohol's boiling point is 173 degrees Fahrenheit, so Catjia brings the pot of water to a boil and turns it off before she heats the tincture, ensuring the alcohol doesn't boil. Taste-neutral vodka is a good choice for infusions that highlight cannabis's flavor, and gin's piney flavor profile works well with most cannabis cultivars.

Makes about 3 cups

THC per serving: 🌿

⅛ ounce cured cannabis flowers
    or trim
750 milliliters (a fifth) of vodka or gin
coffee grinder or mortar and pestle
fine mesh strainer
cheesecloth
heat-ready wide-mouth Mason jar
airtight jar or bottle

Preheat oven to 200°F.

Place cannabis in single layer on baking sheet and bake for 45 minutes.

Remove from oven and let cool slightly.

Using a mortar and pestle or a coffee grinder, grind cannabis to a powder.

Combine cannabis with vodka or gin in a labeled heat-ready wide-mouth Mason jar with an airtight lid. Shake well.

Store in a cool, dark place for at least 4 days (the longer it sits, the stronger it gets). Shake vigorously once a day.

Boil a large pot of water. Turn off heat and let cool down slightly.

Place tincture jar with closed lid in hot water. Water level shouldn't cover top of bottle. Let sit in hot water for 30 minutes.

Line a fine mesh strainer with cheesecloth and place over a bowl, wide-mouth jar, or measuring cup. Pour tincture through strainer to strain out cannabis. You may need to do this more than once to remove all the particles. You want a clear liquid. Twist cannabis with cheesecloth, squeezing out every last drop. Compost cannabis solids.

Return strained tincture to labeled airtight bottle and store in a cool, dark place for up to 1 year.

Cannabis Gin Tincture

Rabib Rafiq

Barkeep Rabib Rafiq says that getting the tincture right might be the most important part of making extraordinary cannabis cocktails. His simple technique calls for combining about ten grams of finely ground cannabis with a liter of fine-quality gin, letting it sit in a cool, dark place for twenty-four hours, and straining out the cannabis. Heating the cannabis in a low oven to convert THC-A into THC, a process known as decarboxylation, maximizes the tincture's strength. Rabib enjoys working with gin because it provides a versatile base for a range of flavors. His gin of choice is Spring44 Old Tom Gin, made from locally sourced botanicals and Rocky Mountain spring water, but that's not always easy to find. Liquor stores are stocking more quality artisanal gins with diverse flavors and botanical combinations, often made locally, so you can experiment until you find one that works well with your favorite cannabis cultivar. Cultivars with pine and eucalyptus flavor profiles such as Headband and Hawaiian Kush are excellent with gin. Rabib uses small amounts of this heady tincture when he mixes drinks, and he warns to be very careful if you choose to drink it straight. Start with no more than one milliliter or about twenty drops.

Makes about 1 liter

THC per serving: 🌿

10 grams (about ½ cup) cured
    cannabis
1 liter fine-quality gin
2 dark glass airtight bottles or jars
mortar and pestle or coffee grinder
fine mesh strainer
cheesecloth

Preheat oven to 200°F.

Place cannabis in single layer on baking sheet and bake for 45 minutes.

Remove from oven and let cool slightly.

Using a mortar and pestle or a coffee grinder, grind cannabis to a powder.

Combine gin and cannabis in glass bottle or jar with tightly fitting lid.

Let sit in a cool, dark place for 24 hours.

Line a strainer with cheesecloth to catch solids and pour liquid into bottle or jar with a tightly fitting lid.

Label jar and store in a cool, dark place for up to 1 year.

Green Cannabis Chartreuse

Rabib Rafiq

Chartreuse has been critical in Rabib Rafiq's evolution as a bartender. The naturally green liqueur—which French monks have been making from a secret recipe involving 130 alpine herbs since the eighteenth century—takes on robust flavor and color as it ages slowly in oak casks. With this tincture, Rabib adds one more alpine herb, cannabis, for a euphoric combination. To make it, he heats six grams of cured cannabis flowers in a low oven to convert THC-A into THC (a process called decarboxylation, see page 79), grinds them, and combines them with ten ounces of green chartreuse. Rabib brings the chartreuse and cannabis to a gentle boil for five minutes, then immediately transfers it to a stainless steel container (the boiling liquid will crack glass) and puts it in the freezer for fifteen minutes to accelerate cooling and prevent evaporation. Chartreuse is strong and herbaceous, and adding poorly cured cannabis or too much cannabis can turn a heavenly liqueur into moonshine. Follow Rabib's measurements; he's been experimenting with this tincture for many years. He uses it in small amounts to make cocktails. If you sip it straight, start with no more than one milliliter (about twenty drops) and sip very slowly.

Makes about 10 ounces

THC per serving: 🌿

6 grams cured cannabis flowers or trim
10 ounces green chartreuse
3 cloves
mortar and pestle or coffee grinder
lidded stainless steel container
fine mesh strainer
cheesecloth
airtight glass jar

Preheat oven to 200°F.

Place cannabis in single layer on baking sheet and bake for 45 minutes.

Remove from oven and let cool slightly.

Using a mortar and pestle or a coffee grinder, grind cannabis to a powder.

Bring chartreuse, cannabis, and cloves to boil in large saucepan. Boil gently for about 5 minutes.

Immediately transfer mixture to a stainless steel container and put in the freezer for 15 minutes.

Line a strainer with cheesecloth and pour liquid through to remove solids.

Transfer to glass bottle or jar with tightly fitting lid.

Label and store in a cool, dark place for up to 1 year.

SWEET INFUSIONS

Honey and vegetable glycerin—a clear, viscous liquid used in cosmetics, toothpaste, herbal remedies, and pharmaceuticals—are excellent solvents for extracting botanical properties from plants, including cannabis. These sweeteners can be used in coffee, tea, and cooking. (They're great for sweet iced tea.)

Cannabis Honey

Lucienne Bercow Lazarus

Infusing raw honey is Lucie Lazarus's favorite way of cooking with cannabis because she enjoys the health benefits and the effects. Raw honey delivers antimicrobial, antiseptic, antibacterial, and anti-inflammatory effects and has been recognized as a healing agent in Greek, Roman, Islamic, and Vedic texts for centuries. In Ayurvedic medicine, it's used to treat imbalances in the body, Egyptians used it to treat wounds, ancient Greeks believed it promoted long life, and the Quran praises its healing qualities. Made of glucose, fructose, and minerals including iron, calcium, phosphate, potassium, and magnesium, honey can soothe coughs, treat wounds, and possibly relieve seasonal allergies. Lucie uses cannabis honey in cooking and cocktails, and she enjoys the elixir's reputed ability to help her body metabolize the alcohol, mitigating its intoxicating effects. Legend has it that beekeepers in the Middle East put their hives near cannabis plants for honey from THC-infused pollen, but Lucie does a simple heat extraction—much like steeping tea—to make hers. She simply combines an ounce of cured, finely ground cannabis flowers or trim with eighty ounces of locally sourced, raw honey in a crockpot and cooks it on low for five hours, stirring occasionally. If you don't have a crockpot, you can put the cannabis and honey in a Dutch oven and warm it in a 180-degree oven instead. Store honey at room temperature rather than in the refrigerator so it doesn't crystallize.

Makes 80 ounces (about 80 1-ounce servings)

THC per serving: 🌿

1 ounce cured cannabis flowers
80 ounces local raw honey
crockpot or Dutch oven
cheesecloth
string
airtight glass jar

If you're using a Dutch oven, preheat oven to 180°F. Bundle cannabis in cheesecloth and tie with string.

Place bundle in crockpot or Dutch oven. Pour honey to cover. Cook on low for 5 hours, stirring with a wooden spoon a few times every hour.

After five hours, turn off crockpot or remove Dutch oven from oven and let cool for up to a day.

Remove cannabis bundle and squeeze out as much honey as you can. Compost cannabis solids.

Ladle into labeled jars. Store in a cool, dark place for up to 1 month.

Glycerin Tincture

Mike DeLao

Readily available online and in health-food stores, vegetable glycerin is naturally sweet but won't spike blood sugar, making it a good choice for diabetics. Mike DeLao puts a couple drops of this tincture under his tongue when he's not feeling well and combines it with fresh juice in morning beverages. The trick to this tincture, made with two ounces of finely ground raw cannabis flowers and four quarts of kosher or food-grade vegetable glycerin, is to keep enough water in the mix to prevent the glycerin from boiling. Mike combines the cannabis, glycerin, and a couple tablespoons of water in a crockpot and lets it simmer, stirring occasionally and adding water as necessary, for two days. Mike uses a wine press to squeeze out every last drop of glycerin from the cannabis solids once the tincture is ready, but you can wear rubber gloves and hand-squeeze it using cheesecloth. Mike warns that this tincture is extremely potent and also a diuretic. When you use this tincture, he says, "drink water, drink water, drink water!"

Makes about 4 quarts

THC per serving: 🌿

2 ounces raw cannabis flowers, finely
   ground
4 quarts kosher or food-grade
   vegetable glycerin
1 cup water
crockpot
fine mesh strainer
cheesecloth
dark glass airtight jar

Combine cannabis, glycerin, and just enough water to keep glycerin from burning (about 2–3 tablespoons) in crockpot.

Simmer on low for 48 hours, stirring often with a wooden spoon. Add water as it evaporates to keep glycerin at an even temperature. It should be as warm as possible without boiling.

When glycerin is dark amber, place cheesecloth inside strainer and place over a bowl. Pour glycerin through strainer to capture cannabis solids. Squeeze cheesecloth to get out every last drop. Compost cannabis solids.

Transfer to labeled dark glass jar with tightly fitting lid. Store in refrigerator for up to 1 year.

Cannabis Agave

Andie Leon

Andie Leon is a fan of agave because it has a low glycemic index and won't spike blood sugar the way refined sugar does. The sweetener, made from the blue agave plant (the same plant that's used to make tequila) is preferable for Andie's vegan catering clients because it doesn't come from bees, but it's high in fructose and could be problematic for people with weight problems, diabetes, or heart disease. You can make this simple infusion with honey if you're not an agave fan. To make her cold infusion, Andie simply pours a twelve-ounce bottle of raw blue agave over an eighth of an ounce of finely ground cured cannabis flowers wrapped in cheesecloth and lets it sit in a cool, dark place (in a labeled jar, of course) for at least five days (the longer it sits, the more potent it will be). After she's squeezed every last drop of agave out of the cheesecloth, Andie pours another bottle of agave over the cannabis bundle to extract whatever THC remains. The second batch is generally less potent than the first, so note that when labeling it for storage. Cannabis agave will keep in a cool, dark place for up to a month.

Makes 12 ounces

THC per serving: ⚕

⅛ ounce cured and trimmed cannabis flowers

1 12-ounce bottle raw blue agave or raw honey

coffee grinder or mortar and pestle

cheesecloth

airtight glass jar

Using a coffee grinder or a mortar and pestle, grind and crush cannabis to a fine powder.

Wrap cannabis in a cheesecloth and tie ends together to make a bundle (or tie with string). Place in a labeled airtight glass container with a tightly fitting lid.

Pour agave over cheesecloth. Seal with lid, label, and let sit in a dark place for at least 5 days.

Remove cannabis bundle and squeeze out every last drop of agave. Compost cannabis solids or use to make another batch.

Store in a cool, dark place for up to 1 month.

Cannabis Simple Syrup

Rabib Rafiq

Simple syrup, a sweetener made from sugar and water, is an essential in any well-stocked bar. To make this (as its name implies) simple infusion, Rabib combines two grams of finely ground cannabis flowers or trim with water and sugar and boils it gently for about twenty minutes, until the cannabis dissolves. Then he stirs in vegetable glycerin, a syrupy liquid sugar alcohol (available at most health-food stores and online) that adds body and improves the syrup's texture while making the syrup more potent because THC binds to it and absorbs quickly into the bloodstream. Even with only two grams of cannabis, this syrup is potent. Rabib uses about two ounces of it to make a moderate to strongly dosed cannabis cocktail, depending on the cannabis's potency. This simple syrup can be refrigerated in a labeled glass jar for up to a month.

Makes about 3 cups

THC per serving: 🍁

3 cups filtered, pure water

3 cups fine granulated sugar

2 grams cured cannabis flowers or trim, finely chopped

2 tablespoons vegetable glycerin (available at health-food stores)

fine mesh strainer

cheesecloth

airtight glass jar

Combine water and sugar in a saucepan and bring to a gentle boil. Using a wooden spoon, stir in cannabis until dissolved.

Cover pot and boil gently for 20 minutes.

Reduce temperature to medium and stir in glycerin. Let simmer for 5–6 minutes, stirring once a minute.

Remove from heat and let cool.

Place cheesecloth inside a strainer and pour syrup through it into a bowl, straining out cannabis. Compost cannabis solids.

Transfer to jar or bottle with tightly fitting lid. Label and store in a cool, dark place for up to 1 month.

MILK

Cannabis milk infusions are simple to make and great to have around for cooking, sipping, or stirring into coffee. Infusions made from organic dairy milk, cream, or any nondairy milk will keep in the refrigerator until the milk's expiration date, or you can pour cannabis-infused milk into labeled ice cube trays and freeze it so that you can pop out one or two cubes and thaw them in the refrigerator whenever you need.

Cannabis Milk

Andie Leon

You can use any kind of milk for this infusion, but Andie Leon prefers to get all the benefits of hemp seed milk when she makes it. Rich in essential fatty acids, essential amino acids, and other vital nutrients, hemp milk is a great alternative for people who can't or don't want to drink cow's milk. Andie blends two ounces of cannabis flowers or trim with sixteen ounces of hemp milk in her food processor, simmers it in a double boiler for an hour, and strains out the cannabis. Andie's infusions are strong. Use this sparingly.

Makes about 2 cups

THC per serving: 🌿 🌿 🌿

2 ounces cured cannabis flowers or trim

16 ounces hemp milk, organic dairy milk, or cream

food processor or Vitamix

double boiler

fine mesh strainer

cheesecloth

airtight jar

In a food processor or Vitamix, combine cannabis and milk. Grind for a minute.

Simmer cannabis and milk in a double boiler for an hour. Let cool.

Line a strainer with cheesecloth and place over a bowl. Pour milk through strainer to catch cannabis solids. Press down firmly on cannabis to strain as much liquid into bowl as possible. Compost cannabis solids.

Transfer to a tightly lidded jar. Seal tightly, label, and store in the refrigerator for up to a week.

Cannabis Cream

Rowan Lehrman

Rowan Lehrman has never infused cream any other way because she's always had success with this secret family recipe (from relatives in Alaska, where cannabis is now legal so the recipe doesn't have to be secret anymore). Rowan simmers an eighth of an ounce of finely ground cannabis flowers and a pint of heavy cream in a double boiler with a slightly cracked lid for about two hours and lets it sit overnight in the refrigerator before straining for a potent, consistent cannabis cream she can rely on when she cooks. Rowan uses only heavy cream because its high fat content makes it more stable and less likely to curdle as it simmers than milk or light cream. (Heavy cream will curdle if you let it boil, so watch your pot closely.) The fat also sucks up fat-soluble THC from the cannabis, which is good to remember if you're stirring this cream into coffee or substituting it for non-infused cream in recipes.

Makes about 2 cups
THC per serving: 🌿

⅛ ounce cured, well-trimmed
    cannabis flowers
1 pint (2 cups) cream
double boiler
fine mesh strainer
cheesecloth
airtight glass container

Using a wooden spoon, combine cannabis and cream in a double boiler.

Bring to a simmer, watching carefully so the cream doesn't boil.

When it has just about reached boiling, reduce heat.

Cover with lid, leaving a slight crack, and simmer on low for about 2 hours.

Remove from heat and let cool to room temperature.

Label pan and place, covered, in refrigerator overnight.

The next day, place cheesecloth inside a strainer and pour cream through strainer into a bowl. Squeeze cheesecloth and compost cannabis.

Store cream in a labeled airtight container in the refrigerator until the cream's expiration date.

BREAKFAST AND BRUNCH

You might want to use an uplifting sativa—which most people prefer for daytime use—when you wake and bake, sauté, stir, or scramble cannabis into your first meal of the day. These nutrient-packed dishes are a healthy way to start the morning, but you can enjoy them at any time of the day

Southwestern Breakfast Buzz with Spicy Black Beans

Donna Shields

Introducing cannabis into breakfast and brunch foods feels slightly decadent to Donna Shields, but she likes to surprise people. Her recipes play with contrasting layers of flavor, texture, temperature, and color, and this combination of crunchy tortilla, cool greens, and gooey egg sautéed in cannabis-infused avocado oil has it all. To make it, Donna quick-fries a tortilla and then an egg in half a tablespoon of cannabis-infused avocado oil. (You can use avocado oil for any of the cannabis oil infusions or simply substitute infused olive oil if you don't want to make a special batch.) She then tops them with cheese, lettuce, avocado, and scallions. This dish is mildly potent on its own, and a small dollop of Spicy Black Bean Spread made with two tablespoons of cannabis-infused avocado oil ups the ante. Offering the black beans on the side is a great way to let everyone control his or her own dosage early in the day.

Serves 1

THC per serving:

With Cannabis-Infused Coconut or Olive Oil (page 101): ☘

With 20-Minute Cannabis Olive Oil (page 103): ☘

With Beginner's Oil (page 100): ☘

½ tablespoon cannabis-infused avocado or olive oil
1 organic corn tortilla
1 egg

1 tablespoon cheddar cheese, grated
¼ cup tomato, chopped
¼ cup lettuce, chopped
1 tablespoon scallions, chopped
2–3 avocado slices
Spicy Black Bean Spread (recipe follows)

Heat oil in small nonstick pan. Fry tortilla on both sides until crispy. Remove tortilla from pan and cook egg in same pan to desired doneness. Place on top of tortilla.

Top with remaining ingredients.

Serve with Spicy Black Bean Spread and hot sauce on the side.

Spicy Black Bean Spread

Donna Shields

This is one of Donna Shields's staples. You can spread it on sandwiches, dip vegetables and crackers in it, stir it into soups, or freeze it in ice cube trays for perfectly dosed black bean popsicles. Avocado oil complements this recipe's Southwestern flavor profile, but it's not mandatory. Feel free to use olive oil if that's what you have on hand.

Makes 1 ¼ cups

THC per serving:

With Cannabis-Infused Coconut or Olive Oil (page 101):

With 20-Minute Cannabis Olive Oil (page 103):

With Beginner's Oil (page 100):

1 cup canned black beans, drained
¼ cup cilantro
2 tablespoons cannabis-infused avocado or olive oil
2 tablespoons red onion, minced
1 tablespoon water
1 tablespoon lime juice
1 tablespoon fresno or jalapeño pepper, finely minced
¼ teaspoon salt
food processor
airtight container

Combine all ingredients in a food processor and puree until smooth.

Transfer to an airtight container, label, and refrigerate several hours before serving.

Highland Yogi Smoothie

Chris Kilham

Chris Kilham has been teaching and practicing yoga (which he calls a delusion-shattering path to spiritual freedom) since 1971. Whether he's at home in Massachusetts or hunting for plant medicines in the Amazon, Chris practices yogic exercises known as the Five Tibetans every morning. Some days that's easier than others. When his energy and divine connection need a pick-me-up—and he has access to an uplifting organic sativa such as Permalos' sun-grown Pura Vida—Chris turns to this smoothie made with an eighth of an ounce of well-trimmed, finely chopped raw cannabis and another of his favorite herbs, maca—a radish cousin that has been used in the Peruvian Andes to improve energy, mental clarity, and sex drive for more than two thousand years. Indians blend raw cannabis into drinks during festivals, and Chris follows their lead. He doesn't decarboxylate (cook) the cannabis before he puts it into the smoothie, and he finds plenty of physical and psychoactive benefit in consuming it raw. If that doesn't work for you, you can heat the cannabis flowers on a baking sheet in a 200-degree oven for forty-five minutes to convert THC-A to THC before you use it. (Chris, a firm believer in the benefits of raw cannabis, doesn't condone this.)

Serves 4

THC per serving: ↘

⅛ ounce cured cannabis flowers, finely chopped

2 cups almond milk

1 heaping tablespoon organic maca powder (or more, to taste)

dash organic vanilla extract

⅓ teaspoon cinnamon powder

1 heaping tablespoon organic Fair Trade cocoa powder (or more, to taste)

10 almonds

4 medjool dates

1 ripe banana

blender

Put all ingredients into blender and blend until well mixed.

Pour into glasses and serve.

Label leftovers and store in the refrigerator.

Raspberry, Apple, and Pear Cannacrisp with Almonds, Cashews, and Walnuts

Leslie Cerier

Leslie Cerier's light, sugar-free fruit crisp made with a quarter cup of cannabis-infused coconut oil is delightful at any time of day. Infused with an uplifting sativa, it's a healthy way to catch a moderate buzz at breakfast. Leslie mixes a quarter cup of cannabis oil and maple syrup with rolled oats, walnuts, and cashews to make a protein-rich topping for raspberries, pears, apples, and blueberries, then bakes the crisp until the fruit is bubbly. You can use whatever combination of organic fruit looks great at your local market for this crisp and you can use frozen berries in the dead of winter.

Serves 4–6

THC per serving:

With Cannabis-Infused
Coconut or Olive Oil
(page 101): ☙ ☙ ☙

With 20-Minute Cannabis
Olive Oil (page 103): ☙ ☙

With Beginner's Oil
(page 100): ☙

¾ cup almonds
2 cups rolled oats
¼ cup plain or black walnuts, halved
¼ cup whole cashews
½ teaspoon sea salt
½ cup maple syrup

¼ cup infused extra-virgin coconut oil, melted
1½ cups fresh or frozen raspberries
1½ cups pears, sliced
1 cup apples, peeled and sliced
½ cup fresh or frozen blueberries
1 cup peach juice or other fruit juice

Preheat the oven to 375°F.

Place almonds in food processor and grind to a meal.

Transfer to large mixing bowl along with oats, walnuts, cashews, and salt. Mix well with a wooden spoon.

Add maple syrup and oil and stir until well blended.

Arrange raspberries, pears, apples, and blueberries in bottom of a 2-quart baking dish. Cover with topping, pour juice on top, and bake 30 minutes or until fruit is hot and bubbly and topping is crisp.

Spoon into bowls and serve warm.

Cannabis, Chai, and Chia Seed Breakfast Pudding

Chad Forsberg

We love the simplicity of Boulder, Colorado-based cannabis chef Chad Forsberg's breakfast pudding (which could, of course, be eaten for dessert or a late-night snack). It takes a few minutes to prep and is ready in less than an hour, so you can take a shower or check emails while the chia seeds set. Made with protein-rich almond milk and unprocessed whole-grain chia seeds—which are packed with essential fatty acids, anti-oxidants, and calcium—the pudding is a healthy way to start the day. If you're not a fan of agave, you can substitute honey for this recipe. Just add a tiny bit more almond milk if the honey makes it too thick to stir. Each serving of Chad's pudding delivers about a teaspoon of cannabis-infused coconut oil, which is a pretty nice buzz first thing in the morning. You can make it less potent by using a teaspoon of non-infused coconut oil and a teaspoon of infused oil.

Serves 2
THC per serving:
With Cannabis-Infused
*   Coconut or Olive Oil*
*   (page 101):* ⚜
With 20-Minute Cannabis
*   Olive Oil (page 103):* ⚜
With Beginner's Oil
*   (page 100):* ⚜

1 cup almond milk (regular or vanilla)
3 tablespoons chia seeds
2 teaspoons agave nectar (or honey)
1–2 chai tea bags, to taste
1 teaspoon cannabis-infused coconut oil

Bring almond milk to simmer in small saucepan. Place tea bags in almond milk and simmer very gently for 5 minutes.

Remove tea bags and stir coconut oil into warm milk.

Remove from stove and let cool to room temperature.

Stir in chia seeds and agave. Let sit for 30–45 minutes so chia seeds can absorb liquid.

Once set, refrigerate or enjoy right away.

Cannabis-Wheel Buns with Goji Berries and Chia Seeds

Andie Leon

Andie Leon's breakfast buns have two-thirds cup of cannabis butter and a one-third cup of cannabis milk, which makes them pretty potent. You can lower the dosage by using non-infused milk. The buns, sweetened with coconut sugar, include many of Andie's favorite superfoods. Bright red-orange, nutrient-rich goji berries have been used for centuries in Asia to promote long life, and studies have found that they can improve mental well-being, athletic performance, and sleep. (They may interact with certain pharmaceuticals for diabetes and high blood pressure, so talk to your doctor if you take that type of drug.) Chia seeds, tiny black and white seeds from the Mexican desert plant *Salvia hispanica,* have been used as energy boosters since Mayan times. Full of omega-3 fatty acids, fiber, antioxidants, and calcium, chia seeds add a mild, nutty flavor to these rolls.

Serves 6

THC per serving:

With Cannabis-Infused Milk (page 121) and Sweet Bonzo Butter (page 109): 🌿 🌿 🌿

With Cannabis-Infused Milk (page 121) and Beginner's Butter (page 106): 🌿 🌿 🌿

With Cannabis-Infused Milk (page 121) and Cannabis Ghee (page 108): 🌿 🌿 🌿 🌿

With Non-Infused Milk and Sweet Bonzo Butter: 10 milligrams

With Non-Infused Milk and Beginner's Butter (page 106): 🌿 🌿

With Non-Infused Milk and Cannabis Ghee (page 108): 🌿 🌿

With Cannabis-Infused Milk (page 121) and Non-Infused Butter: 🌿 🌿

⅓ cup cannabis-infused milk or non-infused low-fat milk

3 ⅓ cups organic all-purpose flour

3 teaspoons dry yeast

⅓ cup warm spring water

2 eggs

½ teaspoon Himalayan sea salt

5 tablespoons organic coconut sugar, plus more for sprinkling

⅔ cup cannabis-infused butter, softened

3 tablespoons chia seeds

2 tablespoons goji berries, washed

2 tablespoons lemon rind

1 tablespoon acai dry freeze powder

2 tablespoons agave nectar

round 9" baking pan

Continued

Cannabis-Wheel Buns with Goji Berries and Chia Seeds

Preheat oven to 350°F.

Warm milk in a small saucepan over low heat.

Sift flour, make a well in the middle, and add yeast, half of water, and half of warm milk. Let yeast ferment for 10 minutes.

Add rest of water, rest of milk, eggs, salt, agave nectar, lemon rind, acai powder, and sugar. Combine well.

Add 8½ tablespoons soft butter and knead for 10 minutes.

Cover and allow to double in size. Punch and knead for a few minutes, then roll into a ball.

Roll out dough into a ¼"-thick rectangle. Let dough rest for 10 minutes.

Melt remaining butter over low heat.

Brush dough with melted butter, sprinkle with coconut sugar, then cover entirely with chia seeds and goji berries.

Roll dough lengthwise and cut into 2" pieces.

Grease a round 9" baking pan. Place rolls into pan and pat each roll down to flatten slightly.

Bake for 20 minutes or until browned.

Remove from oven and cool on rack.

Hemp Protein and Blueberry Muffins

Andie Leon

With a third cup of cannabis-infused coconut oil, these muffins are potent. Andie Leon suggests starting by eating only a quarter of one. Instead of making this batter into muffins, sometimes she spreads it into an 11" x 7" baking pan and bakes it for about 30 minutes, then cuts it into bite-sized pieces for easier dosing. This recipe calls for hemp protein powder made from hemp seeds, which is not cheap but packs a healthy punch. A high-quality protein source because of its easy digestibility, hemp protein powder is rich in omega-3 fatty acids, fiber, and other key nutrients. Hemp, a non-psychoactive cannabis cousin, was outlawed in the United States during the Reefer Madness era. A couple of states now allow farmers to grow hemp and domestic production should soon make it more accessible to people on budgets. The hemp powder and cannabis-infused coconut oil give these muffins a distinct green color; they're great for St. Patrick's Day.

Makes 12 muffins

THC per serving:

With Cannabis-Infused Coconut or Olive Oil (page 101): ⚘ ⚘

With 20-Minute Cannabis Olive Oil (page 103): ⚘ ⚘

With Beginner's Oil (page100): ⚘

⅓ cup cannabis-infused coconut oil
½ cup coconut sugar
1 organic egg
2 organic egg yolks
1 teaspoon pure vanilla extract
1½ cups organic flour
½ cup hemp protein powder
½ teaspoon baking powder or arrowroot
¼ teaspoon Himalayan sea salt
1 cup organic milk
¼ pint blueberries

Preheat oven to 375°F. Grease muffin tin.

Use an electric mixer to beat oil and sugar for 2 minutes. Add whole egg and yolks and beat, rubbing mixture against sides of bowl, until creamy and fluffy. With mixer on low, gently beat in vanilla.

Sift flour, hemp powder, baking powder, and salt. Gradually add flour mixture to egg mixture, alternating with milk, until well combined.

Gently fold in blueberries.

Spoon mixture into muffin tin. Bake for 35–40 minutes.

Remove muffins from oven and let cool.

Cannabis Hemp Seed Scones

Andie Leon

Andie Leon believes in hemp seeds' healing power. She throws the nutritious, protein-rich seeds into almost everything she makes, and she loves pairing them with their psychoactive cousin. These hemp seed scones made with a cup of cannabis-infused almond milk (you can substitute hemp or dairy milk if you prefer) are a classic for Andie's catering clients. She can tailor the dosage to different clients' needs by making them in varying sizes. Andie infuses almond milk just as she would hemp milk (see her recipe on page 121). The almond milk takes an hour to infuse, so give yourself time or make it ahead. These scones have a smaller amount of fat than muffins, so you won't absorb as much THC when you eat them. That makes them great in the morning, but it still pays to make smaller scones as you figure out your dosage. If you have access, a nutty, energetic sativa such as Super Silver Haze is the perfect almond milk infusion for this recipe.

Makes 12 scones

THC per serving:

With Sweet Bonzo Butter
(page 109): 🌿 🌿 🌿

With Beginner's Butter
(page 106): 🌿 🌿 🌿

With Cannabis Ghee
(page 108): 🌿 🌿 🌿

3½ cups organic all-purpose flour
2 teaspoons gluten-free baking powder
½ teaspoon Himalayan pink salt
2 tablespoons coconut sugar or maple sugar
2 ounces cannabis-infused butter
1 cup Cannabis Almond Milk, plus extra for glazing (substitute almond milk for hemp milk in Cannabis Hemp Milk recipe on page 121)
⅓ cup hemp seeds
parchment paper

Preheat oven to 420°F.

Sift flour, baking powder, and salt into a medium bowl. With clean hands, rub butter into flour mixture until it resembles bread crumbs. Add sugar.

Make a well in the middle of the bowl. Add milk and mix until it makes soft dough.

Place dough on a floured flat surface and roll out to ½". Cut out scones with a round cookie cutter or cut into triangles. Place on a baking tray with parchment paper.

Brush with milk and sprinkle tops with hemp seeds.

Bake for 10 minutes or until golden. (Start checking smaller scones after 7 minutes.)

Place scones on baking rack to cool. Store in a labeled airtight container.

Teff Cannabis Waffles

Leslie Cerier

Teff is a tiny grain with a mild, nutty flavor that grows predominantly in Idaho in the United States and in Ethiopia. High in protein, calcium, and amino acids, teff is ground into a gluten-free flour alternative that can be used to make all sorts of baked goods. Its name comes from the Greek phrase, *maskai teff,* which means "the grass of love." Leslie Cerier can't think of anything better to pair with cannabis, that other grass of love. She infuses these healthy waffles with three tablespoons of cannabis-infused coconut oil for a slight morning buzz. If the potency is a little on the mild side, serve these waffles with optional cannabis-infused butter. Infuse the oil or butter with a fruity sativa such as Pineapple Express or Sweet Island Skunk if you have access to them.

Serves 3

THC per serving:

Cannabis-Infused Coconut or Olive Oil (page 101): 🌿 🌿 🌿

With 20-Minute Cannabis Olive Oil (page 103): 🌿 🌿 🌿

With Beginner's Oil (page 100): 3 milligrams

With Bonzo Butter (page 109): 🌿

With Beginner's Butter (page 106): 🌿

4 eggs
¾ cup apple juice or cider
3 tablespoons cannabis-infused extra-virgin coconut oil or butter
3 tablespoons maple syrup
1 tablespoon vanilla extract
1½ cups teff flour
1 tablespoon baking powder
½ teaspoon sea salt
waffle iron

Preheat waffle iron.

Whisk eggs in a large bowl. Stir in juice, oil, maple syrup, and vanilla. Add flour, baking powder, and salt. Stir until well combined.

Brush top and bottom surface of waffle iron with oil, then ladle in enough batter to cover bottom surface of iron. Close waffle iron and cook until steaming stops or the waffle is golden brown.

Serve immediately or keep cooked waffles in a warm oven until ready to serve.

Lemon, Poppy Seed, and Cannabis Pancakes

Grace Gutierrez

Opium poppy seeds—believed to promote sleep, fertility, and abundance—have been used in food and medicine for thousands of years. Delivering calcium, iron, and zinc, the crunchy seeds pair perfectly with tart lemon and one and three-quarters cups of cannabis-infused almond milk in these pancakes inspired by Grace Gutierrez's favorite breakfast muffin. If you can, make the cannabis-infused almond milk the night before. It has to simmer for 45 minutes and come to room temperature before you can use it in the pancake batter, and that's no fun when people are waiting for pancakes. (You can also use the Cannabis Milk recipe on page 121.) Grace recommends using at least a gram of finely ground, cured cannabis flowers, preferably a sweet sativa such as OG Kush, Pineapple Express, or Maui Waui, for the almond milk. You can make pancakes larger or smaller to control dosage.

Makes 12 large pancakes
THC per pancake: ↘

1 32-ounce carton almond milk
2 grams cured cannabis, finely ground
3 cups fresh strawberries
¾ cup granulated sugar, divided
2 cups all-purpose flour
1½ teaspoons baking powder
½ teaspoon baking soda
¼ teaspoon salt
⅓ cup poppy seeds
zest of 2 lemons
2 tablespoons fresh lemon juice
¼ cup plain Greek yogurt
2 eggs
1 teaspoon vanilla
coconut oil or butter for cooking pancakes
cheesecloth

To infuse almond milk, stir together cannabis and almond milk in a saucepan and bring to simmer. Let simmer for about 45 minutes, covered, stirring every 10 minutes or so. Remove from heat and set aside to cool.

Layer about 4 pieces of cheesecloth over a small bowl and secure with a rubber band around the edge. Press very gently to slope the cheesecloth slightly into the glass. Pour milk and cannabis over cheesecloth. Wrap cheesecloth around cannabis flowers and press out all liquid. If making this ahead of time, transfer to a jar or bottle with a tightly fitting lid, label, and refrigerate until ready to use.

Before you make pancake batter, cut strawberries into small pieces and mix with ¼ cup of the sugar in a small bowl. Set aside.

To make pancakes, stir flour, baking powder, baking soda, salt, ½ cup of sugar, and poppy seeds in a large bowl. In a separate medium-sized bowl, mix together lemon zest and juice, 1¾ cups of the infused almond milk, Greek yogurt, eggs, and vanilla.

Combine wet ingredients with dry ingredients. Mix with a wooden spoon until only a few clumps are left in the batter.

Using a ¼-cup measuring cup, pour batter onto greased griddle or pan at medium-high heat. When the pancakes start to bubble around the edges (about 3 minutes), flip and cook other side.

Remove from griddle and serve with syrup and strawberries.

Baked French Toast with Cannabis, Honey, and Pecan Sauce

Herb Seidel

Some days call for breakfast decadence, and Herb Seidel's french toast baked in a quarter cup of cannabis butter is just the ticket. (This recipe is pretty spectacular at midnight, too.) You have to do a little preparation the night before, but that means you don't have to get up quite as early the next day to wake your loved ones to the smell of roasting pecans and gooey brown sugar. With a quarter cup of cannabis butter, this french toast is wake-and-bake potent. Warn your loved ones that it's decadent breakfast day and prepare for them to love you.

Serves 2

THC per serving:

With Bonzo Butter (recipe on page 109): 🌿 🌿

With Beginner's Butter (recipe on page 106): 🌿

With Cannabis Ghee (recipe on page 108): 🌿 🌿

4 large eggs, beaten

¾ cup half-and-half

½ tablespoon brown sugar

1 teaspoon vanilla extract

4 2"-thick slices day-old french bread or crusty bread

¼ cup cannabis-infused butter, cut into pieces

¼ cup brown sugar

¼ cup honey

¼ cup maple syrup

¼ cup pecans, chopped

Combine eggs, half-and-half, brown sugar, and vanilla extract in a small bowl.

Pour half the mixture into a baking dish. Place bread in baking dish and top with other half of mixture, making sure all parts of bread are saturated. Cover and place in refrigerator overnight.

The next morning, preheat oven to 350°F.

Put butter in a 13" x 9" x 2" baking dish and set in oven. When melted, stir in brown sugar, honey, maple syrup, and pecans.

Set soaked bread slices on top of pecan mixture.

Bake for 30–35 minutes, until puffed and golden brown

Remove from oven. Use a spatula to invert bread slices onto plates. Pour excess juices and pecans on top.

Morning Beverages

The "hippie speed ball" (coffee and a spliff) has been popular for decades. With these simple cannabis-laced recipes for chai, coffee, and a traditional Indian beverage known as bhang, you can skip the spliff.

Good Morning Sativa Chai

Chris Kilham

Chai, the honey-sweet tea that has headlined coffee bistro chalkboards in the West for a couple decades, originated in ancient India. The traditional mixture of Ayurvedic healing spices (ginger, cardamom, cloves, and cinnamon) got combined with strong black tea and milk when the British ruled India in the nineteenth century. This chai made with a gram of finely ground cured cannabis flowers, whole milk, black tea, and chai spices is Chris Kilham's contribution to the beverage's evolution. Chris was inspired to combine masala chai spices and cannabis after he watched an Indian *sadhu* (holy man) prepare cannabis for consumption. Chris says the *sadhu* mashed and ground a large pile of fresh cannabis leaves with cardamom and black pepper on a stone to make a fine mash. The *sadhu* dried the preparation in the sun and smoked it. Chris prefers to blend the flavors into this drink, which is euphoric without being overwhelming. Chris doesn't decarboxylate the cannabis before he simmers it with milk for this recipe, and he finds plenty of physical and psychoactive benefit in consuming it raw, especially in the morning. If that doesn't work for you, put the cannabis flowers in a single layer on a baking sheet, cover with foil, and heat in a 200-degree oven for forty-five minutes to convert THC-A to THC before you use it.

Serves 2

THC per serving: 🌿

1 gram cured cannabis flowers, finely chopped

½ cup organic whole milk

2 cups water

2 bags organic black tea (your favorite)

1 tablespoon honey

thumb-sized piece fresh ginger root, peeled

5 cardamom pods, slightly crushed

5 whole cloves

finger-sized cinnamon stick, broken into pieces

double boiler

fine mesh strainer

cheesecloth

In a medium saucepan over a double boiler, stir cannabis into milk. Stir constantly with a wooden spoon, maintaining a low simmer, for 10 minutes.

Meanwhile, combine water, tea bags, ginger, cardamom, cloves, and cinnamon in a saucepan. Simmer slowly for 5 minutes.

Add milk mixture and honey to tea mixture and stir over low heat for a couple of minutes.

Place cheesecloth inside a strainer and pour liquid through to strain out solids. Compost cannabis solids.

Pour into cups and enjoy.

If storing, let cool before pouring into labeled jars with tight lids. Store in the refrigerator for up to 1 week.

Ganja Java Go-Juice

Chris Kilham

Chris Kilham has declared (on *Fox News, The Doctor Oz Show,* and elsewhere) that coffee is a health food, and studies back him up. Full of antioxidants, coffee improves digestion and enhances mental alertness. For added benefit, sometimes Chris stirs sativa-infused milk into his morning or afternoon cup. Chris uses a gram of raw, cured cannabis and an equal mix of Raven's Brew Deadman's Reach and Allegro Organic Mexican Zarazoga coffee beans for this simple pick-me-up. He uses a Melitta slow-drip filter to make his coffee, but any method will do. Chris doesn't decarboxylate the cannabis before he simmers it with milk for this recipe. If that doesn't work for you, heat the cannabis flowers on a baking sheet in a 200-degree oven for forty-five minutes to convert THC-A to THC before you use it.

Makes 2 generous cups

THC per serving: ✺

2 cups pure filtered water
2 large handfuls whole coffee beans, finely ground
½ cup organic whole milk
1 gram cured cannabis, finely ground
sugar or honey, to taste (optional)
fine mesh strainer
cheesecloth

Boil water. Place finely ground coffee beans in unbleached paper filter inside drip filter. Pour boiling water through to make 2 cups of coffee.

Heat milk in a saucepan over low heat. Heating slowly, bring to lowest simmer, stirring constantly with a wooden spoon.

Stir cannabis into milk in saucepan. Stir continuously with wooden spoon over lowest simmer for 10 minutes. Remove milk from stove.

Line fine mesh strainer with cheesecloth and pour liquid through to strain out cannabis. Compost cannabis solids.

Add strained milk to coffee. Sweeten if desired.

Bhang Ki Thandai

Catjia Redfern

Catjia Redfern first experienced *bhang*—a paste made from ghee and cannabis leaves and flowers that Hindus believe to be a gift from Lord Shiva—during Holi Day in Rajasthan. Indian tradition holds that *bhang* makes the mind and body more alert and promotes gaiety. In 1894, the Indian Hemp Drugs Commission Report said it "quickens fancy, deepens thought, and braces judgment." *Bhang* is combined with spices, seeds, nuts, and milk to make creamy, refreshing *Bhang Ki Thandai,* the drink that Catjia now makes at home, usually for special celebrations. Catjia steeps a cup of finely ground fresh cannabis flowers (or a half cup of dried) in simmering water, then adds a quarter cup of cannabis-infused *ghee* to make the *bhang* paste. She blends the paste with almonds, spices, milk (you can substitute almond or hemp milk), and sugar to make a strong drink. Dosages can be diluted by adding milk to the glass when serving. Note that the almonds have to soak the night before you make this drink.

Serves 16–18

THC per serving: 🌿 🌿 🌿

1 cup fresh cannabis flowers or ½ cup dried flowers

1½ cups water

¼ cup Cannabis Ghee (recipe on page 108)

8 teaspoons organic cane or coconut sugar

½ cup almonds, soaked overnight in water, skins removed

2 teaspoons black peppercorns

4 tablespoons rose petals or 2 tablespoons rosewater

1 teaspoon anise seed

1 teaspoon cloves

10 green cardamom pods

½ cup pumpkin, sunflower, watermelon, cucumber, or cantaloupe seeds

½ cup hulled hemp seeds

16 cups milk

fine mesh strainer

cheesecloth

food processor, Vitamix, or mortar and pestle

To make *bhang,* grind fresh or dried cannabis leaves and flowers to a fine powder with mortar and pestle or blender.

Stir cannabis into ½ cup water in a saucepan over medium-high heat and bring nearly to a boil. Just before it boils, lower flame and steep over low heat for 15 minutes.

Remove from stove and cool to room temperature.

Stir ghee into cannabis and water until it forms a thin paste. Stir in 4 teaspoons of sugar until fully integrated into paste.

Place cheesecloth inside a fine mesh strainer. Strain paste through strainer to remove solids. Set aside.

Combine almonds and all the spices and blend in a food processor or Vitamix or mash using a mortar and pestle. Add all the seeds and blend or mash until well integrated into spice mixture.

Add 1 cup water and *bhang* paste. Blend or mash until mixture becomes a thick integrated paste.

Blend in 4 teaspoons sugar, then milk.

Serve warm, chilled, or at room temperature. Keep leftovers in a tightly sealed, labeled jar or bottle in the refrigerator for as long as the milk holds up.

JUICES

Since he began juicing raw fruits, vegetables, and cannabis flowers several years ago, Mike DeLao has felt better every day. Juicing is an important part of Mike's cleansing diet, which he believes heals the body by eliminating its need to expel energy on digestion. Mike uses an Omega juicer, and everyone who juices seems to have a strong personal preference for what's best. Centrifugal juicers, which shred ingredients and strain the bits through a strainer, are less expensive than masticating juicers, which chew up ingredients to extract juice, causing less oxidation. Always drink fresh juice immediately, if possible, and on an empty stomach so the vitamins and minerals can go straight to your bloodstream. If you don't drink the juice right away, store it in a labeled airtight container in the refrigerator and drink within forty-eight hours.

Raw Energy Cannabis Juices

Mike DeLao

Mike DeLao keeps a special patch of cannabis in his backyard that he grows without nutrients (to keep chemicals out of his juices), and every morning he picks two or three good-sized flowers (weighing about an eighth of an ounce) to throw into his juicer along with greens, citrus, fruits, and vegetables. Because Mike's goal is to deliver cannabis's nutrients and healing properties rather than a tremendous high, he doesn't decarboxylate the cannabis before he juices it. He believes cannabis is most healing and nutritious when it's just been picked. The cannabis resins can gum up a juicer, he warns, so wash down the flowers with citrus or another fruit with lots of juice. Mike alternates greens and fruits when he's feeding them into the juicer; you can play around with ingredients based on what's available and your personal preferences. Mike likes bitter greens because he believes they tonify and heal the body and stimulate digestion, and he shies away from too many fruits, which add a lot of sugar and fructose to the mix.

Green Detox

Makes 1 16-ounce serving

⅛ ounce raw cannabis flowers
1 bunch parsley
2 leaves kale
2 cucumbers
1 garlic clove
2 stalks celery
4 grapefruits, peeled
small piece ginger, peeled
small piece of turmeric
¼ cup spinach

Juice parsley, kale, cannabis, and cucumbers.
Add remaining ingredients and juice.
Serve chilled.

Cannabis, Cucumber, and Lime

Makes 1 16-ounce serving

⅛ ounce raw cannabis flowers

½ bunch cilantro

1 mango, peeled

2 limes, peeled

2 oranges, peeled

½ jalapeño, seeds removed

¼ honeydew melon

Alternate feeding cannabis and cilantro into juicer until juiced.

Add remaining ingredients and juice.

Serve chilled.

Cannabis, Citrus, Ginger, and Kale

Makes 1 16-ounce serving

⅛ ounce raw cannabis flowers

1 blood orange, peeled

1 orange, peeled

1 lemon, peeled

½"-piece fresh ginger, peeled

2 leaves kale

3 leaves collard greens

Feed all ingredients into juicer, alternating between cannabis and other ingredients.

Serve chilled.

Sweet Chard and Cannabis

Makes 1 16-ounce serving

⅛ ounce raw cannabis flowers

3 leaves rainbow or Swiss chard

2 kiwi fruits

¼ honeydew melon, rind removed

1 lime, peeled

3 stalks celery

2 green apples

Feed cannabis and chard into juicer.

Once those are juiced, feed in kiwi, melon, and lime.

Add celery and apples. Juice.

Serve chilled.

The Green Standard

Makes 1 16-ounce serving

4 green apples

2 large leaves kale

3 bunches parsley

⅛ ounce raw cannabis flowers

½"-piece ginger

½ lemon

juicer

Alternately feed 2 apples, kale, and parsley into juicer.

Follow with remaining ingredients, alternating with remaining 2 apples. Juice.

Remove foam and serve chilled.

Sunshine and Citrus Cannabis Juice

The citrus in this juice breaks down and activates the glycerin-based tincture, which is stirred in at the end. Mike uses a couple drops of tincture, but you can tailor the dose to your needs. You can also substitute any vegetables you have on hand, though Mike believes this combination provides optimal nutrition and taste.

Serves 1

THC per serving: ↘

2 Meyer lemons, peeled and cut into wedges

2–4 kale leaves

2 whole tangerines, peeled

1 carrot

1 cucumber

1 celery stalk

1 whole ginger root, peeled

½ yellow beet

½ red beet

1–2 drops Glycerin Tincture (recipe on page 117), or preferred dose

juicer

Feed all ingredients into juicer and blend.

Let juice sit for a minute.

Pour preferred dose of glycerin tincture into bottom of glass.

Pour juice into glass and stir vigorously to blend.

APPETIZERS

Cannabis shines in starters such as bruschetta drizzled with cannabis-infused oil and anything dusted in cannabis butter-soaked breadcrumbs. Appetizers are great venues for stronger-tasting cannabis cultivars with citrusy overtones such as the sativa-dominant Lemon Skunk, but careful chefs understand that the party's just getting started and dose appetizers accordingly. It takes anywhere from twenty minutes to a couple of hours for cannabis to take effect after you eat it, which means diners will likely be feeling the appetizers' effects in time to appreciate dessert.

Magic Herb Mushrooms Stuffed with Garlic-Herb Goat Cheese

Donna Shields

Donna Shields likes to introduce people to cannabis food by offering them dishes they're already familiar with, and who doesn't love these cocktail party classics? Donna's mushrooms sautéed in cannabis-infused olive oil and stuffed with garlic-herb goat cheese are compact and contained, so you don't overindulge. The simple recipe calls for two to four tablespoons of cannabis oil for four people, so you might think your chances of overindulging are pretty low. But Donna points out that measurements can be deceiving. The mushrooms absorb a lot of cannabis oil, and the fats in the cream cheese and goat cheese pull out more fat-soluble THC. Donna suggests eating just one mushroom the first time you try them, especially if you're new to cannabis food. You'll know for next time if you can handle two, and it's better not to find out the hard way. (This is great advice that's hard to follow. Donna's mushrooms are delicious.)

Serves 4–8

THC per serving:

With Cannabis-Infused Coconut or Olive Oil (page 101):

With 20-Minute Cannabis Olive Oil (page 103):

With Beginner's Oil (page 100):

8 ounces (about 8–10) baby portabella mushrooms

2–4 tablespoons cannabis-infused extra-virgin olive oil

3 tablespoons garlic-herb goat cheese

2 tablespoons cream cheese

fresh tarragon, finely chopped

Remove stems from mushrooms. Over medium heat, warm oil and heat both sides of mushroom caps until slightly softened, about 5 minutes. The mushrooms absorb a lot of oil; you may need to add more to the pan as they heat.

In a bowl, thoroughly combine goat and cream cheese.

Fill mushroom caps with cheese mixture.

Broil for 2–3 minutes until lightly browned. Garnish with tarragon.

Wild Mushroom, Cannabis, and Hazelnut Pâté with Apple, Bacon, and Sage

Rowan Lehrman

From early spring through early winter, a local picker delivers baskets full of chanterelles, black morels, and other indigenous mushrooms gathered in nearby woods and hillsides to Rowan Lehrman's restaurant on the Oregon coast. That bounty inspired this pâté made with wild mushrooms, eight tablespoons of cannabis-infused butter, apples, bacon, mascarpone, hazelnuts, and dehydrated dried mushrooms (porcinis, shitakes, or whatever Rowan has on hand). Rowan sautés apple, sweet onion, and wild mushrooms in bacon grease, then pours a half cup of brandy into the pan to soak up and dissolve all the yummy bits from the bottom of the pan (a process called deglazing). The resulting sauce is a rich base for this liverless pâté that stands up to but doesn't overwhelm the cannabis. Saturated in flavor, the pâté should be savored. It's great for a party, Rowan says, because people won't eat too much and get too high. During the few months of the season when Rowan can't get fresh wild mushrooms, she substitutes baby portabellas without a problem. The hazelnuts and dried mushrooms need to soak for an hour or overnight, so plan accordingly.

Serves about 12

THC per serving:

With Bonzo Butter
(page 109): ☘

With Beginner's Butter
(page 106): ☘

With Cannabis Ghee
(page 108): ☘

½ cup hazelnuts, chopped
½ cup dried mushrooms

4 strips quality applewood-smoked bacon
1 medium sweet onion, peeled and chopped
1 tart green apple, peeled, cored, and chopped
5 fresh sage leaves, finely chopped
freshly ground nutmeg, to taste
8 ounces fresh wild mushrooms, cleaned and chopped
½ cup brandy or cognac
4 ounces mascarpone cheese
4 ounces (8 tablespoons) cannabis-infused butter, room temperature
kosher salt and freshly ground pepper, to taste
crusty bread for serving
fine mesh colander or sieve
food processor

Continued

Wild Mushroom, Cannabis, and Hazelnut Pâté with Apple, Bacon, and Sage

Combine hazelnuts and dried mushrooms in a medium-sized heatproof bowl and cover with boiling water. Let stand for at least one hour or overnight in the refrigerator.

Meanwhile, place bacon in your largest skillet and cook until crisp. Remove bacon from pan and set aside, leaving the fat.

Place onion and apple in pan with reserved fat and gently sauté over medium-low heat until onion is translucent and apple is tender, taking care not to let the mixture caramelize.

Add sage, nutmeg, and wild mushrooms and continue to cook until mushrooms start to release moisture. Raise heat to medium-high and pour brandy into pan to deglaze it, scraping the bits from the bottom and continuing to cook until most of the liquid is absorbed.

Remove from heat and let cool completely to room temperature or refrigerate for a half hour.

Drain hazelnut-dried mushroom mixture in a fine mesh colander or sieve, or place in a clean dishtowel and gently press or wring out water.

Place drained hazelnut-dried mushroom mixture in the bowl of a food processor. Pulse a few times to achieve a coarse paste.

With a slotted spoon, transfer cooled bacon, apple, and fresh mushroom mixture to food processor and pulse.

Add mascarpone and cannabis butter and purée until smooth, scraping down the sides of the bowl as necessary, until no white streaks of cheese remain. Add salt and pepper to taste.

Transfer pâté to a crock and garnish with edible flowers, fresh herbs, and/or fresh cannabis leaves.

Leftovers keep in a labeled, airtight container in the refrigerator for several days.

Fromage Fondue Infusee

Catjia (Catherine) Redfern

Catjia Redfern's twenty-first-century rendition of the centuries-old dish invented in the Swiss Alps to use up old cheese and stale bread includes half a cup of cannabis-infused ghee swirled into sauce made with white wine, semi-firm Gruyere and Comte cheeses, and pungent Appenzeller, a spicy raw milk semi-hard cheese brined in alpine herbs, roots, seeds, and flowers. The equally pungent cheese and cannabis mellow but don't overwhelm each other in this fondue that smells *outre* and tastes incredible. The trick to the fondue is keeping it smooth and melted without vaporizing the THC or scorching the cheese. You can't let it boil. That's easier in a good ceramic fondue pot with a flat bottom and a gel or electric burner, if you have one, but it can be managed with a heavy-bottomed saucepan or double boiler on the stove. Though the cheese gets very hot (so be careful), the fondue solidifies quickly and must be kept warm over a heating candle or electric burner for serving. You can serve it with cubes of a good Boule or gluten-free bread, but Catjia keeps it local and fresh with an edible palette of that season's vegetables and fruits. (She's partial to golden or Chioggia beets, scallions, radishes, tart apples, sweet peppers, roasted Anaheim chiles, and steamed celeriac root.) Encourage guests to make figure eights with their vegetables as they dip them to keep the cheese stirred and to start with one or two scoops of this potent cheese if they're new to cannabis food. With a little more wine added, leftovers warm up well in a double boiler or microwave. (The kitchen, and possibly the whole house, will reek of ripe cheese and roasted cannabis if you warm it in the microwave.)

Serves 4 or more

THC per serving: 🌿 🌿

2 garlic cloves, peeled

1 cup white wine

2 tablespoons wheat-free flour (amaranth flour strongly suggested)

½ pound Gruyere cheese, grated

½ pound Comte cheese, grated

¼ pound Appenzeller cheese, grated

½ cup Cannabis Ghee, room temperature (recipe on page 108)

fondue pot (or double boiler or heavy pot)

electric burner or heating candle (if not using fondue pot)

fondue forks

Rub inside of fondue pot or a heavy pot with garlic cloves.

Pour wine into pot and bring to a simmer over medium-low heat on the stove.

Mix flour and shredded cheeses in a bowl. Add a small amount of mixture to wine in pot, then a fine drizzle of cannabis-infused ghee. Alternate adding cheese and ghee, stirring constantly in a figure eight movement with a wooden spoon. Whisk cheese with the spoon and wait until cheese is completely melted before adding more cheese and ghee. If mixture is too thin, add more flour.

When cheese, wine, and ghee are fully blended, lower heat and transfer to portable burner. Serve with vegetables or bread cubes.

Baked Artichoke, Crab, and Cannabis Dip

Herb Seidel

Herb Seidel's artichoke dip has less fat and delivers more fun and fresh flavor than the irresistible cheese and artichoke blender goo that's earned a rightful place at every neighborhood and office party potluck. For his artichoke dip, Herb folds peppers sautéed in half of a tablespoon of cannabis-infused olive oil along with artichoke hearts, crab meat, and almonds into mayonnaise, Parmesan cheese, and a quarter cup cannabis-infused butter for a tasty, potent dip that's nothing like the one your grandma made. With mayonnaise, butter, and Parmesan cheese, the dip has a good amount of fat (still less than Grandma's), which ups your absorption of fat-soluble THC when you eat it. Start with one small bite on a tortilla chip, toast point, or carrot stick and wait to see how it hits you before you scoop up more. Because of the fresh crabmeat, this dip doesn't save well if you have leftovers. Make it when you know you'll have a crowd of experienced adult eaters to finish it off. We do not advise bringing it to the next office party, no matter where you work.

Serves 4-6

THC per serving:

With Bonzo Butter (page 109):

With Beginner's Butter (page 106):

With Cannabis Ghee (page 108):

½ tablespoon cannabis-infused olive oil

½ small green pepper, finely chopped

½ small red pepper, finely chopped

1 14-ounce can artichoke hearts, finely chopped

½ jalapeño, finely chopped (optional)

¾ cup mayonnaise

¼ cup cannabis-infused butter, soft

¼ cup scallions, sliced thin

½ cup freshly grated Parmesan cheese

2 teaspoons Worcestershire sauce

½ teaspoon celery salt

½ pound crab meat, picked through to remove shells

¼ cup sliced almonds, toasted

tortilla chips, toast points, or carrot sticks for serving

6"x 9" glass or ceramic baking dish

Preheat oven to 375°F and grease baking dish.

In a small skillet, sauté olive oil and bell peppers until tender.

In a large bowl, combine bell peppers with artichokes, jalapeño, mayonnaise, butter, scallions, Parmesan cheese, Worcestershire, celery salt, crab meat, and almonds. Mix well.

Place mixture in baking dish and sprinkle with toasted almonds.

Bake for 25–30 minutes or until golden brown.

Let cool slightly (so that it's safe to handle) and serve with tortilla chips, toast points, or carrot sticks.

Cannabis Ceviche

Herb Seidel

Ancient Incans in Peru and Ecuador made *ceviche*—fresh fish or shellfish marinated in citrus juice—as a way to prepare and preserve their catch without heat as soon as they brought it in. Most seafood-dependent cultures, especially in Latin America, have some version of fish "cooked" in juice from acidic fruits, which turns it firm and opaque, with supporting ingredients and spices varying from culture to culture. For his version, Herb Seidel combines a quarter of a cup of cannabis-infused olive oil with lemon and lime juice, onions, tomatoes, and chunks of fresh snapper fillet (whatever firm white fish is best in your area will do) and lets the lemon juice cook the fish, which soaks up cannabis oil as the mixture sits in the refrigerator overnight. To accompany this light, refreshing dish—and up the dosage—Herb lightly sprays cannabis-infused olive oil onto tortilla chips, sprinkles them with cumin, paprika, salt, and garlic, and bakes them until golden brown in a 350-degree oven (about 5 minutes).

Serves 6-8

THC per serving:

*With Cannabis-Infused
    Coconut or Olive Oil
    (page 101):* 🌿 🌿

*With 20-Minute Cannabis
    Olive Oil (page 103):* 🌿 🌿

*With Beginner's Oil
    (page 100):* 🌿

2 pounds firm, fresh red snapper
    fillets (or other firm-fleshed fish),
    completely deboned and cut into
    ½" pieces

½ cup fresh-squeezed lime juice
½ cup fresh-squeezed lemon juice
¼ cup cannabis-infused olive oil
½ red onion, finely diced
1 cup fresh seeded tomatoes, chopped
1 serrano chili, seeded and finely diced
2 teaspoons salt
dash ground oregano
dash Tabasco or light pinch cayenne pepper

Gently stir together ingredients until thoroughly mixed. Make sure oil soaks into fish. Refrigerate in a covered, labeled airtight container overnight.

Serve with chips.

Cannabis, Ginger, and Arame Eggrolls with Goji Berries

Leslie Cerier

Leslie Cerier's eggrolls made with two tablespoons of cannabis-infused sesame oil are nutritional power-houses. (You can use any of the oil recipes to infuse sesame oil, or you can use non-infused sesame oil for less potency.) Cabbage and collards are full of Vitamin C, and goji berries deliver antioxidants. Arame (or sea oak), a sweet, mineral-rich brown algae from Japan, delivers fiber, vitamin A, calcium, and magnesium. Sometimes Leslie eschews eggroll wrappers and stuffs this filling into pitas or piles it on top of fresh greens. When she's feeling adventurous, Leslie makes these eggrolls more potent by frying them in cannabis-infused virgin (unrefined) coconut oil. Because the virgin coconut oil has a lower smoke point of 350 degrees Fahrenheit, it won't burn off THC (which begins to degrade if food is cooked above 350 degrees). Heat the coconut oil just enough to fry the eggrolls and use a high-THC cultivar such as Bruce Banner, a hybrid bred from OG Kush and Strawberry Diesel, for the fry oil if you can get it.

Serves 6
THC per serving:
With Cannabis-Infused
    Coconut or Olive Oil
    (page 101): 🌿
With 20-Minute Cannabis Olive
    Oil (page 103): 🌿
With Beginner's Oil
    (page 100): 🌿

⅓ cup arame
¼ cup dried goji berries
1 14-ounce package extra-firm tofu, diced
4 cups green cabbage or collard greens,
    sliced thin
1½ cups cilantro, coarsely chopped
1 cup scallions, coarsely chopped
2 tablespoons cannabis-infused sesame
    oil (optional)
2 tablespoons tamari
1½ tablespoons ginger, peeled and grated
1 tablespoon maple sugar or maple syrup
20 eggroll wrappers (6" squares)

¼ cup cannabis-infused extra-virgin coconut oil (or
    non-infused oil)

Chop arame into thin strips.

Put arame and goji berries in the bottom of a large mixing bowl. Layer tofu on top, then cabbage, cilantro, and scallions. Add sesame oil, tamari, ginger, and maple syrup. Let sit for about 5–10 minutes so tofu can hydrate arame and goji berries. Stir, taste, and adjust seasonings.

Place an eggroll wrapper diagonally on a large cutting board or plate so it looks like a diamond. Place 2 tablespoons of arame mixture in the center. Fold right and left sides of wrapper over filling, then fold up bottom corner. Roll up tightly.

Melt coconut oil in a large frying pan. Add as many eggrolls as will fit, leaving enough room to flip them over. Fry over medium heat for a few minutes until golden on one side, then flip over and fry for about 3 minutes or until most of the surface is golden brown.

Remove from pan and drain on a paper bag or paper towels. Fry remaining egg rolls and add more coconut oil if pan becomes dry.

Arrange egg rolls on a platter and enjoy or serve with your favorite dipping sauce.

Olive and Cannabis Tapenades

Herb Seidel

Olives are an excellent source of copper, iron, fiber, and vitamin E, and very few high-fat foods can match the range of antioxidant and anti-inflammatory nutrients they provide. Herb Seidel plays with their simple goodness in these tapenades made with cannabis-infused extra-virgin olive oil. His black olive tapenade includes a third of a cup of cannabis oil for eight to ten people, and the green olive version has a full half cup of cannabis oil for ten to fourteen. They're great party starters, and you can keep one or both on hand for quick snacks. The tapenades can be spread on crostini or crusty bread, paired with a slice of mild cheese on crackers, and used as a garnish for soup or deviled eggs. Jack Herer, an earthy but spicy sativa, would pair well with the salty, cured olives in these recipes.

Black Olive Tapenade

Serves 8–10

THC per serving:

With Cannabis-Infused
*   Coconut or Olive Oil*
*   (page 101):* 🌿 🌿 🌿

With 20-Minute Cannabis
*   Olive Oil (page 103):* 🌿 🌿

With Beginner's Oil
*   (page 100):* 🌿

3 cups pitted black olives (Gaeta or Kalamata)
⅓ cup cannabis-infused extra-virgin olive oil

Mix ingredients in food processor to a smooth paste.

Transfer to jar with a tightly fitting lid, and cover with a thin layer of additional oil.

Label and store in refrigerator for up to 6 weeks.

Serve at room temperature with crusty Italian bread.

Green Olive Tapenade

Serves 10–14

THC per serving:

With Cannabis-Infused
*   Coconut or Olive Oil*
*   (page 101):* 🌿 🌿 🌿

With 20-Minute Cannabis Olive
*   Oil (page 103):* 🌿 🌿

With Beginner's Oil
*   (page 100):* 🌿

2 5-ounce jars pitted green olives, drained
2 tablespoons toasted blanched almonds
½ cup cannabis-infused extra-virgin olive oil
salt, to taste
pepper, to taste
1 teaspoon dried oregano

Mix ingredients in food processor to a smooth paste.

Transfer to jar with a tightly fitting lid and cover with a thin layer of additional oil.

Label and store in refrigerator for up to 6 weeks.

Serve at room temperature with crusty Italian bread.

Sativa Onion Soup with Ginger and Lemon

Scott Durrah

Scott Durrah owes much of his cooking knowledge to the Jamaican Rastafarians, whose Ital cuisine focuses on fresh, in-season ingredients that enhance vitality (hence the name). Ginger, which has been used for centuries as an anti-inflammatory and pain reliever, is an Ital staple, and it provides a delightful undertone in Scott's onion soup infused with cannabis, another sacred Rastafarian herb. Scott stirs half a cup of cannabis-infused butter and a quarter cup of cannabis-infused extra-virgin oil into this light soup; you can substitute a non-infused version of one or the other to make it less potent. Scott lets diners up their cannabis intake by passing around croutons sautéed in cannabis butter on the side. A tart, sativa-dominant strain such as Super Lemon Haze nicely complements this dish.

Serves 4
THC per serving:
With Cannabis-Infused Coconut or Olive Oil (recipe on page 101) and Bonzo Butter (recipe on page 109):
⚜ ⚜ ⚜

With Cannabis-Infused Coconut or Olive Oil (recipe on page 101) and Beginner's Butter (recipe on page 106):
⚜ ⚜

With Cannabis-Infused Coconut or Olive Oil (recipe on page 101) and Cannabis Ghee (recipe on page 108):
⚜

4 large onions, sliced
½ cup cannabis-infused butter
¼ cup cannabis-infused extra-virgin olive oil
½ teaspoon fresh ginger, peeled and minced
½ tablespoon garlic, peeled and minced
4 cups vegetable or chicken stock
1 tablespoon soy sauce
2 tablespoons lemon juice
salt and pepper to taste

Sauté onions with butter and olive oil until soft and translucent. Add ginger and garlic, then remaining ingredients.

Simmer on low for 30 minutes. Remove from heat and serve.

SALADS

Salads with cannabis-infused dressings are a great way to introduce people to cannabis food because diners can tailor their cannabis intake by using more or less of it. When possible, serve cannabis-infused dressings on the side.

Mixed Greens, Mango, and Pineapple with Cannabis-Curry Vinaigrette

Scott Durrah

If you eat cannabis food, Scott Durrah wants you to take responsibility for your own destiny because you're the only one who understands your own tolerance. With this fresh, bright salad, Scott can feed people of varying tolerance levels by serving the vinaigrette made with a quarter cup of cannabis-infused olive oil on the side. Diners can control the dosage by sprinkling on the dressing with a heavy or light hand. Vitamin C-rich mangoes have high levels of myrcene molecules, which are also the dominant terpenes in cannabis. Because of this, researchers are studying whether mangoes' reputation of increasing, strengthening, and lengthening cannabis's euphoric effects is scientifically true. Our advice? Eat the mango as if that were true. Dress the salad lightly the first time you try it. (Curry powder blends vary. Start out using less than this recipe calls for and taste before you add more.)

Serves 2–4

THC per serving (dressing):

With Cannabis-Infused Coco-
nut or Olive Oil (page 101):

🌿 🌿 🌿 🌿

With 20-Minute Olive Oil
(page 103): 🌿 🌿 🌿

With Beginner's Oil
(page 100): 🌿

To make dressing:
¼ cup cannabis-infused extra-virgin
   olive oil
2 tablespoons apple cider vinegar
1 tablespoon honey
1 teaspoon curry powder

To make salad:
2 cups mixed greens
½ cup mango, sliced
½ cup pineapple, chopped
6 cherry tomatoes
¼ cup cucumbers, sliced

Combine dressing ingredients in a small bowl and whisk to combine.
   Toss salad.
   Serve with dressing on the side.

Grilled Potato Salad with Cannabis-Marinated Oranges and Olives

Lucienne Bercow Lazarus

In the dead of winter, when fresh produce is hard to come by in many parts of the country, Lucie Lazarus makes this elegant salad using winter citrus and always-available potatoes. She prefers to make her salad with spicy arugula, which doesn't show up in farmers' markets until early spring but grows well indoors (if you grow your own) and can usually be found year-round in grocery stores. You can substitute warm spinach in winter. Lucie marinates orange slices and olives in a vinaigrette made with cannabis-infused olive oil, then tosses in grilled potatoes bathed in more cannabis-infused oil. All those layers add up to a full half-cup of cannabis-infused oil, so you don't have to eat a lot of this salad to feel the effects. Lemon Kush, a hybrid with tangy citrus undertones, is ideal for this dish if you can get it.

Serves 6–8

THC per serving (dressing):

With Cannabis-Infused
Coconut or Olive Oil
(page 101): ✹ ✹ ✹

With 20-Minute Cannabis Olive
Oil (page 103): ✹ ✹ ✹

With Beginner's Oil
(page 100): ✹

3 medium navel oranges

½ cup cannabis-infused extra-virgin
olive oil, divided

2 tablespoons fresh rosemary leaves
(3 sprigs), stripped and chopped

1 cup pitted Kalamata olives

3 tablespoons red wine vinegar

6 medium Yukon gold potatoes, sliced
¼" thick

1 teaspoon dried oregano

1 small red onion, thinly sliced

1 tablespoon fresh basil, finely chopped

¼ cup fresh chives, snipped

4–5 cups arugula, chopped (2 bunches)

Peel oranges and cut into 5 crosswise slices (horizontally rather than vertically, so you end up with wheels). Reserve any juice. Transfer to a bowl.

In a separate bowl, combine 5 tablespoons of the olive oil, rosemary, olives, vinegar, and reserved orange juice.

Pour mixture over oranges. Toss well and refrigerate while preparing rest of salad.

Heat grill to medium high.

Place potatoes in a bowl and toss with remaining 3 tablespoons olive oil.

Grill potatoes 4–5 minutes on each side.

Remove potatoes from grill and add to orange mixture. Toss to coat.

Stir in oregano, onion, basil, and chives.

Arrange arugula in bottom of a large salad bowl. Spoon grilled potato mixture on top of arugula and serve.

Crunchy Kumquat Salad with Sweet Cannabis-Garlic Dressing

Lucienne Bercow Lazarus

Lucie Lazarus's festive winter salad combining sweet, tangy kumquats with crisp butter lettuce and crunchy pistachios is perfect for holiday entertaining. Kumquats—tiny, bright orange winter fruits packed with potassium and vitamins A and C—can be eaten with the skins on. Roll them gently with your fingers before slicing to integrate the sweet taste of the rind with the tart pulp. As with any cannabis-infused dressing, it makes good sense to serve this vinaigrette—which includes half of a cup of infused extra-virgin olive oil—on the side so that diners can dose themselves appropriately. (And you can always substitute non-infused oil for some of the infused oil to tone this down.) A citrusy sativa such as Super Silver Haze or an energetic hybrid such as Lemon Kush would nicely complement this salad's bright flavors.

Serves 4

THC per serving (dressing):

With Cannabis-Infused Coconut or Olive Oil (page 101): 🌿 🌿 🌿 🌿

With 20-Minute Cannabis Olive Oil (page 103): 🌿 🌿 🌿

With Beginner's Oil (page 100): 🌿

To make dressing:
¼ cup white balsamic vinegar
2 teaspoons spicy Dijon mustard
1 tablespoon honey
1 clove garlic, finely chopped
½ cup cannabis-infused olive oil
salt, to taste
pepper, to taste

To make salad:
⅓ cup kumquats, sliced
1 head butter lettuce, roughly torn
¼ cup salted pistachios

Whisk together balsamic, Dijon, honey, and chopped garlic. Add salt and pepper to taste, then gradually whisk into ½ cup of infused olive oil.

Toss salad ingredients.

Serve salad with dressing on the side.

Grilled Romaine Hearts with Olive Cannabis Dressing

Herb Seidel

Brushing Romaine lettuce with cannabis-infused extra-virgin olive oil before grilling it gives the lettuce crunch and a subtle charred flavor and infuses it with THC and healthy fats. Romaine, an excellent source of fiber, omega-3s, folic acid, vitamins C and K, calcium, manganese, potassium, copper, and iron—is surprisingly high in complete protein with nearly eight grams per head. Herb Seidel combines Romaine hearts and rustic bread grilled with cannabis-infused olive oil and passes around a garlicky olive dressing made with a quarter of a cup of cannabis-infused olive oil to finish this salad. In addition to getting them high, the oil-based dressing boosts the availability of fat-soluble carotenoids, including pro-vitamin A beta-carotene, in the Romaine.

Serves 6-8

THC per serving:

With Cannabis-Infused Coconut or Olive Oil (page 101): 🌿 🌿

With 20-Minute Cannabis Olive Oil (page 103): 🌿

With Beginner's Oil (page 100): 🌿

½ cup pitted black olives, not too salty

2 cloves garlic, roughly chopped

zest and juice of 1 lemon

¼ cup cannabis-infused extra-virgin olive oil, plus more for grilling bread and Romaine

4 pieces rustic bread

4 Romaine lettuce hearts, halved lengthwise

1 small cucumber, thinly sliced

1 ripe tomato, sliced

a few thin slices red onion or shallot

a few shavings of Parmigiano-Reggiano

salt, to taste

freshly ground black pepper, to taste

Continued

Grilled Romaine Hearts with Olive Cannabis Dressing

In a mini food processor, thoroughly purée olives and garlic. Add lemon zest and juice. Process for 20 seconds.

Add olive oil, 2 teaspoons at a time, processing for 15 seconds after each addition to emulsify. Let rest, taste, and adjust acid and salt. Set aside. (If you make dressing ahead of time, bring to room temperature before serving.)

Heat a grill pan over a medium-high flame. Brush both sides of bread with cannabis olive oil and toast on each side until nicely browned and marked by the grill. Push down on it slightly to get nice marks.

Cut Romaine hearts in half lengthwise. Brush each half with cannabis olive oil and sprinkle with salt and pepper.

Place lettuce on grill and push down on it gently. When lettuce starts to char (about 30 seconds), use tongs to flip it over and char other side. Remove from grill.

To assemble salad, put each piece of bread on a plate. Top with two Romaine halves and some cucumber, tomato, red onion, and Parmigiano-Reggiano.

Serve with dressing on the side and finish with a grind of black pepper.

Entrees

People in cultures across the world add cannabis to their cuisine for its taste as much as its health and entertainment value. Indonesians in the Aceh region often flavor a spicy noodle dish known as *mie aceh* with chopped marijuana leaves. Savory cultivars such as White Widow blend delightfully with pungent ingredients like garlic, ginger, and curry in sophisticated renditions of old and new classics that take full advantage of cannabis's distinct flavor profile.

Cannabis-Roasted Chicken with Onions, Carrots, and Fennel

Joey Galeano

Roast chicken is festive and easy to infuse with cannabis. Joey Galeano slathers a 5- to 6-pound bird with six tablespoons of cannabis-infused olive oil and four tablespoons of cannabis-infused butter and roasts it with carrots, fennel, and onions brushed with cannabis-infused oil for a psychoactive feast. Joey's goal is to layer every plate so that it includes somewhere between 75 and 100 milligrams of cannabis, which is a pretty high dose for some people. You can make this less potent by substituting non-infused olive oil or butter. (If you use non-infused oil, the vegetables will be mostly cannabis-free.) If you can get it, a classic sativa with lemon undertones such as spicy, full-bodied Lamb's Breath nicely complements this classic dish.

Serves 6
THC per serving:
With Cannabis-Infused
  Coconut or Olive Oil
  (recipe on page 101) and
  Bonzo Butter (recipe on
  page 109): ✻ ✻ ✻
With Cannabis-Infused
  Coconut or Olive Oil
  (recipe on page 101) and
  Beginner's Butter (recipe on
  page 106): ✻ ✻ ✻
With Cannabis-Infused Coconut
  or Olive Oil (recipe on
  page 101) and Cannabis
  Ghee (recipe on page 108):
  ✻ ✻ ✻

1 5–6 pound roasting chicken
4 tablespoons (½ stick) cannabis-infused butter, melted
6 tablespoons cannabis-infused extra-virgin olive oil
1 tablespoon garlic powder
4 tablespoons poultry seasoning
3 tablespoons pink Himalayan salt + 3–4 teaspoons
  pink Himalayan salt
1 tablespoon freshly ground black pepper
1 large bunch fresh thyme (about 30 sprigs)
1 Meyer lemon, halved
1 bulb garlic, cut in half crosswise
1 large yellow onion, thickly sliced
20–25 baby carrots
1 bulb fennel, tops removed, cut into wedges (optional)
3–5 garlic cloves, mashed and finely chopped
pinch red pepper flakes (optional)

Continued

Cannabis-Roasted Chicken with Onions, Carrots, and Fennel

Preheat oven to 350°F.

Remove everything inside chicken. Rinse chicken inside and out. Remove excess fat and leftover pin feathers on back of chicken and pat outside dry.

Whisk butter, half of oil, garlic powder, and poultry seasoning together in a small bowl and rub liberally onto chicken skin. Sprinkle inside of chicken with 3 tablespoons of Himalayan salt and pepper.

Stuff chicken cavity with 20 to 27 sprigs of thyme, both lemon halves, and garlic bulb.

Tie legs together with kitchen string and tuck wing tips under body of chicken.

Place onions, carrots, and fennel in a 9" x 13" roasting pan. Toss with remaining oil, salt, pepper, remaining sprigs of thyme, and optional red pepper flakes. Spread around the bottom of pan and place chicken on top.

Roast chicken for 1½–2 hours or until the internal temperature reaches 160°F.

Remove chicken and vegetables; transfer to a platter. Cover with aluminum foil for about 20 minutes.

Slice chicken and serve with vegetables.

Seared Wagyu New York Strip with Cannabis Rub

Joey Galeano

When you just need a good steak, Joey Galeano is the guy to make it for you. Joey has dreamed up about thirty signature dry rubs he uses to infuse meats with flavor—and cannabis. Joey uses decarboxylated cannabis flowers as a base in many of his rubs, including the 10-Hour Flower Power Steak Rub that gives these New York strips their deep, nutty flavor. Joey massages seven tablespoons of cannabis-infused extra-virgin olive oil and six tablespoons of the rub, made with a generous half cup of cannabis flowers, into both sides of the steaks before he quickly sears and then grills them. Joey's rub—a lively blend of cannabis, dried lavender, mustard seeds, and other herbs and spices—keeps for months and makes a great gift for friends who eat cannabis food. You can make it in a coffee grinder or blender, but using a mortar and pestle brings out more of the herbs' and spices' essential oils and ensures that you won't over-process them. Wagyu, which means "Japanese cow," is a type of beef (also called kobe) known for its intense marbling. If you can't find Wagyu New York strips for this dish, look for cuts with visible veins of fat running through. As the fat melts, it naturally tenderizes the meat and enhances its flavor. Allow the steaks to come to room temperature before you work with them and cook them on the hottest part of the grill. Remember that steaks will continue cooking after you take them off the grill, so cook them just a bit less than you think you should and let them sit for five minutes before serving to let the juices from the center infuse the entire steak. When he's making this for a special occasion, Joey tops the steaks with shrimp scampi and serves them with broccoli rabe for a restaurant-style classic.

Serves 4

THC per serving:

With Cannabis-Infused
  Coconut or Olive Oil
  (page 101): 🌿 🌿 🌿 🌿

With 20-Minute Cannabis Olive
  Oil (page 103): 🌿 🌿 🌿

With Beginner's Oil
  (page 100): 🌿

2 boneless 2"-thick Wagyu New York Strip steaks
7 tablespoons cannabis-infused olive oil
6 tablespoons 10-Hour Flower Power Steak Rub (recipe follows)
meat thermometer (optional)

Turn grill on high.

Cut each steak in half so you have 4 steaks of equal size.

In a medium-sized bowl, massage 3 tablespoons olive oil onto steaks and generously sprinkle with about half of the rub.

Continued

Seared Wagyu New York Strip with Cannabis Rub

Heat 4 tablespoons olive oil in a large sauté pan on medium-high for 60–90 seconds.

Place steaks into pan one at a time and sear for 90 seconds on each side.

Remove from pan and place on serving dish.

Apply rest of rub to steaks.

Sear on grill over high heat for 2 minutes on each side. To determine whether steak is done, insert an instant-read thermometer into center. If it reads 110–115°F, steak is rare; 120°F, medium rare; 125–130°F, medium; 130–135°F, medium-well; and 140°F, well.

Remove to a plate and pour leftover oil from pan over steaks. Let rest for 5 minutes. Transfer to serving plates.

10-Hour Flower Power Steak Rub

Joey Galeano

Joey Galeano's method for decarboxylating cannabis is on page 79.

Makes about 1 cup

Total THC content: ✹ ✹ ✹ ✹ ✹

14 grams (a generous ½ cup) decarboxylated cannabis flowers
4 tablespoons coarse sea salt
2 tablespoons freshly ground coarse black pepper
1 tablespoon dehydrated garlic
1 tablespoon dehydrated onion
½ tablespoon dried thyme
1 teaspoon mustard seed
½ tablespoon dried rosemary
½ tablespoon dried coriander
½ teaspoon cayenne
½ teaspoon turmeric
½ teaspoon paprika
½ teaspoon crushed red pepper
¼ teaspoon dried dill
2 kaffir lime leaves
2 tablespoon dried lavender
mortar and pestle or food processor

Place all ingredients into a bowl and crush with a mortar and pestle or in a food processor and pulse 10 times for 1 second each time.

Store in a labeled jar in cool, dark place.

Smoked Apple-Glazed Roast Pork Loin with Walnut and Cannabis Leaf Stuffing

Scott Durrah

For this feast-like main dish, Scott Durrah mixes a half cup of chopped cannabis fan leaves into stuffing made from walnuts, apples, and raisins. Fan leaves, which are all too often thrown away or composted at harvest, have a stronger, spicier taste than cannabis flowers. They give Scott's stuffing an earthy undertone that infuses his pork loin as it slow roasts in cannabis butter. (If you don't have access to fan leaves, you can leave them out or use a green of your choosing; it won't destroy the dish.) Scott rubs the entire loin with cannabis butter and includes it in the stuffing, adding up to a full cup of butter. The fan leaves add very little THC, so this entrée is just right for eight experienced eaters. People who want more buzz can eat more stuffing; people who don't can eat less. If you're making this for a dinner party, be aware that the pork has to be refrigerated for at least three hours after it's been rubbed with the butter. Give yourself time.

Serves 8

THC per serving:

With Cannabis-Infused Coconut or Olive Oil (page 101): 🌿 🌿 🌿 🌿

With 20-Minute Cannabis Olive Oil (page 103): 🌿 🌿 🌿 🌿

With Beginner's Oil (page 100): 🌿 🌿

1 6-pound whole pork loin, with a little fat
1 cup cannabis-infused butter or coconut oil

1 cup organic brown sugar, plus some for sprinkling pork
½ cup fresh cannabis fan leaves, chopped
1 teaspoon cinnamon
1 teaspoon allspice
1 cup walnuts, finely chopped
¼ cup pure maple syrup
6 sweet red apples, diced and peeled
¼ cup raisins (optional)
string to wrap pork loin
apple or hickory wood for smoking pork (optional)
kitchen string
roasting pan
meat thermometer

Continued

Smoked Apple-Glazed Roast Pork Loin with Walnut and Cannabis Leaf Stuffing

Completely wash pork loin and split down the middle on belly side, about halfway through the pork loin. This is where you'll place the stuffing.

Using about ¼ cup of butter, rub entire loin (top, bottom, and inside). Sprinkle with brown sugar and refrigerate for 3 hours minimum.

To make stuffing, combine cannabis leaves, brown sugar, cinnamon, allspice, walnuts, maple syrup, apples, and raisins in a warm skillet over low heat. Simmer on low, stirring occasionally with a wooden spoon, until sugar melts and apples soften.

Add remaining butter to skillet and simmer for 10 minutes on low. Remove from heat and set aside to cool. Once stuffing has cooled, separate and remove any oil or butter that has solidified on top of skillet and place in a bowl for later.

Refrigerate stuffing until completely cool.

To roast pork loin, heat oven to 300°F.

Stuff entire loin, starting in the middle and working outward. You may want to save a little stuffing to put on top of the loin before you place in oven or to pass as a topping when you serve it.

Once loin is stuffed, wrap tightly with kitchen string and place in roasting pan. Pour remaining butter evenly over top. Sprinkle with brown sugar and cinnamon.

Roast for 1–1 ½ hours, basting every 20 minutes. Use meat thermometer to ensure loin is cooked completely to an internal temperature of at least 145°F. Let rest for at least 5 minutes before slicing and serving.

If smoking loin, place in smoker on low for one hour, then in oven until fully cooked to at least 145°F.

Hemp Seed–Crusted Chinook Salmon with Cannabis Cream

Rowan Lehrman

To make this special-occasion dish, Rowan Lehrman bakes deboned Chinook salmon fillets coated with hemp seeds and serves them with a rich cream sauce made with a quarter of a cup of cannabis-infused cream. Because the cannabis is in the cream sauce, diners can moderate their doses by dolloping on more or less of the sauce. Rowan gets to work with fresh wild-caught Chinook salmon (also known as king salmon) nearly every day from April through September at her restaurant on the Oregon coast, but she's still in awe of and inspired by the highly prized fish that spawns in rivers from central California to northwest Alaska. Loaded with protein, omega-3 fatty acids, vitamin D, and tryptophan (a natural sedative), bright orange Chinook salmon is tastier and healthier than farmed salmon, which is often fed pesticide-laden GMO soy and corn and antibiotics, swims in water treated with fungicides, and is dyed with food coloring. An advocate of cooking with only the freshest, healthiest organic ingredients, Rowan says farmed salmon will not work for this dish. Similarly, she only uses Frey Vineyards' biodynamic chardonnay for the cream sauce because cheap cooking wine would sully the taste. "Chinook salmon and cannabis are both rare treats," Rowan says. "It's important to let them shine with other top-shelf ingredients."

Serves 4

THC per serving: ☘

For the salmon:
¼ cup hemp seed oil
½ cup raw shelled hemp seeds
4 4-ounce wild-caught Chinook
    salmon fillets
kosher salt and freshly ground pepper
lemon slices (optional)
basil springs (optional)

For the cannabis cream:
2 medium shallots, minced
1 ½ cups organic white wine
1 cup Cannabis Cream (recipe on page 122)
½ cup Thai basil leaves
kosher salt and freshly ground pepper to taste
parchment paper

Continued

Hemp Seed–Crusted Chinook Salmon with Cannabis Cream

Preheat oven to 375°F.

Pour hemp seed oil in a small flat dish. Place hemp seeds in a separate dish.

Line a baking sheet with parchment paper and set aside.

Working one at a time, take each fillet and dip, flesh side down, first in hemp oil and then in hemp seeds, gently pressing to coat. Carefully transfer each crusted fillet and place skin-side down on parchment-lined baking sheet.

Put shallots in a large, wide saucepan. Add white wine and cook over medium-high heat until reduced to about ¼ cup. Add cannabis cream. Season with salt and pepper and keep warm.

Place baking sheet with salmon fillets in oven and cook for approximately 10–15 minutes or until salmon is firm. Do not overcook.

Transfer fillets to a large serving platter. Finely chop or tear basil and sprinkle over the fillets.

Pour cream sauce over fillets, garnish with lemon slices and basil sprigs, and serve.

Sesame-Crusted, Cannabis-Seared Ahi Tuna with Wasabi, Soy, Cannabis, and Citrus Sauce

Joey Galeano

When he's home on Florida's west coast, Joey Galeano can find fresh line-caught yellowfin tuna (*ahi*, Hawaiian for yellowfin, is a marketing name) in seafood markets almost every day. When he's in Seattle for MagicalButter, Joey picks up fresh-off-the-boat yellowfin at Pike Street Market and sears the firm, sweet, deep red meat in sesame and sunflower oil infused with Super Lemon Haze for a super special local treat. (You can infuse sesame and sunflower oil using any of the recipes for olive and coconut oil.) Joey drizzles the tuna, a rich source of lean protein, omega-3s, vitamins, and minerals, with a beer-reduction wasabi-citrus sauce that he may or may not make with cannabis-infused orange blossom honey. In Seattle, whether Joey infuses the honey depends largely on the local cannabis harvest. (Seattleites enjoy their cannabis, like their coffee, dense and potent.) If Joey's concerned that the sauce might be the extra bit of cannabis that puts someone over the edge, he makes half of it with cannabis and half without. Diners can decide for themselves whether they want more. Joey is the executive chef for MagicalButter, which makes microprocessor-controlled botanical extraction machines, and he lets his wasabi-citrus sauce amalgamate with precision in the machine. You can make the sauce in a saucepan on the stovetop then refrigerate it for an hour if you don't have a MagicalButter machine.

Serves 4

THC per serving:

With Cannabis-Infused Coconut or Olive Oil (page 101): 🌿 🌿 🌿 🌿 🌿

With 20-Minute Cannabis Olive Oil (page 103): 🌿 🌿 🌿 🌿

With Beginner's Oil (page 100): 🌿 🌿

12–16 ounces sushi-grade ahi tuna, 1 solid piece 4–6" in diameter
¼ cup cannabis-infused toasted sesame oil
4–6 tablespoons black and white sesame seeds
¼ cup cannabis-infused sunflower seed oil
8 ounces lager-style beer (Stella Artois or Sapporo)
Wasabi-Soy-Citrus Sauce (recipe follows)
baby cilantro sprigs (or chopped cilantro)
pickled Thai red chili slivers (or red jalapeño)
lime wedges

Continued

Sesame-Crusted, Cannabis-Seared Ahi Tuna with Wasabi, Soy, Cannabis, and Citrus Sauce

Brush tuna on both sides with sesame oil. Cover with black-and-white sesame seeds.

Place tuna on a plate and cover with aluminum foil. Refrigerate for 15 minutes.

Place half of sunflower oil in a large heavy-bottomed sauté pan over medium-high heat and coat pan until oil is scorching hot.

Take tuna out of refrigerator and sear on each side for 45–60 seconds per side in sauté pan.

Remove tuna from pan, put on a plate, cover with aluminum foil and let rest in refrigerator while you make Wasabi-Soy-Citrus Sauce.

Add beer to sauté pan and cook over medium heat until reduced by half. You will use this in the Wasabi-Soy-Citrus Sauce.

Serve tuna topped with Wasabi-Soy-Citrus Sauce, cilantro, chilies, and limes.

Wasabi-Soy-Citrus Sauce

THC content: ↘

½ cup soy sauce

4–8 tablespoons crystallized ginger (about 5–10 pieces)

3 tablespoons cannabis-infused or non-infused honey (recipe on page 116)

2–3 tablespoons prepared wasabi

2 tablespoons fresh orange juice

1 tablespoon fresh lime juice

1 kaffir lime leaf (or substitute 1 teaspoon fresh lime zest)

Place all ingredients plus the beer reduction from the tuna pan inside MagicalButter machine. Set temperature at 160°F and press the "1 Hour/Oil" button. Pour into a serving dish until ready to use.

If you don't have a MagicalButter machine, whisk ingredients together in a bowl and transfer to a small saucepan. Simmer over medium-low heat, stirring frequently, until thickened, about 4 minutes. Let refrigerate for at least an hour so flavors can meld.

Fresh Fan Leaf Pesto

Andie Leon

Too many growers throw away or compost cannabis's large fan leaves because they have a lot less THC than the inner leaves and flowers. Whenever she can get them from growers, Andie Leon eats raw fan leaves because she believes they help her overall health and well-being. Raw fan leaves deliver antioxidants, cannabinoids, vitamins, minerals, and chlorophyll. Andie juices the leaves, tosses them into green salads, and blends them into this pesto. The best fan leaves are picked from the plant when it's about three months old, and they have somewhere between 3 percent and 7 percent THC (usually closer to the low end). They impart a gentle high, if any. Andie ups her pesto's dosage with a half cup of cannabis-infused coconut oil. If your coconut oil is strong, you may want to dilute it with non-infused coconut oil to temper the dosage. If you're making this pesto strictly for the health benefits from the raw leaves and don't want psychoactive effects, use non-infused oil. The pesto keeps in the refrigerator (in a labeled jar, of course), so you can pull it out to serve over pasta, rice, or vegetables. Andie pours hers into labeled ice cube trays and freezes it so she can pull out a perfect pesto dose for months.

Makes about 2 cups

THC per serving:

With Cannabis-Infused Coconut or Olive Oil (page 101): 🌿 🌿 🌿 🌿 🌿

With 20-Minute Cannabis Olive Oil (page 103): 🌿 🌿 🌿 🌿 🌿

With Beginner's Oil (page 100): 🌿 🌿

½ cup cannabis-infused coconut oil
½ cup Parmesan
30 fresh marijuana leaves, torn
10 basil leaves, torn
⅓ cup hazelnuts
½ teaspoon Himalayan sea salt

Combine all ingredients in a blender or food processor and pulse into a paste.

Transfer to a labeled jar. Pesto will keep for a week or so in the refrigerator.

Bring pesto to room temperature before serving.

Mellow Shrimp Cappellini Finished with Cannabis Oil

Mike DeLao

Mike DeLao is more interested in getting healthy than getting high. He keeps the ingredients fresh and the cannabis dosage minimal in this simple, healthy dish. Experienced eaters can eat a whole serving of this pasta without a lot of worry—and they'll want to. The only cannabis in this recipe is in the tablespoon of olive oil that Mike uses to finish it, making it easy to serve non-infused "custom orders" to people who don't wish to imbibe (just finish theirs with plain old extra-virgin olive oil). Mike uses about 1 ounce of cannabis sugar leaf trim from his harvest—which he prefers because it's not as potent as whole flowers—to infuse sixteen ounces of extra-virgin olive oil. An oil infusion made with flowers will have stronger effects.

Serves 4

THC per serving:

With Cannabis-Infused
  Coconut or Olive Oil
  (page 101): 🌿 🌿

With 20-Minute Cannabis Olive
  Oil (page 103): 🌿

With Beginner's Oil (page
  100): 🌿

2 tablespoons extra-virgin olive oil
16 large deveined shrimp
sea salt, to taste
fresh pepper, to taste
4 cloves garlic, sliced lengthwise, paper
  thin
1 tomato, diced and seeded (optional)
fresh basil chiffonade*
24 ounces angel hair pasta, cooked
1 tablespoon cannabis-infused extra-
  virgin olive oil

Heat a sauté pan over medium-high heat. Coat evenly with olive oil.

Place shrimp in pan and season with a pinch of salt and pepper.

When shrimp start to cook, add garlic and tomato. Season again with salt and pepper. Add basil chiffonade and toss until well combined.

When sauce has come together, take it off heat and add cannabis-infused olive oil. Toss to combine and set aside.

While sauce is resting, cook pasta according to package directions.

Toss hot pasta with sauce and stir until evenly coated.

Serve in a large pasta bowl. Garnish with fresh basil, if desired.

*Chiffonade is a cooking technique in which herbs or leafy green vegetables are cut into long, thin strips. Stack leaves, roll them tightly, then cut across the rolled leaves with a sharp knife, producing fine ribbons.

High Ho Pottanesca

Chris Kilham

As he's whipping up this lively sauce made with a quarter cup of cannabis-infused olive oil, Chris Kilham loves to tell people that its name means "in the style of the whore." Believed to be a staple for the ladies and their clients in Nepalese brothels, Puttanesca has a storied history—and it's hard to know which stories are true. Some say a restaurant owner made the first Puttanesca in the 1950s when he had to feed late-night diners with the only ingredients he had on hand: tomatoes, olives, and capers. A quarter cup of cannabis-infused olive oil feeds six people in this recipe, so it's not overwhelming in potency. That's good news, but also be aware that its zingy taste masks the taste of the cannabis. Don't forget that it *is* in there.

Serves 6

THC per serving:

With 20-Minute Cannabis Olive Oil (page 103): ☙

With Cannabis-Infused Coconut or Olive Oil (page 101): ☙ ☙ ☙

With Beginner's Oil (page 100): ☙ ☙ ☙

¼ cup 20-Minute Cannabis Olive Oil (recipe on page 103)

2 medium red onions

8–10 cloves organic garlic

1 28-ounce can crushed organic tomatoes

handful black pitted oil-cured olives

2 or 3 whole hot chilies (whatever looks good)

salt, to taste

handful of capers

dash tamari sauce

1 bunch fresh basil, finely chopped

handful of fresh oregano, finely chopped

splash of organic red wine

parmesan cheese, grated (as much as you like)

2-ounce can anchovies, mashed

1 package quality spaghetti, cooked

In a large skillet, heat cannabis-infused olive oil over medium-high heat.

Stir in onions and garlic. Sauté until caramelized, about 6 minutes.

Stir in tomatoes and remaining ingredients. Simmer until sauce is thickened and slightly reduced, about 30 minutes. Adjust seasonings to taste, cover, and set aside.

Make spaghetti and drain.

Add sauce to cooked pasta and toss.

Salmon and Rice Cheese Risotto with Sesame and Chia Seeds

Andie Leon

Risotto, the creamy slow-cooked rice that can take on a range of flavors from pumpkin to mushroom, is relatively quick and easy to make, but Andie Leon warns that it isn't for multi-taskers. You can't walk away from stirring the rice, even for a quick text. You have to stand at the stove, keep the stockpot hot, and stir while you add fish stock a slow cup at a time, letting the rice absorb flavors and dissolve slowly into garlic, leek, and onion sautéed in a quarter cup of cannabis butter to make a creamy sauce. If you skip this part and dump in all the broth at once, you'll make a tasty but gloppy cannabis rice casserole that will get you high but won't impress your friends. Andie finishes this risotto with chunks of Alaskan, chum, sockeye, coho, pink, or Chinook salmon seared in another quarter cup of cannabis butter along with a handful of healthy seeds and spices for a potent main dish that should be served as an appetizer if you're new to cannabis food. (You can cut the dosage in half or more by searing the salmon in regular butter or olive oil.) Instead of throwing away the omega-3-packed salmon skin when she trims the fillets, Andie brushes them lightly with olive oil, sprinkles on a little salt, and bakes them on a parchment-lined baking sheet in a 375-degree oven for about ten minutes. Andie tosses the toasted skin pieces into a simple salad of greens and pomegranate seeds and serves it with this risotto for a quick, complete meal.

Serves 6

With Bonzo Butter: 🌿
With Beginner's Butter: 🌿
With Cannabis Ghee: 🌿

4 4-ounce salmon fillets
½ cup cannabis-infused butter
3¾ cups fish stock
3 garlic cloves, finely chopped
1 leek, white part only, sliced
1 small red onion, finely chopped
2 cups white Arborio or Bomba rice, washed

½ cup white wine
¼ cup fresh dill
2 tablespoons sesame seeds
2 tablespoons chia seeds
1 cup mozzarella-flavor rice cheese (or mozzarella)
1–2 tablespoons plain yogurt
Himalayan sea salt, to taste
pepper, to taste
parchment paper

Remove skin from salmon (save it to toast later) and cut fillets into cubes. Lightly salt both sides of salmon.

Continued

Salmon and Rice Cheese Risotto with Sesame and Chia Seeds

Heat ¼ cup of the butter in a large, nonstick sauté pan. When butter is just starting to bubble, sear salmon chunks for 1 minute on each side. Set aside.

Bring fish stock to boil in a medium saucepan. Lower heat to keep warm.

In a large saucepan, heat remaining ¼ cup of butter. Add garlic, leek, and onion. Lightly sauté, stirring occasionally, over medium heat for 30 seconds.

Add rice, stirring thoroughly to coat with butter. Add wine and stir continually until fully absorbed into rice.

Raise heat to high. Add 1 cup of fish stock and stir constantly until stock has been completely absorbed. Continue to add stock 1 cup at a time, stirring over medium-high heat until stock is absorbed, about 20 minutes.

Add seared salmon with the last of the stock.

Turn heat to low and add dill, sesame seeds, chia seeds, cheese, and yogurt. Stir thoroughly.

Serve immediately, topped with salt and freshly ground cracked pepper.

Jamaican Chicken Stir-Fry with Curry Coconut Milk

Scott Durrah

Scott Durrah's cooking is heavily influenced by the time he's spent in Jamaica, where goat curry is a national staple and every good cook has a heavily guarded recipe for it. Because goat meat isn't easy to find in the States, Scott makes his curry with organic chicken breasts when he's at home in Denver, and he sautés them along with onions and peppers in a tablespoon of cannabis-infused butter and two tablespoons of cannabis-infused extra-virgin olive oil. Curries have been an important part of Jamaican cuisine since they were brought over by East Indians working the Jamaican sugar plantations in the mid-nineteenth century. Jamaicans tailored their curries to include locally grown allspice along with some combination of turmeric, coriander seeds, cayenne, and fenugreek. You can find Jamaican curry powder at the grocery or online, or you can make your own blend. (Curry powder blends vary. Start out using less than this recipe calls for and taste before you add more.)

Serves 2–4

THC per serving:

With Cannabis-Infused Coconut or Olive Oil (recipe on page 101) and Bonzo Butter (recipe on page 109):

🌿 🌿

With Cannabis-Infused Coconut or Olive Oil (recipe on page 101) and Beginner's Butter (recipe on page 106):

🌿 🌿

1 tablespoon cannabis-infused butter
2 tablespoons cannabis olive oil
½ cup onions, diced
½ cup bell peppers, sliced
2 organic chicken breasts, cut into strips

1 tablespoon Jamaican curry powder
1 teaspoon garlic, minced
½ teaspoon Lawry's seasoning salt
½ teaspoon allspice
1 cup organic chicken or vegetable stock
½ cup coconut milk
1 teaspoon soy sauce
salt and pepper, to taste
Cooked white or brown rice

Heat cannabis butter and oil in a large sauté pan or wok over medium-high heat. Sauté onions and peppers until onions are translucent and peppers are soft.

Add chicken, curry powder, garlic, seasoning salt, and allspice. Sauté for 1–2 minutes.

Add stock, coconut milk, and soy sauce. Simmer for 5–10 minutes.

Serve with rice.

Spinach, Potato, and Cannabis Curry

Scott Durrah

Pungent curry overpowers any cannabis taste from an eighth of a cup of infused olive oil in Scott Durrah's vegan stew, which is great for people who don't like the taste of cannabis, but is also a little bit dangerous. It's easy to forget you're eating cannabis without the taste, and that makes it easy to eat too many tender potatoes simmered with spinach in cannabis olive oil, coconut milk, curry, and onions. Start with a bite or two if you're new to cannabis food and label any leftovers clearly. For simplicity's sake in this recipe, Scott sticks with potatoes and spinach, the classic combination in the Indian curry *aloo palak*. When he makes it himself, Scott combines whatever vegetables and greens look best and make him hungry. Sometimes he uses sweet potatoes, sometimes kale or mustard greens. Any good cook can—and should—play with this and all recipes, Scott says, as long as they stick to organic, whole foods, preferably in season, when they do. Cannabis is a healing, helping herb, but only in the company of healing, helping food. (Curry powder blends vary. Start out using less than this recipe calls for and taste before you add more.)

Serves 4-6

THC per serving:

*With Cannabis-Infused
    Coconut or Olive Oil
    (page 101):* ☘

*With 20-Minute Cannabis Olive
    Oil (page 103):* ☘

*With Beginner's Oil
    (page 100):* ☘

⅛ cup cannabis-infused extra-virgin
    olive oil
1 small onion, diced
6 small potatoes, not peeled, large dice
4 cups washed spinach, chopped
    roughly
2 tablespoons curry powder
1 tablespoon green curry paste

2 tablespoons flour
1 13.5-ounce can coconut milk
2 tablespoons tamari or soy sauce
1 cup vegetable broth
salt, to taste
4 tablespoons cilantro, chopped
4 cups cooked white or brown rice

Heat a Dutch oven or large skillet over medium heat. Add oil and onion and stir together over medium heat for a few moments. Add potatoes and spinach, stir, and let cook for a few more minutes.

Add curry powder, then green curry paste. Add flour and mix well.

Add coconut milk, tamari, and vegetable broth. Taste for salt.

Let simmer for at least 15 minutes or until sauce thickens and potatoes are tender.

Garnish with cilantro and serve over rice.

Eggplant, Lentil, and Cannabis Curry

Leslie Cerier

Leslie Cerier grinds half of a cup of cured cannabis flowers in a coffee grinder and sautés them with cinnamon, cayenne, cumin, fennel, and turmeric to get this vegan lentil stew started. Leslie warns that grinding and handling the cannabis can leave a sticky residue on your hands (sometimes the only tool that will get the last of the goo out of the grinder) and that "if you're licking your hands, anything on your hands counts." Leslie says she's been sent into outer space because she didn't consider that when she ate this stew later. When Leslie cooks with cannabis, she likes to include it as a layer of flavor, like basil or garlic, but rarely makes it the dominant theme. Coconut and curry are the standout tastes in this delightful meal that won't put you over the edge. You can play with Leslie's all-seasons recipe, swapping out vegetables according to what's good at the market. If the eggplant or potatoes look dodgy, try carrots, sweet potatoes, or cauliflower. Throw in zucchini when your garden gives you the bounty.

Serves 4

THC per serving:

3 tablespoons extra-virgin coconut oil

½ cup cured cannabis flowers, ground into a fine powder

1 cinnamon stick

1 tablespoon cumin seeds

1 teaspoon fennel seeds

½ teaspoon cayenne

¼ teaspoon turmeric

1 13.5-ounce can whole coconut milk

1 cup red lentils, rinsed

3 cups water

1½ cups potatoes, coarsely chopped

1½ cups eggplant, coarsely chopped

1 cup red onions, coarsely chopped

1 cup cilantro, coarsely chopped

½ teaspoon sea salt

cooked rice

coffee grinder

Heat oil in a 6-quart stockpot over medium heat. Add cannabis, cinnamon stick, cumin seeds, fennel seeds, cayenne, and turmeric. Sauté for about 15–20 minutes over a very low flame to infuse oil with spices.

Stir in coconut milk, followed by lentils, water, potatoes, eggplant, and onions.

Bring ingredients to a boil. Reduce heat to medium low. Cover and simmer for about 15–20 minutes or until lentils soften and begin to melt.

When potatoes are as tender as you like, stir in cilantro and salt. Taste and adjust seasonings.

Ladle into bowls and serve with rice.

Store leftovers in a labeled container in the refrigerator.

Bok Choy, Cashews, and Scallions Stir-Fried in Cannabis-Ginger Red Palm Oil

Leslie Cerier

Ready in less than half an hour, Leslie Cerier's fresh, nutritious stir-fry is a quick, healthy way to get your vegetables—and a slight buzz. Leslie flavors two tablespoons of cannabis-infused virgin organic red palm oil with ginger, giving this vegan, gluten-free dish a nice bite. Leslie is a huge fan of red palm oil, a sacred healing food for civilizations dating to the ancient Egyptians. Derived from the fruit of the oil palm tree—not to be confused with palm kernel oil, which comes from oil palm kernels—red palm oil is rich in powerful anti-oxidants and vitamin E and has been proven to fight heart disease and lower cholesterol. Red palm oil gives this stir-fry extra-rich flavor and has a low smoke point of about 150 degrees to 300 degrees Fahrenheit, so it won't degrade the THC in this dish. (You can use cannabis-infused unrefined virgin coconut oil if that's what you have on hand.) Bok choy, a mild-flavored cabbage cousin, contains more than seventy antioxidants and is rich in vitamin A. With a lower fat content than many other nuts, cashews deliver protein, antioxidants, vitamins, and important minerals including iron, magnesium, phosphorous, zinc, copper, and manganese. Mirin, a Japanese condiment made from rice wine, gives it a bright flavor.

Serves 4

With Cannabis-Infused Coconut or Olive Oil (page 101): 🌿 🌙

With 20-Minute Cannabis Olive Oil (page 103): 🌿

With Beginner's Oil (page 100): 🌙

2 tablespoons cannabis-infused virgin organic red palm blend oil, coconut oil, or sesame oil
2 tablespoons ginger, grated
2 tablespoons mirin
1 tablespoon tamari

1 cup cashews
1 cup red bell pepper, sliced
6 cups bok choy, sliced
1 cup scallions, sliced
2 cups cooked rice

Warm a wok over medium-high heat. Add oil, ginger, mirin, tamari, and cashews. Stir-fry 2 minutes to flavor cashews with ginger.

Add red bell pepper, bok choy, and scallions. Stir fry for 3 minutes or until pepper turns bright red and bok choy wilts slightly.

Taste and add more tamari for a saltier flavor, if desired.

Serve with rice, if desired.

Kushie Tomato Soup with Grilled Boursin and Gruyere Croutons

Joey Galeano

Afghani A-1 would be Joey Galeano's cultivar choice for this recipe because the euphoria it gives him matches the euphoria he feels when he eats this soup, just like when his grandma made it for him. Joey makes tomato soup using his grandmother's recipe—with a slightly different herbal infusion. Joey infuses his soup and the Boursin cheese (which is great on its own) for the croutons with cannabis butter and sautés the croutons in four tablespoons of cannabis butter. If you eat all those layers—"and why wouldn't you?" Joey asks—you'll get a nice buzz. You can also leave out the croutons (or eat fewer of them) to temper your dosage. Joey is the executive chef for MagicalButter, which sells microprocessor-controlled botanical extraction machines, and he's taken his grandmother's recipe high tech by making this soup inside the machine. You can make this comfort food the old-fashioned way if you don't own the gadget.

Serves 4-6

THC per serving:

With Bonzo Butter (recipe on page 109): ☘

With Beginner's Butter (recipe on page 106): ☘

With Cannabis Ghee (recipe on page 108): ☘

6 tablespoons cannabis-infused butter or coconut oil

1 medium yellow onion, chopped

5–8 garlic cloves, minced

2 cups chicken stock (preferably homemade)

1 28-ounce can crushed tomatoes (preferably San Marzano)

½ cup heavy cream

1 tablespoon pink Himalayan salt

freshly ground black pepper, to taste

large pinch saffron threads

Grilled Boursin and Gruyere Croutons (recipe follows)

Heat butter or oil over medium heat in a large sauté pan.

Add onion and cook 10–15 minutes, stirring occasionally, until golden brown.

Add garlic and cook for 1 more minute.

Remove from heat and place in MagicalButter machine with rest of ingredients and close top. Set temperature at 160°F and time for 1 hour.

If you don't have a MagicalButter machine, place all ingredients in a large heavy-bottomed pan over medium-high heat. Bring to a simmer, stirring constantly. Reduce heat to low, cover and simmer for 40 minutes.

Serve hot with Grilled Boursin and Gruyere Croutons scattered on top.

Boomin' Boursin Cheese

Joey Galeano

Makes about 3 ¾ tablespoon servings
With Cannabis-Infused Coconut or
Olive Oil (page 101): 🌿 🌿 🌿
🌿 🌿 🌿
With 20-Minute Cannabis Olive Oil
(page 103): 🌿 🌿 🌿 🌿
With Beginner's Oil (page 100): 🌿
½ cup cannabis-infused olive oil

6–12 garlic cloves, minced
4 tablespoons (12 ounces) cream cheese
4 ounces goat cheese
4 tablespoons fresh Italian parsley, finely
  chopped
4 tablespoons fresh basil, finely chopped
4 tablespoons fresh chives, finely chopped
2 tablespoons fresh rosemary, finely chopped
2 tablespoons fresh oregano, finely chopped

Heat oil in a small sauté pan over medium heat, add garlic, and cook for 5 minutes. Set aside to cool for 5 minutes.

Combine garlic oil and all the other ingredients in mixer bowl and blend with electric mixer on low for 45–60 seconds. Turn the speed to 5 or 6 for 1–2 minutes. Cheese should be well mixed but still dense.

Transfer to a labeled storage dish and refrigerate until you're ready to use.

Grilled Boursin and Gruyere Croutons

Joey Galeano

Makes about 12 croutons
With Bonzo Butter (recipe on page 109):
  1.95 milligrams per crouton
With Beginner's Butter (recipe on
  page 106): 1.5 milligrams per crouton
With Cannabis Ghee (recipe on
  page 108): 2 milligrams per crouton

4 tablespoons cannabis-infused butter
4 slices multigrain country bread, crusts
  removed
garlic salt and fresh ground pepper, to taste
½ cup Boomin' Boursin Cheese (recipe
  above)
6–8 ounces Gruyere cheese, grated
4 slices white American cheese

Butter both sides of bread. Spread 2 slices each with half Boursin, sprinkle with half of Gruyere, and top each with 2 American cheese slices. Top with remaining 2 bread slices. Sprinkle with garlic salt and pepper.

Heat a large sauté pan over medium heat. Place sandwiches in pan and cook both sides until sandwiches are golden brown and cheese is melted.

Remove from pan and let rest for 2 minutes. Cut into 1" square pieces.

Crab and Mahi-Mahi Sliders with Cannabis, Turmeric, and Garlic Sauce

Grace Gutierrez

Only the spicy sauce is infused in this recipe, so it's easy to control the dosage by slathering a lot or a little onto sliders made with crab cakes and almond-crusted mahi-mahi. Turmeric, a ginger relative with anti-inflammatory properties, gives the sauce its rich yellow color and ups the therapeutic value. The sauce can, and probably should, be made several hours or the night before as it needs to chill before you use it. It's key to the dish, but let guests know that it's also the rocket fuel. (If they're new to cannabis food, you might want to serve the sauce on the side.) Though they're indica-dominant, which could be a bit heavy if you're serving these at the start of a meal, earthy Cheese cultivars are delicious for the sauce infusion if you have access to them.

Serves 4

With Cannabis-Infused Coconut or Olive Oil (page 101): 🌿 🌿 🌿

With 20-Minute Cannabis Olive Oil (page 103): 🌿 🌿

With Beginner's Oil (page 100): 🌿

Cannabis, Turmeric, and Garlic Sauce (recipe follows)
½ cup raw almonds, toasted
¼ cup shredded coconut
1 teaspoon toasted sesame oil
2 teaspoons honey
½ teaspoon salt
½ teaspoon freshly cracked pepper
4 2-ounce mahi-mahi fillets, patted dry
2 tablespoons olive oil
4 2-ounce crab cakes
8 slider buns
2 avocados, sliced
½ cup mango, very thinly sliced strips (make sure it's not overly ripe)
food processor

Continued

Crab and Mahi-Mahi Sliders with Cannabis, Turmeric, and Garlic Sauce

At least an hour before you plan to serve sliders, make Cannabis, Turmeric, and Garlic Sauce. Refrigerate.

Place almonds and coconut in food processor bowl and pulse until finely ground. Pour into a small bowl and stir in sesame oil, honey, salt, and pepper. Combine well. Pat mixture onto both sides of mahi-mahi fillets.

Over medium heat in a large skillet, heat olive oil. When oil is hot, cook crab cakes and mahi-mahi fillets until golden brown for 3 minutes; turn and cook until just opaque and golden brown, about 3–4 minutes.

While fish cooks, lightly toast slider buns under broiler. Place top halves of slider buns on a platter and spread evenly with about 2 teaspoons Cannabis, Turmeric, Garlic Sauce.

Place bottom halves of slider buns on a platter and place a mahi-mahi fillet, then a crab cake, on each one. Place another small dollop of sauce on top, then top with avocado slices, mango strips, and bun tops.

Serve with remaining sauce on the side.

Cannabis, Turmeric, and Garlic Sauce

Grace Gutierrez

Makes about 1 cup

¾ cup mayonnaise
2 large garlic cloves
¼ cup cannabis-infused olive oil
2 teaspoons turmeric powder
2 tablespoons fresh parsley, chopped
1 small jalapeño pepper, seeded and chopped

Combine mayonnaise, garlic, olive oil, and turmeric in the bowl of a food processor and process until well combined.

Add chopped parsley and jalapeño. Pulse until combined. Do not over-process.

Chill before serving. Store in a labeled airtight container in the refrigerator for up to 1 month.

Holy Mole!

Chris Kilham

As with most legendary dishes, the origin of sienna-colored, chocolate-tinged *mole poblano* is the subject of some dispute. Some say the Aztec king Moctezuma served it to the conquistadors; some say an angel inspired nuns in Puebla de los Angeles when they had nothing to serve a visiting archbishop in the seventeenth century. Whatever its true roots might be, mole has become a staple. Every good Mexican cook has his or her own secret mole recipe, and variations are rife from village to village. Medicine Hunter Chris Kilham, who seeks out spectacular traditional foods when he's tracking indigenous plants, says the best mole he ever ate was made by a grandmother in San Luis Potosi in southern Mexico. He's been tinkering with his own mole recipe ever since, and he's created a delicious, psychoactive variation by sautéing onions, garlic, chilies, and chocolate in a quarter cup of cannabis-infused oil for the sauce's base. This sauce is excellent on chicken and other meats or on tempeh and tofu for vegans. Slather it on and roll it up in a tortilla with cheese and lettuce for a satisfying meal. In Mexico, mole can be—and often is—served with every meal.

Serves 4-6

With Cannabis-Infused Coconut or Olive Oil (page 101):

With 20-Minute Cannabis Olive Oil (page 103):

With Beginner's Oil (page 100):

¼ cup 20-Minute Cannabis Olive Oil

1 large red onion, coarsely chopped

10–12 cloves garlic, coarsely chopped

2–3 fresh hot chilies (habanero are best but whatever looks good), chopped coarsely

2 heaping tablespoons organic dark Fair Trade cocoa powder

1 teaspoon cumin powder

1 teaspoon chili powder

2–3 dashes habanero sauce

small bunch fresh cilantro, relatively finely chopped

¼–½ cup red wine

salt, to taste

Heat olive oil in a large skillet. Add onion and garlic. Sauté until soft and translucent.

Add chopped hot chilies and cook until chilies are tender.

Add cocoa powder and stir constantly with a wooden spoon.

Add a small bit of water, just an ounce or two, to make sauce less thick.

Add cumin, chili powder, habanero sauce, cilantro, and red wine. Stir continuously for at least 20 minutes.

Remove from heat. If not serving immediately, let cool and transfer to a labeled jar or bottle with a tightly fitting lid and store in the refrigerator for a few weeks or the freezer for up to 6 months.

SIDES

Cannabis-infused side dishes add to a meal without overdoing it, and it's easier for people to control their doses. Serving an infused side dish during a dinner party is a great way to provide feel-good food only for those who opt for it. Try toasting and salting fan leaves and serving them with drawn butter or lightly dusting buds with a little flour and sautéing them. Whip a little cannabis-infused butter into mashed potatoes just as you might use wasabi butter. The possibilities are endless.

Winter Squash Roasted in Cannabis Oil with Pomegranate Seed and Dried Cherry Stuffing

Donna Shields

When Donna Shields needs an ideal vessel for a stuffed, roasted side dish or vegetarian main dish, she turns to winter squash. High in vitamins C and K, beta-carotene, and other antioxidants, winter squash has anti-inflammatory properties and is great for fighting off colds and flu. For this dish, Donna bathes acorn and Hubbard squashes (any striped round or oblong winter squash would do) with cannabis-infused coconut oil, fills them with sweet, savory stuffing made using creamy coconut milk, and roasts them. This recipe calls for only two tablespoons of infused coconut oil, but Donna warns that the coconut milk gives the dish a pretty high fat content and makes it more potent. THC, a fat-soluble molecule, binds to fat, exacerbating its psychoactive effects. "Fat does potentiate the cannabis's effect," Donna says. "A recipe with more high-fat ingredients will be more kickass."

Serves 4

*With Cannabis-Infused Coco-
nut or Olive Oil (page 101):*

🌿 🌿

*With 20-Minute Cannabis Olive
Oil (page 103):* 🌿

*With Beginner's Oil
(page 100):* 🌿

1 2–3 pound winter squash

2 tablespoons cannabis-infused coconut oil

1 cup fresh whole-grain breadcrumbs

½ cup cilantro

¼ cup sunflower seeds, unsalted

¼ cup dried tart cherries

¼ cup coconut milk (preferably
canned)

1 teaspoon garam masala

½ teaspoon salt

fresh ground pepper

sour cream

pomegranate seeds

Preheat oven to 375°F.

Prick squash several times with fork and microwave on high 3–5 minutes until slightly soft to the touch. If you don't have a microwave, pierce squash with a fork and bake for 20 minutes in a 350°F oven until just soft enough to easily cut open.

Cool, cut in half, and discard seeds. Drizzle coconut oil onto both cut sides.

In a bowl, combine breadcrumbs, cilantro, sunflower seeds, dried cherries, coconut milk, garam masala, and salt.

Stuff both squash cavities and sprinkle with pepper.

Bake for about an hour or until squash is fork tender. If needed, cover with foil during roasting to prevent too much browning.

To serve, top with a dollop of sour cream and pomegranate seeds.

Cinnamon-Cannabis Roasted Sweet Potatoes

Joey Galeano

Sweet potatoes deliver an enormous amount of beta-carotene, a powerhouse antioxidant. Just like cannabis, beta-carotene is more effectively absorbed into the bloodstream when it's combined with fat, so the quarter cup of cannabis butter and the quarter cup of cannabis coconut oil do double duty—upping the THC *and* the antioxidant levels—in Joey Galeano's cinnamon- and agave-roasted sweet potatoes. (If you don't care for agave, you can substitute honey in this recipe. Just add a little water if that makes the oil hard to whisk.) Joey's reduction sauce, made from the oil that the potatoes roasted in, is pretty potent and best served on the side so diners can be responsible for their own destinies. The sauce adds a rich gooiness, but the potatoes are also delicious without it. Joey uses Pineapple Kush, a sweet, buttery-tasting hybrid, to infuse the oils for this dish when he can get it.

Serves 8

With Bonzo Butter (recipe on page 109): 🌿

With Beginner's Butter (recipe on page 106): 🌿

With Cannabis-Infused Coconut or Olive Oil (page 101): 🌿 🌿

4 sweet potatoes
¼ cup cannabis-infused butter
¼ cup cannabis-infused coconut oil, liquefied
⅓ cup agave syrup
1 teaspoon fresh ground cinnamon, plus more for topping
½ teaspoon pink Himalayan salt
⅛ teaspoon organic ground cayenne pepper (optional)

Preheat oven to 325°F.

Wash sweet potatoes thoroughly and leave skins on. Cut in half lengthwise and put sweet potatoes, face up, into a roasting pan.

In a mixing bowl, whisk butter, coconut oil, agave, and cinnamon together. Pour on top of potatoes, cover with aluminum foil, and place in preheated oven for 35 minutes.

Remove from oven and drain leftover liquid into a saucepan. Cook on stovetop over medium heat until liquid reduces and thickens into a syrupy consistency, about 5 minutes.

Cut sweet potatoes into 1–2-inch-thick wedges. Serve with sauce on the side.

Dijon and Cannabis Green Beans with Pecans

Herb Seidel

There's nothing like picking up a mess of fresh green beans at the market when they're at their best in mid-summer. Herb Seidel's recipe for tangy green beans tossed with toasted pecans and Dijon-lemon vinaigrette made with a third of a cup of cannabis olive oil Is a simple and unexpected way to make the most of green beans and a great accompaniment for poultry, fish, or meat. It's easy to temper the potency of this dish because the secret's in the sauce. If a tablespoon of cannabis oil per serving seems like a lot for the occasion, just use a lighter hand with the dressing and put what you don't use in a labeled jar in the refrigerator for another day. Herb steams his green beans, keeping them crispy tender and full of nutrients, for three to five minutes. He uses a steamer, but if you don't have one, you can just place the beans in a colander inside a Dutch oven full of water and simmer with the lid on tightly.

Serves 4-6

*With Cannabis-Infused
    Coconut or Olive Oil
    (page 101):* 🌿 🌿 🌿

*With 20-Minute Cannabis
    Olive Oil (page 103):* 🌿 🌿

*With Beginner's Oil
    (page 100):* 🌿

2 tablespoons peanut oil
2 cups shelled pecan halves
½ cup lemon juice, freshly squeezed (2–3 whole
    lemons)
1½ teaspoons sugar
1½ teaspoons Dijon mustard
1 cup grapeseed oil
⅓ cup cannabis-infused olive oil
salt, to taste
pepper, to taste
2 pounds green beans
steamer or Dutch oven and colander

Continued

Dijon and Cannabis Green Beans with Pecans

Heat peanut oil over medium heat. Add pecans and salt to taste. Toast lightly, stirring constantly. (Nuts cook quickly. Be careful not to burn them.) When pecans are golden and fragrant, remove from heat and set aside.

To make dressing, whisk lemon juice, sugar, and mustard together. Slowly drizzle in grapeseed and olive oil until emulsified. (Use a hand blender if you have one for faster better emulsification.) Add salt and pepper to taste. Set aside.

Trim beans and cut into 3" lengths. Place in a steamer and steam until crisply tender, about 3–5 minutes.

Rinse beans with water to arrest cooking process. Drain thoroughly and transfer to a bowl.

Whisk dressing if it has settled and lightly coat beans with dressing. Toss in the nuts. Adjust salt and pepper.

Serve at room temperature.

Cannabis Sweet Potato Fries with Hemp Seeds and Kelp Flakes

Leslie Cerier

Leslie Cerier's sweet potato fries are a healthy way to be a little decadent. Sweet potatoes are loaded with beta-carotene and other vitamins and minerals; hemp seeds, a complete protein, are rich in omega-3s, fatty acids, fiber, minerals, and vitamins; and kelp has Vitamin C, calcium, iron, manganese, and magnesium. These are three of Leslie's favorite foods, and crisp-frying the sweet potatoes in three tablespoons of cannabis-infused virgin coconut oil seals the deal. Virgin coconut oil, made from fresh coconut meat, has more nutrients than refined coconut oil, made from dried coconut meat, and a lower smoke point of 350 degrees Fahrenheit. That's just right for cannabis fries, as conventional wisdom holds that THC will degrade if food is cooked above 350 degrees. The THC in Leslie's fries doesn't degrade, so tread lightly. Don't eat them like they're from Umami Burger. Two or three make for an enjoyable meal; six is probably too many; nine lands most people on the sofa for the night.

Serves 6 or more
THC per serving:
With Cannabis-Infused
    Coconut or Olive Oil
    (page 101): 🌿 🌿
With 20-Minute Cannabis
    Olive Oil (page 103): 🌿
With Beginner's Oil
    (page 100): 🌿

3 cups yams or sweet potatoes, peeled
3 tablespoons cannabis-infused virgin
    coconut oil
¼ cup hemp seeds
1 tablespoon kelp flakes

Cut sweet potatoes into 4 or 5 vertical pieces, then cut each piece into french fry sticks. Set aside.

Melt and heat coconut oil in a large skillet. After a few minutes, stick the end of a wooden spoon into the oil. When bubbles form around the wood and start floating to the top, the oil is ready for frying.

Add sweet potatoes and fry, covered, for 5 minutes or until potatoes are almost yellow. Flip over and fry for about another 2–3 minutes or until tender. Fork test for doneness.

Garnish with hemp seeds and kelp flakes. Serve immediately.

Smokin' Grilled Corn, Zucchini, and Cilantro Salad

Herb Seidel's Smokin' Grilled Corn (page 224) smothered in cannabis-spice butter, always a hit at summer parties, is a treat all by itself. Because it's wrapped in foil, the corn is easy to prepare and serve at large gatherings. But with a full half-cup of cannabis-infused butter, it's potent—and your guests should take it slow. You might end up with leftovers, and you won't want to waste all that buttery corn and cannabis goodness. We combined a couple ears of Herb's leftover corn with zucchini, peppers, and *cotija* cheese to make a side dish that works alongside breakfast eggs, dinnertime tacos, or on its own for lunch. To re-up the dosage, because the cannabis corn gets diluted by the rest of the salad ingredients, you could use cannabis-infused olive oil in the salad dressing. We found the salad just right for lunch without it.

Serves 4-6

With Cannabis-Infused Coconut or Olive Oil (page 101): 🌿 🌿 🌿

With 20-Minute Cannabis Olive Oil (page 103): 🌿 🌿

With Beginner's Oil (page 100): 🌿 🌿

olive oil for grill
2 tablespoons cannabis-infused or non-infused extra-virgin olive oil
1 large red bell pepper
1 5"-long zucchini, sliced lengthwise
2 ears grilled corn on the cob
½ cup red onion, chopped
½ cup cilantro, chopped
1 serrano chili pepper, seeded and minced

1 teaspoon ground cumin
¼ cup cotija cheese
2 tablespoons lime juice
salt, to taste
freshly ground pepper, to taste

Preheat grill for high heat and brush with oil.

Rub bell pepper and zucchini with infused or non-infused oil. Place pepper on grill and heat until skin has blistered, about 20 minutes.

During last 5 minutes of cooking, grill zucchini for about 2 minutes on each side.

Remove pepper's blistered skin, seeds, and stem. Chop into small pieces.

Chop zucchini into small pieces.

Remove corn kernels from cobs using a sharp knife and long downward strokes.

In a large bowl, combine corn, bell pepper, zucchini, onion, cilantro, and chili pepper.

Add cumin, ½ tablespoon oil, lime, and *cotija*. Mix gently.

Transfer to serving bowl and serve.

Smokin' Grilled Corn

Herb Seidel

Serves 4

THC per serving:

With Bonzo Butter (recipe on page 109): ✹

With Beginner's Butter (recipe on page 106): ✹

With Cannabis Ghee (recipe on page 108): ✹

olive oil for grill
1 tablespoon chili powder
⅛ teaspoon dried oregano
cayenne pepper, to taste
garlic powder, to taste
1 pinch onion powder
salt, to taste
pepper, to taste
½ cup cannabis-infused butter, softened
4 ears corn, husked and cleaned

Preheat grill for high heat and rub with oil.

In a medium bowl, mix together chili powder, oregano, cayenne, garlic powder, onion powder, salt, and pepper. Blend in butter.

Apply mixture to each ear of corn and place each ear onto a piece of aluminum foil big enough to wrap the corn. Wrap like a burrito and twist ends to close.

Place wrapped corn on preheated, oiled grill and cook 20–30 minutes, until tender when poked with a fork. Turn occasionally. Remove and let cool.

Spring Vegetables Sautéed in Cannabis Butter

Herb Seidel

This fresh mix of asparagus, sugar snap peas, radishes, and chives sautéed in three tablespoons of cannabis butter is always a crowd pleaser when Herb Seidel does cooking gigs at cannabis conventions. Herb's recipe couldn't be simpler, and that simplicity is key to its magic. Herb parboils the vegetables, then sautés them for about five minutes in the cannabis butter until they're crispy tender. That's just enough to give this dish a rich, earthy cannabis undertone without overwhelming the tasty spring vegetables, and it makes for a nice, light dosage. If you can get hold of one, try a Cheese cultivar, which has subtle notes of radish and chive, for the oil infusion.

Serves 4–6

THC per serving:

With Bonzo Butter (recipe on page 109): ☘

With Beginner's Butter (recipe on page 106): ☘

With Cannabis Ghee (recipe on page 108): ☘

2 pounds asparagus, trimmed and cut into 1½" pieces

8 ounces sugar snap peas, strings removed

3 tablespoons cannabis-infused butter

1 pound radishes, cut into quarters

½ teaspoon salt

⅝ teaspoon freshly ground black pepper (or to taste)

4 tablespoons fresh chives, snipped

Fill a large, covered stockpot with water and add salt to taste. Heat over high heat until water boils.

Fill large bowl with ice water; set aside.

Add asparagus and snap peas to saucepot; cook 4 minutes. Drain vegetables; transfer to ice water to cool. Drain vegetables well.

Meanwhile, in 12" skillet, heat butter on medium heat until melted. Add radishes, salt, and pepper. Cook 10 minutes or until tender-crisp.

Transfer to bowl; keep warm. To serve, garnish with chives.

To same skillet, add asparagus, snap peas, ¼ teaspoon salt, and ½ teaspoon freshly ground black pepper; cook 5 minutes or until tender-crisp, stirring occasionally.

Stir in 2 tablespoons chives.

Transfer to serving bowl; arrange radishes around edge. Sprinkle with remaining chives.

Red Beans and Ricely Yours

Herb Seidel

Traditionally eaten on Mondays using ham from Sunday dinner, red beans and rice is a staple in New Orleans. Every cook in the Crescent City—and beyond—has his or her own take on the best mix of vegetables, herbs, and spices for this comfort food. It was a staple for Louis Armstrong, who signed his letters "Red Beans and Ricely Yours." Coincidentally, cannabis was the jazz great's favorite herb; he called it "a friend" and "a thousand times better than whiskey." In Armstrong's honor, Herb Seidel found a way to subtly infuse cannabis (which also happens to be Herb's favorite herb) into this refreshingly light version of the Creole classic. Herb sautés onion, green pepper, garlic, and cilantro in two tablespoons of cannabis olive oil to flavor his vegetarian red beans and rice. At about half a tablespoon of cannabis oil per serving, they're not overwhelmingly potent, but you might find listening to Louis and his orchestra play "Muggles" *really* interesting after eating them.

Serves 4-5

THC per serving:

*With Cannabis-Infused
    Coconut or Olive Oil
    (page 101):*

*With 20-Minute Cannabis
    Olive Oil (page 103):*

*With Beginner's Oil
    (page 100):*

2 tablespoons cannabis-infused olive oil

1 medium onion, chopped

½ cup green pepper, chopped

2 garlic cloves, minced

⅓ cup fresh cilantro, minced

3 16-ounce cans red beans, rinsed and drained

½ teaspoon salt

½ teaspoon ground cumin

⅛ teaspoon pepper

3 cups hot cooked rice

Warm oil in a large nonstick skillet. Add onion, green pepper, and garlic. Sauté in oil until tender.

Add cilantro; cook and stir until wilted, about 1 minute.

Stir in beans, salt, cumin, and pepper. Cover and simmer for 10–15 minutes.

Serve over rice.

Black Chinese Heirloom Rice with Coconut Milk and Cannabis

Joey Galeano

Joey Galeano stir-fries black Chinese heirloom rice in half a cup of cannabis coconut oil, then lets it blossom in chicken broth and coconut milk for this simple but sexy side dish that can dress up the plainest entrée. Black Chinese heirloom rice (which is really deep purple) is high in antioxidants, cooks quickly without sticking, and has a sweet undertone that pairs nicely with cannabis and coconut oil. Cannabis Cup perennial favorite Girl Scout Cookies, with its own sweet earthiness, is great with this dish.

Serves 8

THC per serving:

With Cannabis-Infused
Coconut or Olive Oil
(page 101): 🌿 🌿 🌿

With 20-Minute Cannabis Olive
Oil (page 103): 🌿 🌿

With Beginner's Oil
(page 100): 🌿

½ cup cannabis-infused coconut oil
½ red bell pepper, diced
½ yellow bell pepper, diced
3–4 scallions, chopped
3 garlic cloves, minced
salt, to taste
freshly ground pepper, to taste
1 cup black Chinese heirloom rice
1½ cups homemade chicken broth
1 cup coconut milk

Heat oil in a heavy-bottomed medium saucepan over medium heat until liquid. Add peppers, scallions, garlic, salt, and pepper. Sauté, stirring occasionally, for 8–10 minutes.

Add rice and stir for another 2 minutes, coating all grains of rice with oil.

Add broth and coconut milk. Bring to a boil.

Cover tightly, reduce heat to low, and simmer for 25–30 minutes.

Let rest for 5–10 minutes. Fluff with a fork and serve.

Broccoli, Bacon, and Almonds in Cannabis Mayonnaise Vinaigrette

Herb Seidel

When President Barack Obama told student journalists that his favorite food was broccoli and insisted to Jay Leno that he ate it all the time, he wasn't talking about the green mush he (and a lot of other people) hated as a kid. Michelle Obama grows broccoli in the White House kitchen garden, so the Obamas eat only fresh organic stalks, and chefs have learned a lot about bringing out the best in the crisp cabbage cousin since President George H. W. Bush banned it from Air Force One in 1990. Herb Seidel's combination of raw broccoli, bacon, and almonds with creamy dressing made from mayonnaise and a third of a cup of cannabis olive oil is a fine example, though the cannabis-laced dish isn't likely to be served in the White House anytime soon (Willie Nelson for President!). Herb's masterful combination of sweet and savory ingredients makes the most of the powerhouse vegetable, packed with fiber, vitamins A and C, potassium, phytochemicals, and antioxidants. This salad needs to be chilled in the refrigerator for at least an hour before serving. The longer it sits, the more time the strong flavors and aromas have to commingle into a complex dish with seasoned cannabis undertones.

Serves 6–8

THC per serving:

With Cannabis-Infused Coconut or Olive Oil (page 101): 🌿 🌿

With 20-Minute Cannabis Olive Oil (page 103): 🌿 ⌇

With Beginner's Oil (page 100): ⌇

½ pound bacon
2 heads fresh broccoli
1 red onion
¾ cup raisins
¾ cup sliced almonds
1 cup mayonnaise

⅓ cup cannabis-infused olive oil
½ cup white sugar
2 tablespoons white wine vinegar

Place bacon in a deep skillet and cook over medium-high heat until evenly brown on both sides. Cool and crumble.

Cut broccoli into bite-sized pieces and cut onion into thin bite-sized slices. Combine in a bowl with bacon, raisins, and almonds. Mix well.

To make dressing, mix mayonnaise, olive oil, sugar, and vinegar until smooth.

Stir dressing into salad, let chill for at least an hour, and serve.

Desserts

As you wind down a full-course meal, dessert is the perfect time to introduce a relaxing indica cultivar. Sweet-tasting cultivars are abundant—and ideal for decadent desserts. Stay away from the more pungent cultivars to avoid giving your sweet treats a skunky flavor.

Buttermilk Panna Canna

Catjia Redfern

Catjia Redfern stirs half a cup of cannabis flowers into heavy cream and lets it infuse in a low oven for up to three hours for her version of panna cotta, the rich Italian pudding that has become a restaurant staple. Panna cotta is a simple, elegant dessert (really, just cooked cream) that chefs love because it can take on fresh fruits and flavors as they're in season or in vogue. The cannabis in Catjia's version, in a buttermilk base with vanilla accents, is detectable but not overwhelming. Her pudding is a great foundation for experimenting with whatever berries and cannabis cultivars are in season and in your neighborhood. Catjia uses kosher beef gelatin (dehydrated collagen from cattle bones), but it's fine to use agar (cooked and pressed algae) instead. It's not fine to substitute coconut sugar for the white sugar (the panna canna won't set right), but it's more than fine to use frozen berries if you don't have fresh ones and brighten up the berries with a splash of rum. On that note, you could up the dosage on this dessert by greasing the ramekins with cannabis-infused ghee. Only you know whether that's a good idea for you.

Serves 4-6

THC per serving: 🌿 🌿 🌿

1 cup organic heavy cream
⅓ cup cured and trimmed cannabis flowers, finely
    ground
2 teaspoons vanilla bean paste or fresh vanilla bean
2 teaspoons unflavored gelatin or agar
2 cups organic buttermilk
½ cup sugar
1–2 tablespoons raw honey
assorted frozen or fresh berries such as red currants,
    gooseberries, black or red raspberries
Dutch oven
cheesecloth
fine mesh strainer

Continued

Buttermilk Panna Canna

Preheat oven to 170°F.

Combine heavy cream and cannabis in Dutch oven and place, covered, on center rack of oven for 1–3 hours. (The longer the mixture cooks, the stronger the cream is likely to be.) Place cheesecloth inside a strainer. Strain out cannabis solids and set aside cream.

Lightly oil 6 ramekins or custard cups.

If using fresh vanilla bean, split pod and scrape seeds from pod into a small bowl. Save seeds and pod. Set aside.

In the top of a double boiler, sprinkle gelatin or agar over 1 cup of buttermilk. Do not heat.

Meanwhile, combine cannabis-infused cream and sugar in a saucepan. Bring to a boil over medium-high heat.

As soon as cream and sugar boil, pour mixture into gelatin mixture in double boiler. Heat, stirring constantly with a whisk, until gelatin dissolves, about 5 minutes.

Whisk in remaining cup of buttermilk and vanilla and remove from heat.

Divide among ramekins and chill until set, about 4 hours.

Just before serving, warm raw honey in saucepan, careful not to overheat. Add semi-frozen berries and heat gently until berries reach room temperature.

To serve, slip a knife around the edges of each ramekin and invert onto plates. Top each panna canna with berries and honey.

Kheer with Green Cardamom, Mango, and Pistachios

Rowan Lehrman

Rice pudding was Rowan Lehrman's favorite dessert when she was growing up in Fairfield, Iowa, in the 1970s. Her parents were Transcendental Meditators at Maharishi International University, not Midwesterners, so her mom made the pudding with cracked green cardamom seeds instead of raisins and called it by its Indian name, *kheer*. Rowan stirs half a cup of cannabis-infused cream into her adult version of kheer, a staple in Indian homes and temples for centuries, giving woody depth to the mild pudding made from basmati rice, coconut milk, and cracked green cardamom pods. Rowan serves her kheer with pistachio sprinkles and mango slices. Because they're high in myrcene molecules, which are also the dominant terpenes in cannabis, mangoes are reputed to increase, strengthen, and lengthen cannabis's euphoric effects. If you're making this for dessert, a citrusy indica such as Orange Kush is delicious with this pudding, but bear in mind that most people feel a more intense high with indicas. High-fat dairy and coconut milk enhance absorption of fat-soluble THC, so it delivers more than the half cup of cannabis cream suggests. Don't scoop it into your bowl like you're at the Indian buffet. Start with a couple spoonfuls. If you find that it's not strong enough for your liking, you can infuse the milk using the recipe on page 121.

Serves 4-8

THC per serving: ↘

1 heaping cup cooked basmati rice

1 cup organic whole milk

5 whole green cardamom pods, shells lightly cracked

pinch salt

¾ cup unsweetened coconut milk (roughly half of a 13.5-ounce can)

½ cup granulated cane sugar

½ cup Cannabis Cream (recipe on page 122)

1 ripe fresh mango, peeled and diced

⅓ cup unsalted pistachios, chopped

In a large, heavy-bottomed saucepan over medium heat, combine cooked rice, milk, cardamom pods, and salt. Bring to a simmer, stirring frequently until mixture begins to thicken.

Add coconut milk, sugar, and Cannabis Cream. Continue to stir frequently over medium heat until mixture thickens again, about 5–10 minutes.

Transfer kheer to individual serving dishes. Serve warm or chilled, garnished with mango and pistachios.

Store leftovers in a labeled, airtight container in the refrigerator.

Cannabis Avocado Mousse with Cashews and Lavender

Lucienne Bercow Lazarus

Sweetened with maple syrup and a quarter cup of cannabis-infused honey, Lucie Lazarus's mousse made from ripe avocados, coconut milk, and Greek yogurt is a dessert you can feel good about eating. (It's great for breakfast as well.) With more protein (about 4 grams per avocado) and less sugar than most fruits, creamy avocados are high in omega-3 fatty acids, antioxidants, vitamins B and K, magnesium, phosphorous, iron, and potassium. Lactose-free coconut milk, the cream that rises to the top when coconut flesh is soaked in water, delivers vitamins and minerals including iron, selenium, sodium, calcium, magnesium, and phosphorous. This healthy recipe couldn't be easier. Lucie whips up the ingredients in a blender, pours them into ramekins, and lets the mousse set in the refrigerator for two hours. With their high fat content, avocados and coconut milk absorb plenty of fat-soluble THC in this dish, so it's more potent than the two milligrams of THC per serving implies. If it's not strong enough for your taste, you can up the THC content by infusing the coconut milk with cannabis using the milk recipe on page 121.

Serves 4

THC per serving: ⬊

2 ripe avocados

2 teaspoons vanilla

¼ cup pure maple syrup

¼ cup Cannabis Honey (recipe on page 116)

1 cup coconut milk

½ cup plain Greek yogurt

pinch salt

chopped cashews and lavender for garnish

blender or food processor

ramekins

Peel and pit avocados.

In a blender or food processor, combine avocado, vanilla, maple syrup, infused honey, coconut milk, and yogurt.

Blend until mixture is smooth and creamy.

Spoon into 4-ounce ramekins or serving glasses and refrigerate for 2 hours.

Top with cashews and lavender. Serve.

Matcha and Cannabis Crème Brûlée

Rowan Lehrman

This recipe isn't for everybody. It's green and requires a kitchen blowtorch. The instructions include the words *taking great care not to burn yourself with melted sugar*, which means you shouldn't make it if you've eaten cannabis food for dinner (or breakfast or lunch). But if you have an open mind, a clear head, and a kitchen blowtorch, Rowan Lehrman's crème brûlée made from three-quarters of a cup of cannabis cream and antioxidant-rich Japanese green tea is worth the effort it takes to melt a little sugar—and you can make the crème without the brûlée if you're intrigued by the flavors but intimidated by the blowtorch (call it custard). Rowan has created a perfect balance of dank green cannabis and bright green matcha in this not-too-sweet dessert; green tea mellows cannabis's heavier undertones and tastes brighter against it. It's a treat if you enjoy the taste of cannabis (and matcha, but chances are pretty good that if you enjoy one, you enjoy the other). The fat content makes this dessert more potent than you might think, so use 4" ramekins the first time you make it. That's likely enough for a fine buzz; you can use 6" ramekins or use more Cannabis Cream and less non-infused cream if you need more green next time.

Serves 6-8

THC per serving: ↘

3 ¼ cups heavy cream
¾ cup Cannabis Cream (recipe on
    page 122)
1 tablespoon matcha
6 large organic egg yolks
½ cup granulated cane sugar plus
    6 teaspoons for caramelizing
fine mesh sieve
mixer with whisk attachment
ramekins
roasting pan
kitchen blowtorch

Preheat oven to 325°

Place both creams and matcha in a heavy-bottomed saucepan and whisk to incorporate. Over medium heat, bring to a low boil. Watch closely and do not let mixture boil over. Remove from heat, cover, and let sit for 15 minutes.

In the bowl of a mixer fitted with a whisk attachment, whisk together egg yolks and ½ cup sugar.

With mixer running on low, slowly add matcha cream in a steady stream.

Set a fine mesh sieve over a clean large bowl. Pour mixture through strainer into bowl.

Transfer mixture to 4" or 6" ramekins.

Continued

Matcha and Cannabis Crème Brûlée

Place ramekins into a large roasting pan. Carefully pour enough hot water into the pan to come halfway up the ramekins' sides and place roasting pan in oven.

Bake until crème is set but still trembling in the center, approximately 40 minutes.

Remove from oven and let sit until cool enough to handle.

Remove ramekins from water and refrigerate for at least 2 hours.

Pull ramekins from the refrigerator 30 minutes before you plan to serve them.

Sprinkle a teaspoon of granulated sugar on each ramekin and spread to evenly coat the top of the custard.

Using a kitchen blowtorch, melt the sugar on top to form the crispy brûlée, taking great care not to burn yourself with melted sugar.

Let sit for 5 minutes before serving.

Pumpkin Praline Mousse Cups with Cannabis Coconut Nectar

Scott Durrah

Not a fan of processed sugar, Scott Durrah keeps it to a minimum in this dessert, using it only to lightly coat pecans for the top of each mousse cup. Scott folds a half cup of cannabis coconut oil into vegan, sugar-free mousse made from pumpkin meat and coconut nectar in these nicely contained desserts. The mousse tastes like pumpkin pie, with a slight cannabis undertone that's largely masked when it's piped into chocolate cups. Scott sweetens the mousse with coconut nectar, low-glycemic syrup made from coconut blossom sap that delivers vitamins and amino acids, and thickens it with Irish moss gel, seaweed that's high in antioxidants, vitamins, minerals, calcium, and iodine. All of that gives this mousse beyond-dessert nutritional value, but Irish moss isn't always easy to find. You can order it online if you can't find it locally, and Scott's stumped for substitutions. He always has the seaweed—which is prolific on rocks around his beloved Jamaica—on hand at his restaurant in Denver. (In Jamaica, Irish moss is blended into an energy drink that many believe is also an aphrodisiac.) Scott points out that when you're cooking with fine cannabis, it's worth the effort to track down specialty ingredients that match it in benefits and quality. (It wasn't always easy to find cannabis, but we managed.) If you can't find Irish moss or don't want to use it, Scott encourages you to play with his recipe until you find the right solution for you. (You might want to use non-infused coconut oil until you get it right. Making mistakes with cannabis oil gets expensive.) This recipe also requires a decorating bag, blissfully easy to find at your local grocer.

Serves 6
THC per serving:
With Cannabis-Infused
    Coconut or Olive Oil
    (page 101): 🌿 🌿 🌿 🌿
With 20-Minute Cannabis Olive
    Oil (page 103): 🌿 🌿 🌿
With Beginner's Oil (page 100):
    🌿 🌿 🌿 🌿

2¾ cups pumpkin meat (4–5-pound pumpkin)
¾ cup Irish moss
1½ cups water + ¼–½ cup water
7 tablespoons coconut nectar or maple syrup
4 drops liquid stevia
2 tablespoons pumpkin pie spice
⅛ teaspoon sea salt
½ cup cannabis-infused coconut oil, melted
¼ cup sugar
splash of lemon juice
6 whole pecans
chocolate cups (available in grocery stores or online)
decorating bag
parchment paper

Continued

Pumpkin Praline Mousse Cups with Cannabis Coconut Nectar

Preheat oven to 350°F.

Cut pumpkin in half, scoop out seeds and pulp (save the seeds for roasting). Place pumpkin, cut side down, on parchment-lined baking sheet. Bake until flesh is easily pierced with a fork, about 45 minutes. Remove from oven and scoop out flesh into a bowl.

Rinse Irish moss well. Place in saucepan with 1½ cups water and boil on medium-high heat for 15 minutes. Remove pan from heat and let cool for 15 minutes.

In a blender, mixer, or food processor, blend Irish moss, cooked pumpkin, coconut nectar or maple syrup, stevia, pumpkin pie spice, and sea salt until completely smooth and creamy. Add coconut oil and blend to incorporate.

Peel paper liner from chocolate cups and arrange on a platter.

Place mousse in decorating bag fitted with small star tip. Pipe mousse into chocolate shells. Refrigerate.

Place sugar and lemon juice in a pot and add enough water to make the mixture resemble wet sand. Stir to combine and cook over medium-high heat until mixture is a nice amber color. Remove from heat.

Use a fork to dip pecans into sugar water and soak until pecans are well-coated. Transfer to a plate lined with waxed paper and let cool.

Take mousse cups from refrigerator and place a pecan on top of each one.

Refrigerate in a labeled container until set, about 30 minutes or up to 1 day before serving.

Cannabis Sugar Cookie Stacks with Orange, Kumquat, and Ginger Confit

Lucienne Bercow Lazarus

Lucie Lazarus's impressive cookie stack takes some planning but isn't all that hard to pull off. You have to make the confit the night before, so you might as well make the cookies then, too. Those are the two most time-consuming tasks when making this dessert, however, so it's a breeze to assemble for a dinner party once they're out of the way. Confit is sugar-cured fruit, derived from ancient practices of salting meat for long-term storage. The curing process exaggerates the flavor of chewy oranges, kumquats, and ginger in Lucie's confit, giving it just the right bite to complement but not overpower sugar cookies made with half a cup of cannabis butter. (If you can get it, use Lemon Kush—one of Lucie's favorite sweet and tangy hybrid cultivars—to infuse the butter.) This dessert uses only twelve of the cookies you'll bake (because it would be silly to go to all that trouble for just a dozen), but you can halve the cookie recipe or freeze extras in a labeled, airtight container to snack on or use to make this dessert again. You'll also have extra confit, which keeps in the refrigerator (in a labeled, airtight container, of course) for up to six months. You can easily temper the dose of this dessert by how many cookies you stack.

Serves 4

THC per cookie: ⬎

½ cup Orange, Kumquat, and Ginger *Confit* (recipe below)

Buttermilk Cannabis Cookies (recipe below)

½ cup crème fraiche or whipped cream

8 raspberries

4 whole kumquats, thinly sliced

mint leaves

Set out four dessert plates and place a cookie on each one.

Pour confit into a wide bowl. Finely chop orange, kumquat, and ginger slices in confit to make a small dice.

Spoon 1 tablespoon confit onto each cookie and top with another cookie.

Spoon 2 tablespoons crème fraiche or whipped cream on top.

Gently place another cookie on top.

Spoon 1 tablespoon confit on top.

Garnish with raspberries, kumquats, and mint leaves.

Orange, Kumquat, and Ginger Confit

Makes about 1 cup

1 cup sugar
1 cup water
1 small orange, unpeeled, halved and thinly sliced crosswise
1 3" piece fresh ginger, peeled and thinly sliced
12 kumquats, thinly sliced

In a small pan, combine sugar and water and bring to a boil over medium-high heat, stirring often. Boil, stirring often, for about 1 minute.

Add orange slices, ginger, and kumquats to boiling sugar-water. Turn off heat and cover pan with foil. Let cool and transfer to an airtight, labeled container. Refrigerate overnight.

Keeps in the refrigerator for up to 6 months.

Cannabis Sugar Cookies

For more potent cookies, replace the regular butter with cannabis-infused butter.

Makes about 48 cookies

THC per cookie: ⬎

2¾ cups all-purpose flour
1 teaspoon baking soda
½ teaspoon baking powder
½ cup cannabis-infused butter, softened

½ cup unsalted butter, softened
1½ cups white sugar
1 egg
1 teaspoon vanilla extract
¼ teaspoon almond extract
3–4 tablespoons buttermilk
raw sugar

Preheat oven to 375°F.

In a small bowl, stir together flour, baking soda, and baking powder. Set aside.

In a large bowl, cream together butters and sugar until smooth. Beat in the egg and extracts.

Slowly add dry ingredients to wet ingredients and blend until just combined. Add enough buttermilk to moisten dough so it's soft but not wet. Roll teaspoons of dough into about 48 evenly sized balls. Roll balls in raw sugar, place on an ungreased cookie sheet, and slightly flatten tops.

Bake for 8–10 minutes or until light golden brown. Do not over bake! Let stand for 2 minutes before removing to cooling racks.

Super Lemon Haze Banana Rum Surprise

Scott Durrah

Jamaica's soil, water, and climate are ideal for growing cannabis and also sugarcane, which Jamaicans have been distilling into rum for centuries. Durrah has tasted some fine rum, and some fine cannabis, in both Jamaica and in Denver. In this dessert—a toasted-butter-caramel-cannabis bananas Foster without shooting flames—Scott combines five teaspoons of strong, aged Jamaican dark rum and a quarter cup of melted butter infused with Super Lemon Haze, pours it over sliced bananas, pops the bananas in the oven for about twenty minutes, and tops them with ice cream and cinnamon. (You don't have to use a citrusy cultivar if it's hard to find, but they're best at picking up a good Jamaican rum's citrus undertones.) Even in small amounts, alcohol exacerbates the body's THC absorption, so start with small servings. People can always have more, and you can refrigerate leftover sauce in a labeled airtight container in the refrigerator to drizzle over pancakes or stir into oatmeal, yogurt, or rice for the next couple of days.

Serves 4
THC per serving:
With Cannabis-Infused
    Coconut or Olive Oil
    (page 101): 🌿 🌿 🌿
With 20-Minute Cannabis
    Olive Oil (page 103): 🌿 🌿
With Beginner's Oil
    (page 100): 🌿

6 ripe bananas
4 tablespoons brown sugar
¼ cup cannabis-infused butter or
    coconut oil, melted
5 teaspoons dark rum
½ teaspoon lemon rind, grated

vanilla ice cream
cinnamon
9"x 13" glass baking pan

Preheat oven to 275°F.

Peel and cut ripe bananas slant-wise and place in glass baking pan. Cover lightly with brown sugar.

Combine melted butter, rum, and lemon rind. Beat together with a whisk until creamy.

Pour melted butter and rum mixture over bananas.

Place in oven for 20–25 minutes.

Remove from oven and let stand for 5 minutes.

Scoop into individual bowls and top with vanilla ice cream and a pinch of cinnamon.

Flourless Superfood Cannabis Chocolate Cake

Andie Leon

Andie Leon wants everyone to eat chocolate cake in peace. She's healed herself from an eating disorder with a superfoods diet, and this gluten-free (vegan if made with coconut oil) cake is a staple that has become a favorite of her catering and restaurant clients. Andie packs this cake with nutritious, low-glycemic superfood sweeteners, including powder from Peruvian lucuma fruit, which is high in beta-carotene, iron, zinc, vitamin B3, calcium, and protein; powder from Amazonian açai berries, which delivers antioxidants, omega fats, and fiber; and powder from the tart Chilean maqui berry, an abundant source of polyphenols and anti-inflammatory compounds. (These are all available in health-food stores and online.) Andie beats the eggs for this cake for a good ten minutes, giving them enough structure to make up for the lack of flour. Well-beaten eggs bind the cake and improve its texture. She throws in whatever organic berries are in season and available to give the cake texture and tartness, and she folds a full cup of cannabis-infused butter (or coconut oil) into the batter. This cake is potent. Andie cuts it into inch-by-inch pieces and keeps them in a labeled container in the freezer so she can enjoy a couple bites at a time. Even with a high tolerance for cannabis, Andie never eats more than three pieces (and she absolves herself of responsibility for anyone else who does). If you're new to this cake, she suggests starting out with a piece the size of your thumb.

Serves 20
THC per serving:
With Cannabis-Infused Coconut or Olive Oil (page 101): ꙮ ꙮ ꙮ
With 20-Minute Cannabis Olive Oil (page 103): 14 milligrams
With Beginner's Oil (page 100): ꙮ
With Bonzo Butter (page 109): ꙮ
With Beginner's Butter (page 106): 4 milligrams
With Cannabis Ghee (page 108): ꙮ

1 cup gluten-free vodka
2 tablespoons dried lavender
13 eggs
1 teaspoon baking powder
⅓ cup lucuma powder
2 cups coconut sugar
½ pound (1 cup) cannabis-infused butter or coconut oil
1½ pound dark organic chocolate (60 percent cacao)

Continued

Flourless Superfood Cannabis Chocolate Cake

2 tablespoons açai powder
2 tablespoons maqui berry powder
1 teaspoon vanilla
½ cup organic berries
cheesecloth
fine mesh strainer

Combine vodka and lavender in a jar and shake. Set aside.

Preheat oven to 350°F.

In a mixing bowl, using a hand or electric mixer, beat eggs for 10 minutes. Add baking powder, lucuma, and coconut sugar. Beat mixture for 2 more minutes until well mixed.

In a medium-sized saucepan, combine butter and chocolate. Melt slowly over low heat, stirring constantly. Stir in açai powder, maqui, and vanilla.

Remove butter and chocolate from heat and pour into egg mixture. Fold together gently until well mixed.

Line a strainer with cheesecloth and pour vodka through to strain out lavender.

Fold vodka and berries into batter.

Pour batter into 9" x 9" baking pan. Bake for 1 hour.

Remove from oven and let cool on rack.

Cut into 1" pieces and serve or store in a labeled container in the freezer for up to a month.

Lemon Candy Cannabis Cake

Grace Gutierrez

Tart, sweet lemons are Grace Gutierrez's favorite flavor. For this special-occasion pound cake, she folds crushed hard lemon candies into a batter made with half a cup of cannabis olive oil, fresh lemon, and Greek yogurt. Topped with an almond milk glaze and more crushed lemon candies, the cake is dense, moist, and potent. Cut it into 1" x 1" pieces so people can test it and enjoy it slowly. You can substitute a few tablespoons of regular olive oil for some of the cannabis-infused oil if you want to eat bigger pieces. If you're a hardcore (and we're not responsible for you), use Cannabis Milk (recipe on page 121) for the glaze. Grace uses a sweet-smelling indica such as Blue Berry or White Rhino when she makes this cake as a dessert and an uplifting sativa such as her favorite, OG Kush, when she makes it for brunch.

Serves 8 or more

THC per serving:

With Cannabis-Infused
   Coconut or Olive Oil
   (page 101): ☘ ☘ ☘

With 20-Minute Cannabis
   Olive Oil (page 103): ☘ ☘

With Beginner's Oil
   (page 100): ☘

¾ cup hard lemon candies, divided

1½ cups flour

¾ teaspoon salt

2 teaspoons baking powder

½ cup fresh lemon juice (about 3–4 small lemons)

1 cup plain Greek yogurt

¾ cup granulated sugar

¼ cup light brown sugar

3 large eggs

2 teaspoons lemon zest (from about 2 small lemons)

½ cup cannabis-infused olive oil

1 cup powdered sugar

¼ cup vanilla almond milk

hammer

aluminum foil

Continued

Lemon Candy Cannabis Cake

Preheat oven to 350°F. Grease a 9"x 5" loaf cake pan with cooking spray. Dust a small amount of flour over cooking spray.

Put lemon candy into a medium-sized plastic food-storage bag, wrap in a small dishtowel, and place on sturdy cutting board. With a small hammer, pound candies until they're coarsely crushed. Do not break them up so much that they turn into powder. Divide into ¼ cup and ⅛ cup portions. Set aside.

In a small bowl, mix flour, salt, and baking powder.

In another medium bowl, mix together fresh lemon juice, Greek yogurt, sugars, eggs, and lemon zest.

Hand-mix dry ingredients into lemon juice and egg mixture. Once the two are fully incorporated, fold in infused olive oil. Mix in ¼ cup crushed hard lemon candies. Pour into prepared pan.

Bake cake for 35–40 minutes. When top of cake gets golden but cake is not fully cooked inside, tent a small piece of aluminum foil over cake and continue baking for another 10–15 minutes.

While cake bakes, whisk together powdered sugar and almond milk in a small bowl until all powdered sugar clumps are gone.

Once cake comes out with a clean cake tester, remove from oven and let cool about 15 minutes. Turn out of baking pan onto a plate.

Pour glaze over cake. While glaze is still wet, sprinkle ⅛ cup crushed lemon candies on top of cake.

Cut into 1" x 1" slices and serve. Store leftovers in a labeled airtight container.

Go Phish! Deconstructed Brownies

Lucienne Bercow Lazarus

Lucie Lazarus turns garden-variety treats into dessert art. Phish Food, one of Lucie's favorite Ben & Jerry's ice cream flavors (chocolate with marshmallow and caramel swirls and Goldfish dipped in fudge), inspired this dish. Lucie bakes Goldfish crackers and marshmallows into gooey brownies made with eight tablespoons of cannabis butter, then scoops a spoonful on top of whipped cream in a sugar cone for a treat that would make Ben and Jerry smile. With eight tablespoons of cannabis butter for twelve servings, this dessert won't take you out (if you eat just one and don't sneak little bites of brownie while you assemble the cones). If you know you have the tolerance, you can use Cannabis Cream (recipe on page 122) for some or part of the whipped cream to make the dessert stronger. You can also temper the potency by spooning in more or less brownie when you assemble the cones. Cultivar taste is less important when choosing cannabis to infuse the butter for this dessert because the strong chocolate taste overwhelms it. Lucie uses her favorite hybrid, OG Kush, because it makes her happy.

Serves 12

THC per serving:

With Bonzo Butter: ↘

With Beginner's Butter: ↘

With Cannabis Ghee: ↘

Butter to grease foil
8 tablespoons cannabis-infused butter
¾ cup unsweetened chocolate, chopped
1 cup sugar plus 2 tablespoons more for whipped cream
2 eggs
½ cup flour
½ cup cheddar-flavored Goldfish crackers
½ cup mini marshmallows
¼ cup milk chocolate chips
pinch salt
½ teaspoon vanilla extract
1 cup heavy whipping cream
12 sugar cones
aluminum foil
electric mixer

Continued

Go Phish! Deconstructed Brownies

Heat oven to 350°F. Line a 9" baking pan with foil. Grease the foil with butter.

Combine butter and chocolate in a small saucepan over low heat. When chocolate is nearly melted, remove from heat and stir until smooth.

Transfer chocolate mixture to a bowl and stir in 1 cup sugar.

Break one egg at a time into chocolate and beat mixture to fold in each egg.

Gently add flour, Goldfish, marshmallows, and chocolate chips. Stir to combine.

Add salt and vanilla. Stir.

Pour into prepared baking dish and place in preheated oven. Brownies will bake for about 20–25 minutes.

While brownies are baking, prepare whipped cream. Using an electric mixer, whip heavy cream in a bowl until it begins to thicken. Add 2 tablespoons sugar and continue beating until soft peaks form.

Remove brownies from oven when middle has just barely set. Cool completely on a rack before cutting into 12 pieces.

To serve, scoop a dollop of whipped cream into the bottom of a sugar cone and top with a heaping spoonful of brownie.

Cannabis, Chia, Almond, and Goji Berry "Pot Brownie" with Cranberry, Chocolate, and Red Wine Sauce

Andie Leon

Andie Leon transforms gluten-free brownies made with two-thirds of a cup of cannabis butter, mesquite flour, coconut sugar, cacao nibs, chia seeds, coconut, and goji berries into a full-on dessert when she smothers them in cranberry, chocolate, coconut, and red wine sauce made with a third of a cup of cannabis agave. Cacao nibs, "nature's chocolate chips," provide pure chocolate flavor from whole cacao beans as well as antioxidants, vitamins, minerals, and fiber. Andie makes the brownies with a combination of wheat flour and gluten-free mesquite flour, which is made from ground dried pods of the mesquite tree and is rich in soluble fiber, calcium, and magnesium. You could substitute mesquite flour for all the flour in this recipe to make it gluten-free, or you could substitute wheat flour for the mesquite flour if you prefer. The brownies are strong on their own, so start with 1" x 1" pieces (people who know they have tolerance can have more than one) and temper the dosage by drizzling on more or less sauce. The chocolate in this dessert overwhelms the taste of cannabis butter, so the taste of the cultivar you use isn't all that important.

Serves 4-6

THC per serving:

With Bonzo Butter: 🌿 🌿

With Beginner's Butter: 🌿

With Cannabis Ghee: 🌿 🌿

1 ⅓ cups flour, sifted

⅔ cup mesquite powder (or flour)

⅔ cup cocoa powder

1 teaspoon baking powder

2 eggs

2 tablespoons vodka

¼ cup raw almonds (or almond flakes)

½ cup cacao nibs

1 teaspoon cannabis-infused agave or honey (recipe on page 118)

⅔ cup cannabis-infused butter, softened

⅔ cup coconut sugar

¼ cup black chia seeds

½ cup grated coconut

½ cup goji berries

Cranberry, Chocolate, and Red Wine Sauce (recipe follows)

food processor

Preheat oven to 350°F. Lightly spray an 8" x 8" baking pan with cooking spray.

In a small bowl, mix flour, mesquite flour, cocoa, and baking powder. Set aside.

Lightly beat eggs and vodka together.

Grind almonds in a food processor.

Continued

Cannabis, Chia, Almond, and Goji Berry "Pot Brownie" with Cranberry, Chocolate, and Red Wine Sauce

In a small bowl, combine cacao nibs with agave or honey. Combine until cacao nibs are well coated.

In a cake mixer or large bowl, beat together butter and coconut sugar until it becomes a smooth paste. Alternating between the flour mixture and the egg mixture, add one cup at a time of each, continuing to beat until all ingredients are completely combined into a batter. Add almonds, agave cacao nibs, chia seeds, coconut, and goji berries. Beat thoroughly.

Pour batter into baking dish and bake for 40 minutes. Brownie is ready when a toothpick inserted into center comes out clean.

While the brownie bakes, make Cranberry, Chocolate, and Red Wine Sauce.

Remove brownie from oven and set pan on a rack to cool slightly.

Cut brownie into 1" x 1" squares.

Serve brownie warm with warm Cranberry, Chocolate, and Red Wine Sauce on top.

Cranberry, Chocolate, and Red Wine Sauce

Andie Leon

Makes about 3 cups

THC per serving: ↘

2 cups light coconut milk

½ cup red wine

⅓ cup cannabis-infused agave (recipe on page 118)

2 cups fresh cranberries

4 ounces (8 tablespoons) dark chocolate

1 cup grated coconut

Combine coconut milk, wine, agave, and cranberries in a small saucepan over medium heat and bring to a boil.

Add chocolate, lower heat, and stir continually with a wooden spoon while chocolate melts.

Simmer for 20 minutes, stirring occasionally.

Stir in coconut and remove from heat.

Serve warm over brownies.

Store leftovers in a labeled, airtight glass jar in the refrigerator for up to a week.

SAVORY SNACKS

Cannabis-infused snacks are portable, convenient, easy to measure—and nice to nibble on when you don't feel like committing to a whole meal.

Trippy Trail Mix

Donna Shields

Nomadic tribes mixed together dried meat, dried berries, and nuts to make a low-maintenance, high-energy food for long treks, and variations on the portable snack have been showing up as "trail mix" ever since. The main characters threw together trail mix before hiking in Jack Kerouac's 1958 novel *The Dharma Bums*, and '60s surfers relied on it when waves were gnarly. By the 1970s, trail mix, made with everything from chocolate candies to pretzels so people would eat it, could be found in every convenience store. Donna Shields's nutritious mix of raw nuts, seeds, and dried fruit baked in cannabis- and turmeric-infused coconut oil and maple syrup is more like the nomads' and less like the plastic-bag trail mix from 7-Eleven. In addition to a slight buzz, Donna's trail mix delivers turmeric's anti-inflammatory properties as well as protein, healthy fats, and antioxidants without empty calories, extra salt, or sugar. When she infuses the coconut oil for this recipe with cannabis, Donna adds a quarter teaspoon of ground turmeric for every tablespoon of coconut oil. The trail mix isn't terribly potent, though it's always a good idea to start slowly and try it at home before you eat it and hit the trails.

Makes 2 ½ cups

THC per serving:
With Cannabis-Infused
  Coconut or Olive Oil
  (page 101): ⚘ ⚘
With 20-Minute Cannabis
  Olive Oil (page 103): ⚘
With Beginner's Oil
  (page 100): ⚘

½ cup almonds
½ cup walnuts
½ cup dried goji berries
½ cup dried mulberries
¼ cup pumpkin seeds
¼ cup sunflower seeds
1 tablespoon real maple syrup
2 tablespoons cannabis-infused
  turmeric coconut oil*

Preheat oven to 350°F.

Combine almonds, walnuts, goji berries, mulberries, pumpkin seeds, and sunflower seeds in a bowl.

In a separate bowl, mix together syrup and cannabis-turmeric oil.

Pour syrup and oil mixture over nuts and berries. Stir with a wooden spoon to coat mixture.

Spread trail mix in a single layer on baking sheet.

Bake for 5 minutes until lightly browned.

Cool and transfer to a labeled, airtight container.

Store in the refrigerator.

* When infusing coconut oil for this recipe, add ¼ teaspoon ground turmeric for every tablespoon of oil.

Pemmicannabis

Catjia Redfern

Native Americans prepared pemmican—a dense mixture of dried meat, rendered fat, and dried berries or fruit—as a way to preserve meat for traveling. Fur traders and explorers adopted the compact, protein-rich snack and counted on it to feed expeditions. Pemmican is the ultimate paleo and primal snack, and Catjia Redfern has created a version made with a cup of cannabis flowers that delivers protein, nutrients, and a nice buzz. To make it, Catjia dehydrates grass-fed beef, bison, moose, deer, or elk at a very low temperature, then crushes it into a powder and mixes it with cannabis flowers, dried fruit, and tallow (rendered fat that's available from butchers, farmers, and online). Tallow from grass-fed animals is richer in carotenoids, the fat-soluble vitamin A precursor that gives carrots their orange color, and contains nearly 50 percent more healthy omega-3 fatty acids than tallow from grain-fed animals. Catjia presses the mixture into the bottom of cupcake tins, and freezes it to set. Pemmican can keep in the freezer for up to a year in a labeled, airtight container.

Serves 18

THC per serving: 🌿 🌿 🌿

1 pound tallow
1 pound top round or bottom round redmeat
1 cup decarboxylated, well-trimmed cannabis flowers, finely ground
2 teaspoons Himalayan sea salt
1 cup dried fruit (organic tart cherries, currents or blueberries)
strainer
food processor
cookie sheet or cupcake tin
parchment paper
string

Preheat oven to 225°F.

Cut tallow into small pieces, about ½" square. Place in a roasting pan and slow roast for 12 hours or longer. Remove from oven when all popping noises have stopped and all moisture is removed. The opaque white fat should be broken down to a liquid.

Line a strainer with a cloth or paper towel and place over a bowl. Pour fat from roasting pan through strainer, pressing down on the cracklings to extract as much fat as possible. Set aside fat to cool. Refrigerate.

Place meat in the freezer and let it firm up partially, about 15–30 minutes. You want meat to be firm but not completely frozen. Remove and slice as thinly as possible.

Set oven on lowest heat. Lay meat pieces directly on oven racks and place a tray on the bottom rack to catch any fat that falls. Keep oven at lowest temperature and allow meat to dry out completely, about 10 hours or more depending on the moisture and fat level in the meat.

Remove meat from oven and grind in a food processor.

Finely mince dried fruit in a food processor or Vitamix until granular.

Slowly warm tallow in a pan over low heat.

In a large bowl, combine tallow, ground meat, dried fruit, cannabis flowers, and salt, incorporating warm fat slowly into powdered meat and berries.

Press or roll into forms on a cookie sheet or cupcake tin.

Freeze to firm, about 1 hour. Wrap in parchment and tie with a string. Store in freezer or refrigerator.

Popcorn with Cannabis Butter and Spicy Hemp Furikake

Rowan Lehrman

When Rowan Lehrman lived in Funabashi City, Japan, as a teenager, she introduced her host family to stove popped popcorn, and the family introduced her to *furikake*, a mixture of dried fish, seeds, and seaweed that every Japanese family keeps on hand to pickle, spice, and sprinkle on rice. That exchange led Rowan to dream up this snack: popcorn drizzled with two teaspoons of cannabis butter and sprinkled with her own version of *furikake* made with seaweed, dried orange peel, and lavender, Aleppo pepper flakes, hemp, poppy, and sesame seeds. The sweet-salty furikake stands up to earthy cannabis butter, and the Aleppo peppers, while fairly mild, prevent Rowan from eating too much popcorn too quickly. If you have cannabis fan leaves, you could cut a handful into 1½" pieces, toss them with olive oil to coat, and crisp them in a 275-degree oven for about 20 minutes to make cannabis chips as a substitute for nori in the furikake. They won't add a lot of THC, but they'll add nutritional value. With roughly a teaspoon of cannabis butter per person, this popcorn is just right for enjoying a movie but won't leave you stuck on the sofa watching infomercials for the rest of the night. You can increase or decrease the popcorn's potency (and calories) by drizzling on more or less cannabis butter or substituting a teaspoon of regular butter.

Serves 2

THC per serving:

With Beginner's Butter (recipe on page 106): ↘

3 tablespoons coconut oil
⅓ cup organic popcorn
2 teaspoons cannabis-infused butter
unsalted butter, to taste
Spicy Hemp Furikake (recipe below)

Continued

Popcorn with Cannabis Butter and Spicy Hemp Furikake

Have a large serving bowl handy.

In a 2-quart lidded saucepan, melt coconut oil over medium-high heat. Add popcorn and place lid slightly askew to let steam escape. At roughly 10-second intervals, begin shaking the pan by moving it gently back and forth across the burner. As the corn starts to pop, shake more vigorously. When popping slows to a few seconds between pops, remove pan from burner and place popped corn in serving bowl.

Add cannabis butter and regular butter to the same saucepan and melt. Pour melted butter over popcorn, season liberally with furikake, and mix with your hands to evenly distribute.

Store leftovers in a labeled, airtight jar.

Spicy Hemp Furikake

Rowan Lehrman

This Japanese staple can be sprinkled on popcorn, rice, eggs, or fish.

Makes roughly ½ cup

2 tablespoons hemp seeds
2 tablespoons Aleppo pepper flakes
1 tablespoon dried orange peel
2 tablespoons sesame seeds
2 tablespoons poppy seeds
½ teaspoon dried lavender
1 sheet toasted nori or a handful of toasted cannabis leaf chips
1 tablespoon sea salt
2 teaspoons sugar

Make furikake in batches by combining hemp seeds, pepper flakes, orange peel, sesame seeds, poppy seeds, and lavender in an electric spice grinder, pulsing until almost a powder but leaving some of the spices intact so that the mixture has texture.

With your fingers or kitchen shears, finely crumble or snip nori (or cannabis chips, if using) into a bowl.

Add ground spices, sugar, and salt. Stir to combine.

Store in a labeled, airtight container for up to 1 year.

Roasted Garlic, Cannabis, and White Bean Dip

Herb Seidel

Herb Seidel says this dip made with five tablespoons of cannabis olive oil is an incredible start to any party, and it's great to have around for snacking. Whether served with toasted bread, baked pita wedges, celery sticks, or red pepper wedges, this dip is a tasty alternative to hummus. Incorporate it into sandwiches, stir a spoonful into scrambled eggs, or spread it on pizza. Herb uses an entire garlic bulb, which gives the dip antioxidant and anti-inflammatory properties. With about a tablespoon of cannabis-infused olive oil per serving, it delivers a nice buzz and a hint of cannabis flavor. Oil infused with a lemony sativa such as Super Lemon Haze or Lemon Thai is perfect in this dip.

Serves 4-6

THC per serving:

With Cannabis-Infused Coconut or Olive Oil (page 101): 🌿 🌿 🌿

With 20-Minute Cannabis Olive Oil (page 103): 🌿 🌿

With Beginner's Oil (page 100): 🌿

1 19-ounce can cannellini beans
1 large head garlic, roasted
5 tablespoons cannabis-infused extra-virgin olive oil
1 teaspoon lemon juice
dash hot red pepper flakes (optional)
salt, to taste
pepper, to taste
chicken broth, as needed
2 tablespoons chopped tomatoes or red peppers, to garnish
food processor

Drain beans in a strainer and rinse with water. Drain well.

Place beans in a food processor and squeeze roasted head of garlic on top. Add olive oil, lemon juice, red pepper flakes (if using), salt, and pepper.

Pulse until smooth, adding as much chicken broth as needed to create a smooth dip.

Fresh Cannabis Flower Guacamole

Scott Durrah

Scott Durrah's goal as a cannabis chef is to help people find a dosage that's comfortable while delivering the health benefits they seek. With guacamole, people can start slow (one chip) as they learn how much or little they can handle. For this favorite party snack made from simple, whole foods, Scott uses two tablespoons of cannabis olive oil and also folds in two teaspoons of finely chopped raw cannabis flowers. Without decarboxylation, the raw flowers don't increase the guacamole's psychoactive effects (for many people), but they're loaded with anti-inflammatory antioxidants and taste great in this dip. You can omit the raw flowers if you don't have them. Avocados, an excellent source of fiber, vitamins, and antioxidants, are also high in oleic acid, which increases the body's absorption of fat-soluble nutrients such as carotenoids—and THC. Even with just two tablespoons of cannabis oil for six servings, this guacamole gets you pleasantly, moderately high (unless you eat more than your share, and then we can't be responsible).

Serves 6

THC per serving:

With Cannabis-Infused Coconut or Olive Oil (page 101):

With 20-Minute Cannabis Olive Oil (page 103):

With Beginner's Oil (page 100):

1 red chile, finely chopped
juice of two limes
2 tablespoons cannabis-infused olive oil
2 teaspoons cured cannabis flowers, finely chopped
3 ripe avocados, diced
½ cup onion, finely chopped
tortilla chips

Mix ingredients with a wooden spoon in a medium-sized mixing bowl until well mixed but still chunky.

Transfer to a serving bowl and serve with chips.

Store in a labeled, airtight container in the refrigerator for 1–2 days or the freezer for 3–4 months.

SWEET SNACKS

There's beauty in figuring out that a quarter of a brownie or cookie will bring on the relaxation, creative stimulation, or sleep (depending on the cultivar you use) you're craving. Once you know your dose, these snacks are convenient, discreet, and easy to portion consistently.

Majoon Love Balls

Chris Kilham

Chris Kilham discovered *majoon*, an Arabic word for cannabis candy, when he read Richard Burton's translation of *The Arabian Nights* in the 1980s. He found a footnote describing an aphrodisiacal confection made from "ganja or young leaves, buds, capsules, and florets of poppy seed and flowers of the thorn-apple (*datura*) with milk and sugar-candy, nutmegs, cloves, mace, and saffron, all boiled to the consistency of treacle, which hardens when cold." The Indians used highly intoxicating "gum of hemp," collected by hand or by passing a blanket over cannabis plants early in the morning. Intrigued, Chris tinkered with the recipe for decades, and he's perfected these beauties. Made from dried fruits, nuts, and a cup of Chris's cannabis-honey butter, but without poppies or delirium-inducing *datura*, Chris's balls are perfect little cannabis snacks. You can temper their dosage by rolling them larger or smaller, and they'll keep in the freezer for weeks or even months. The first time you make them, roll them small.

Makes about 20 balls

THC per serving: 🌿

10–12 dried dates (preferably medjools)
8–10 dried figs
10 dried apricots, organic and sulfur-free
½ teaspoon ground cinnamon
½ teaspoon ground cloves
½ teaspoon cardamom powder
½ cup almonds
½ cup shelled pistachios
1 cup Bonzo Butter, softened (recipe on page 109)
crushed coconut

Fine-chop all ingredients except Bonzo Butter and coconut by hand on a wooden cutting board.

Put all ingredients into a bowl and mix thoroughly with a wooden spoon.

Add Bonzo Butter and knead with hands. Roll into balls about 1" in diameter (larger or smaller will make them more or less potent).

Roll balls carefully in crushed coconut until coated.

Store in a labeled, airtight container in the refrigerator or freezer.

Hash Hive Cookies

Emily Sloat

You may know these balls of chocolate, butterscotch, nuts, and chow mein noodles as no-bake or haystack cookies. Ready without an oven in less than half an hour, they're a cookie swap favorite with endless ingredient variations (oatmeal, corn flakes, dried fruit). Emily Sloat's version includes a tablespoon and a half of coconut oil infused with Chemdawg hash. The indica hybrid has as much as 20 percent THC, so a tablespoon and a half of oil makes Emily's cookies plenty potent. You'll make milder cookies if you use oil infused with plant material and a lighter sativa. The chocolate, butterscotch, and peanuts overwhelm any cannabis taste in these cookies, which makes them dangerous. It's easy to overindulge on cookies that look and taste just like the ones your mom made for holidays. Make the cookies small (about the size of a silver dollar), label the container you store them in, and clearly label them if you take them to parties.

Makes 18 cookies
THC per serving:
With Solventless Hash and
  Coconut Oil (page 104): ⬎
With Cannabis-Infused
  Coconut or Olive Oil
  (page 101): ⬎
With 20-Minute Cannabis Olive
  Oil (page 103): ⬎

1 5-ounce can crunchy chow mein
  noodles
⅓ cup roasted salted peanuts
⅓ cup mini marshmallows
1½ tablespoons cannabis-infused
  coconut oil
6 ounces butterscotch chips
6 ounces semisweet chocolate chips
wax or parchment paper

Line 2 baking sheets with wax or parchment paper.

Combine noodles, peanuts, and marshmallows in a large bowl and set aside.

Melt oil, butterscotch, and chocolate chips over a double boiler, stirring until melted and well combined.

Pour mixture on top of noodles, peanuts, and marshmallows and stir to coat completely.

Drop tablespoons of mixture onto prepared baking sheets. Place in the freezer to set for 15 minutes.

Store in a labeled, airtight container for 3 to 4 days at room temperature or up to 3 months in the freezer.

Alice B. Toklas Carrot Cupcakes

Catjia Redfern

Alice B. Toklas's "brownie"—really fudge made with hash and dried fruit—became an icon when she published the recipe in her cookbook in the 1950s. Pot brownies resurged again in the 1970s after eating one changed Peter Sellers's life in the 1968 film *I Love You, Alice B. Toklas.* Sixty-some years later, Catjia Redfern pays homage to Toklas with carrot cake, another 1970s icon that has yet to be claimed. Catjia blends a cup and a half of cannabis-infused ghee (which she prefers, but you can use coconut oil) in a batter with grated carrots, pecans, and golden raisins and pours it into cupcake tins for a portable snack (like a brownie, but better) that's great to take to parties (invited and clearly labeled, of course). The frosting has half a cup of cannabis ghee, giving it a green cast and pleasant grassy taste. You can temper the cupcakes' potency by smearing on a little or a lot of frosting or leaving cannabis oil out of the frosting altogether. To make these cupcakes gluten-free, Catjia suggests a blend of glutenless flours or Pamela's gluten-free flour mixture (omit the baking powder and baking soda if you use Pamela's). Sometimes she substitutes goat cheese for the cream cheese to fancy up the frosting. One cupcake is a solid dose for experienced cannabis eaters and five or more doses according to Colorado's ten-milligram dosing regulations. Beginners should start with a sliver and go easy on the frosting.

Makes 12 cupcakes

THC per serving:

With Cannabis-Infused Coconut
  or Olive Oil (page 101): ☘
  ☘ ☘ ☘ ☘

With 20-Minute Cannabis
  Olive Oil (page 103): ☘ ☘
  ☘ ☘ ☘

With Beginner's Oil (page 100):
  ☘

1 cup organic cane sugar

1 cup coconut sugar

2 cups cannabis-infused ghee or coconut oil, chilled

4 large eggs

2½ cups flour

2 teaspoons baking powder

2 teaspoons baking soda

1 teaspoon salt

1 teaspoon cinnamon

¾ teaspoon nutmeg

2 teaspoons pure vanilla extract

Continued

Alice B. Toklas Carrot Cupcakes

3 cups carrots, grated (about 1 pound)
1 cup pecans, lightly roasted and chopped
½ cup golden raisins or currants
2 8-ounce packages cream cheese (or soft goat cheese)
1 cup ricotta cheese
½ cup confectioner's sugar
2 teaspoons lemon rind, grated
4 teaspoons lemon juice
muffin tins
electric mixer or whisk

Preheat oven to 325°F. Lightly grease muffin tins.

Beat cane sugar, coconut sugar, and 1½ cups ghee or oil in large bowl until well combined. Add eggs one at a time, beating after each one.

Place flour, baking powder, baking soda, salt, cinnamon, nutmeg, and 1 teaspoon vanilla into sugar and oil mixture. Fold in carrots, chopped pecans, and raisins.

Pour batter into prepared tins. Bake until a toothpick inserted into the center of each cupcake comes out clean and cakes begin to pull away from the sides, about 45 minutes.

Cool in pans on racks for 15 minutes. Turn out cupcakes onto racks and cool completely.

To make frosting, use an electric mixer or whisk to beat cream cheese, ricotta cheese, ½ cup of ghee, confectioner's sugar, 1 teaspoon vanilla, lemon rind, and lemon juice in bowl until smooth and creamy.

With a spatula, spread frosting over tops of cupcakes.

Store in a labeled, airtight container in the refrigerator or at room temperature.

Oatmeal, Almond, and Coconut Ganja Cookies

Shaman Cuervo

Chris Killham insisted that we include this recipe for "the very finest pot cookies anywhere, period" from his Amazonian friend Shaman Cuervo. Chris knows his pot cookies, and these are quite fine. Shaman Cuervo simmers a quarter- to a half-ounce of cured cannabis flowers in butter for fifteen minutes, then stirs in maple syrup for a quick infusion that sweetens the sugar-free cookies. Maple-sweet with a hint of cannabis, the cookies have fiber-rich oatmeal and coconut, brain-food almonds, and wheat germ, which is great for the immune and cardiovascular systems. The cookies are potent, and Chris advises starting with half of one. The first time you make them, spoon out dough balls about the size of a silver dollar and start checking them in the oven after seven minutes. It's better to start small and not overindulge with "just one cookie."

Makes 24-36 cookies

THC per serving: 🌿

½ cup (1 stick) butter

¼–½ ounce well-trimmed, cured cannabis flowers, finely ground

½ cup pure maple syrup

1 cup almonds, ground in a blender into coarse flour

⅓ cup oatmeal, ground in a blender into coarse flour

⅓ cup shredded, dried coconut

⅓ cup wheat germ

1 cup pastry flour

¼ teaspoon powdered cinnamon

pinch of salt

strainer

cheesecloth

Preheat oven to 350°F.

Place butter in pan and melt at low heat. When butter is thoroughly melted, stir in cannabis and simmer on low heat for 10–15 minutes.

Remove cannabis butter from stove. Line a strainer with cheesecloth and pour butter into bowl to strain out cannabis. Squeeze cheesecloth and compost plant matter.

Stir in maple syrup. Stir until syrup is thoroughly integrated. Set aside.

In a mixing bowl, use a wooden spoon to combine almonds, oatmeal, coconut, wheat germ, pastry flour, cinnamon, and salt.

Stir in maple-cannabis butter.

When ingredients are thoroughly mixed, use a tablespoon to scoop out dough and fashion dome-shaped cookies on cookie sheets.

Bake for 10–12 minutes, until golden brown. Cool on racks.

White Chocolate, Walnut, and Cannabis Bars

Herb Seidel

Herb Seidel blends more than two sticks of cannabis butter into these bars, and they're potent. Mixed with brown sugar into a rich butterscotch base, the butter loses most of its cannabis flavor. That can be disastrous for unwitting snackers, so label these bars conspicuously when you store them. Made with your favorite sativa, they offer quick inspiration; with indica, a nighttime snack. The blondies do well at the bottom of an ice cream sundae, but for the most part they're nibbling bars. A bite or two gives you a working buzz and a sugar fix when you need it. Cut these into one-by-one inch pieces and bear in mind that Herb calls them "extreme." Treat them like you would energy shots, with appreciative moderation.

Serves 15–20
THC per serving:
With Bonzo Butter (page 109):

With Beginner's Butter
(page 106):
With Cannabis Ghee
(page 108):

4 cups all-purpose flour
2 teaspoons baking powder
1½ teaspoons salt
1⅓ cups (2⅓ sticks) unsalted cannabis-
    infused butter, room temperature
3 cups packed light brown sugar
4 teaspoons vanilla
4 eggs
2½ cups walnuts, coarsely chopped
1¼ cups white chocolate chips
2 9" square baking pans
aluminum foil

Heat oven to 350°F. Line baking pans with enough foil to extend over two sides.

Combine flour, baking powder, and salt in a bowl.

In a large bowl, use electric or hand mixer to beat together butter, sugar, and vanilla in large bowl until creamy. Beat in eggs, one at a time. On low, beat in flour mixture.

Stir in 2 cups walnuts and 1 cup chips.

Divide batter into pans. Divide remaining nuts in half; sprinkle half over each pan.

Bake for 40 minutes, until toothpick tests clean.

Remove pans from oven. Sprinkle tops with remaining chips; lightly press down chips with spatula to melt slightly.

Cool in pan on rack. Cut into 1" x 1" squares (or smaller).

Store in a labeled, airtight container.

Green Tea, Cannabis, and Coconut Brownies

Andie Leon

Brownies remain the most popular way of eating cannabis because they work. They're easy to infuse with cannabis butter or oil, can be cut into any size pieces, and travel well. All of that is crucial for a caterer delivering cannabis food, and Andie Leon is a huge fan of the brownie. Andie's brownies, made with coconut sugar, two-thirds of a cup of cannabis butter, and a teaspoon of cannabis agave (or honey), are nothing like the ones that Hyde and Eric made on *That '70s Show*. They deliver the taste and health benefits of almonds, black chia seeds, goji berries, coconut, and matcha—a grassy, antioxidant-rich green tea powder that pairs well with cannabis. Mesquite flour adds flavor and nutrition depth, and Andie substitutes it for all the flour when she makes these brownies for gluten-free clients. (You can substitute wheat flour for the mesquite flour if you can't find it or don't want to buy it.) Non-infused agave makes these brownies less potent (always our choice so we can eat more), and infused vodka (recipe on page 112) turns these brownies into serious medicine (do this at your own risk). Andie suggests testing your tolerance by eating a piece of brownie the size of your thumb. You can always eat more later, and there's no going back if you underestimate these brownies' strength.

Serves 4-6

THC per serving:

With Bonzo Butter (page 109):

    🌿 🌿

With Beginner's Butter
(page 106): 🌿

With Cannabis Ghee
(page 108): 🌿 🌿

1⅓ cups flour, sifted
⅔ cup mesquite powder
⅔ cup cocoa powder
1 teaspoon baking powder
2 eggs
2 tablespoons vodka
¼ cup raw almonds (or almond flakes)
½ cup cocoa nibs
1 teaspoon cannabis-infused agave (recipe on page 118)
⅔ cup cannabis-infused butter, softened
⅔ cup coconut sugar
¼ cup black chia seeds
½ cup goji berries
½ cup grated coconut

Continued

Green Tea, Cannabis, and Coconut Brownies

Preheat oven to 350°F. Lightly spray an 8" x 8" baking pan with cooking spray.

In a small bowl, mix flour, mesquite powder, cocoa, and baking powder.

In a separate bowl, lightly beat eggs and vodka together.

Grind almonds in a food processor.

In a small bowl, combine cocoa nibs with agave and stir until nibs are well coated.

In a cake mixer or large bowl, beat together butter and coconut sugar until mixture becomes a smooth paste. Alternating between flour and egg mix, add one cup at a time of each, continuing to beat until all ingredients are completely combined.

Add almonds, agave cocoa nibs, chia seeds, goji berries, and coconut. Beat thoroughly.

Pour batter into baking dish and bake for 40 minutes. Brownies are ready when a toothpick inserted into center comes out clean.

COCKTAILS

Be careful! Alcohol is an extremely efficient method of extracting cannabis. These aren't cocktails for people who like to knock back a couple cocktails (or more). These are for people who want one carefully thought-out, ritually made infusion of cannabis and fermentation.

Buzzy Bee's Knees

Catjia Redfern

This cocktail of gin, honey, and lemon was born to mask the nasty taste of bathtub gin when the rotgut was one of few spirits available during Prohibition (like brownie mix when schwag was the only cannabis around). Catjia Redfern celebrates the end of another Prohibition (in her state) with this embellished Bee's Knees, a summertime cocktail that combines three of her favorite local Colorado ingredients: Jack Herer cannabis, Peach Street Distillers' Jackalope organic gin, and orange blossom honey. To make this cocktail for two, Catjia stirs two tablespoons of cannabis-infused honey into two ounces of cannabis-infused gin or vodka and the juice of a lemon in a shaker until the honey dissolves, then mixes in the water from a young coconut, shakes, and pours the mixture over cracked ice (you can do this in the palm of your hand with the back of a spoon). (Honey can be difficult to stir. If yours is too thick to dissolve, make a simple syrup by combining one part honey with one part boiling water and boiling until honey is dissolved.) Catjia's cocktail is an opportunity to see how products from your neighborhood grower, distiller, and beekeeper interact. You may want to choose cultivars based on effects (indica for nightcaps, sativa before dinner), because the honey and lemon mask the cannabis taste in this cocktail. Don't let that fool you. With two different infusions, this cocktail has an ounce of cannabis honey and an ounce of infused gin per serving. You can make it less potent—so you can drink more on a hot summer day—by using non-infused honey. Infuse your honey and gin or vodka with the same cultivar so your brain doesn't have to unscramble indica, sativa, *and* alcohol.

Serves 2

THC per serving: 🌿

2 tablespoons Cannabis Honey (recipe on page 116)

2 ounces Gin or Vodka Infusion (recipe on page 112)

juice of 1 large lemon

1 cup raw coconut water

8 or more ounces tonic water, to taste

sliced lemon

mint basil (or basil)

shaker

strainer

tall glasses

Phillips screwdriver (if using fresh coconut)

If you're using fresh coconut, place it on a cutting board. Find the soft "eye" (if there are two or more, find the softest one). Puncture the screwdriver through the soft "eye." Drain out water into a bowl.

In shaker, stir with a spoon to dissolve honey into gin or vodka and lemon juice. Stir in coconut water. Shake vigorously. Place cracked ice, lemon slices, and basil leaves in tall glasses. Pour honey, gin, and lemon through strainer over cracked ice. Add tonic water to taste. Stir. Garnish with lemon slices and basil mints or herbs of your choice.

Melamine

Rabib Rafiq

Rabib Rafiq's twenty-first-century take on the Bijou cocktail (*bijou* means "jewel" in French), a herbaceous, full-flavored combination of green Chartreuse, gin, and vermouth that was popular at the turn of the twentieth century, has the sweet, viscous appeal of the original martini relative—with two important twists. Rabib infuses the green Chartreuse with an ounce of decarboxylated cannabis (see recipe on page 79), and he uses rum instead of vermouth for big, deep flavor. Green Chartreuse, one of Rabib's favorite liqueurs, is an intense, aromatic spirit that adds a spicy, sweet layer to cocktails without being cloying. Rabib mixes the Chartreuse, bitters, and Ron Zacapa 23 rum (his choice, but any high-quality aged *rhum agricole*, or rum made with sugar, will do) with ice and strains it into a champagne coupe or martini glass. This can be served as a cocktail and is a great after-dinner drink as the herbal spirits help ease digestion.

Serves 1

THC per serving: ☘

1 ounce cannabis-infused green
    Chartreuse (recipe on page 114)
1½ ounces gran classico bitters
    (or 25 milliliters Campari)
1 ounce *rhum agricole*
mixing glass
strainer
champagne coupe or martini glass
ice

Fill a mixing glass ⅔ full with ice.
Vigorously stir together ingredients until very cold.
Strain into a champagne coupe (a shallow, broad-bowled, stemmed glass) or martini glass with no garnish.

Central Park North

Rabib Rafiq

Every bartender makes a Central Park differently. Some use bourbon, some tequila. The original version, said to have been mixed at Portobello, a vegan restaurant in Portland, Oregon, calls for bourbon, boysenberry liqueur, and Ramazzotti Amaro, an herbaceous Italian liqueur. Rabib Rafiq's version includes two cannabis-infused liquors—three quarters of an ounce of gin and a couple drops of aromatic green chartreuse—along with gin, bitters, and Dolin Rouge, a sweet vermouth with a brandy-like quality. Rabib's preferred gin for this cocktail is Spring44 Old Tom Gin, made from locally sourced botanicals and Rocky Mountain spring water, but you can use your favorite local artisanal gin. (Every fine gin has a unique mix of botanicals, so the label you choose makes a difference in the taste of this gin-dominant drink.) For the tinctures, Rabib infuses a liter of gin with ten grams of decarboxylated cannabis and ten ounces of green Chartreuse with six grams of decarboxylated cannabis. Just before serving this cocktail, Rabib flames an orange zest into the glass, lightly caramelizing the essential oil and enhancing its flavor as he twists it. (Use the freshest orange you can find for the most oils and the brightest flame.) Keep the flame a good three to six inches from the liquid's surface to avoid making the cocktail taste like lighter fluid, at a forty-five degree angle pointing up toward the glass rim. Flaming makes for an impressive presentation, but do it before you've had your own cocktail. This mixture of herbal infusions is *potent*.

Serves 1

THC per serving: ↘

orange zest

½ ounce Spring44 Old Tom Gin

¾ ounce Cannabis Gin Tincture (see page 113)

1¼ ounces gran classico bitters (or 20 milliliters Campari)

½ ounce Dolin Rouge

2 drops Chartreuse Cannabis Tincture (recipe on page 114)

mixing glass

strainer

large rocks glass

ice

matches

Using a sharp paring knife, cut a 1" diameter circle of orange zest.

Fill a mixing glass ⅔ full with ice.

Vigorously stir together all ingredients except for orange until very cold.

Strain into glass.

Light a match and hold it about 6" away from rim of glass. Hold orange peel with skin toward glass, about 2" above the match and pointing toward it so that the oils will spurt toward the glass. Twist and squeeze the peel. It will flame up briefly.

Rub the zest around the rim of the glass and use as garnish.

Serve in a large rocks glass with one large rock.

Mary Jane Daiquiri

Rabib Rafiq

The daiquiri, a blend of rum, sugar, water, and citrus, was invented in the seventeenth century as a way to dilute rum rations on British navy ships in the Caribbean—not because rum was scarce but because sailors drank too much of it. It was called grog until an iron magnate living in Cuba during the Spanish–American War named his version after Daiquiri, a village on Cuba's eastern coast. The cocktail found its way to ports around the world. By the 1920s, the characters in F. Scott Fitzgerald's novels were drinking daiquiris, and Ernest Hemingway created his own in the 1930s. Later, Middle America customized the cocktail with a new invention, the blender, but that's not the daiquiri we're talking about here. Rabib Rafiq's shaken daiquiri is old school with a twist, combining three quarters of an ounce of cannabis-infused simple syrup with pineapple and lime juices and Diplomatico Reserva Exclusiva, a rich, fruity molasses-distilled Venezuelan rum that's aged in bourbon casks for twelve years. Diplomatico Reserva Exclusiva's sugar-and-spice flavor profile is ideal in this cocktail, but you can use the aged rum of your choice. (Aged rum adds important vanilla and toffee notes.) To make his simple syrup, Rabib simmers together two grams of decarboxylated cannabis flowers or trim with three cups of water and three cups of sugar (his recipe is on page 119). He serves the cocktail in a champagne coupe, the broad, shallow glasses often used to serve champagne at weddings. You can use a martini or cocktail glass if you don't have coupes.

Serves 1

THC per serving: ↘

1¾ ounces aged rum
½ ounce lime juice
¼ ounce pineapple juice
¾ ounce Cannabis Simple Syrup
pineapple leaf for garnish
mixing glass
strainer
champagne coupe
ice

Fill a mixing glass ⅔ full with ice.

Vigorously stir together all ingredients until very cold.

Strain into champagne coupe.

Submerge pineapple leaf diagonally in glass, letting tip hang over the edge.

High Monk Swizzle

Rabib Rafiq

The exact formulation for Fernet Branca, an Italian liqueur made from 27 herbs including aloe, gentian root, and rhubarb, has been a family secret since Bernardino Branca first sold it as a tonic in 1845. (Fernet Branca's claims to handle everything from menstrual cramps to parasites allowed it to stay on the shelves as medicine during Prohibition.) The liqueur's secret ingredient is rumored to be saffron, the same herb that makes yellow Chartreuse yellow. The recipe for Chartreuse is also tightly held by Carthesian monks who have been crafting the "elixir of long life" from 130 alpine herbs since 1605. Combined in Rabib Rafiq's icy cocktail, the mysterious *digestifs* are irresistible. Honey-sweetened yellow Chartreuse, which still has the spicy bite of the green Chartreuse that spawned it, has the heft to mellow Fernet Branca's bitter edges, while cannabis-infused simple syrup and orange bitters mimic the dance between the two liqueurs and soften both big flavors. To make it, Rabib stirs together three-quarters of an ounce of cannabis simple syrup, an ounce and a half of Fernet Branca, three quarters of an ounce of yellow Chartreuse, and two dashes of orange bitters with ice cubes, strains it into a glass with crushed ice, and piles more crushed ice on top for a snow-cone effect. If you don't have an ice crusher, you can use a food processor or blender. If your blender doesn't have a "crushed ice" option, add about a quarter cup of water when you blend the ice.

Serves 1

THC per serving: ↘

1½ ounces Fernet Branca

¾ ounce yellow Chartreuse

¾ ounce Cannabis Simple Syrup (see page 119)

crushed ice

4–5 mint sprigs

mixing glass

strainer

swizzle stick

large rocks glass

2 dashes orange bitters

ice

Put ice cubes and all ingredients except bitters in a mixing glass.

Shake until cold and strain into large rocks glass.

Place swizzle stick inside glass.

Add crushed ice to fill glass, leaving enough room to stir.

Swizzle to mix all ingredients.

Fill top of rocks glass with more crushed ice for a snow-cone look.

Garnish with mint. Add dash of bitters on top for enhanced flavor and color contrast.

Pine Forest Fizz

Rabib Rafiq

The gin fizz, a vigorously shaken cocktail made from gin, egg white, citrus, sugar, and soda water was a smash at the turn of the twentieth century and remained popular throughout Prohibition. As an act of disobedience at the start of Prohibition, New Orleans nightclub owner Henry C. Ramos encouraged home bartenders when he leaked the secret gin fizz recipe with orange flower water that had made his club famous. In the recipe, Ramos urged people to keep experimenting until they got the cocktail right and concluded: "The secret in success lies in the good care you take and in your patience, and be certain to use good material." Rabib Rafiq follows in Ramos's footsteps with this minimalist gin fizz infused with Cannabis Simple Syrup. Rabib can't serve Pine Forest Fizzes at his bar yet, but he can, and does, make them at home in Massachusetts. He's played with this mix of infusions for years, and this cocktail delivers complex taste and a pleasant, moderate buzz. To make it, Rabib shakes egg whites and lemon juice in an airtight stainless steel shaker for a full minute, then hard shakes that with Cannabis Simple Syrup, gin, raspberry liqueur, and a dash of bitters. (If you have a milk frother, use that to foam the mixture.) He pours the mixture over ice, refrigerates it for two minutes to solidify the foam, and tops it off with a pour of soda water. Rabib uses a Collins ice mold, which makes ice that fits into tall Collins glasses, and highly recommends using St. George Terroir gin, a mix of juniper, California bay laurel, and coastal sage that pairs well with cannabis. If that's hard to find, you could experiment with one of the handmade, organic spirits being made by craft gin makers everywhere.

Serves 1

THC per serving: ↘

1 egg white
¾ ounce lemon juice
1½ ounces St. George Terroir gin
¾ ounce Cannabis Simple Syrup
    (recipe on page 119)
½ ounce St. George raspberry liqueur
1 dash angostura bitters
ice cubes
soda water
shaker
tall Collins glasses
Collins ice mold (optional)
ice

Extract egg white from egg into shaker. Add lemon juice. Dry shake (shake without ice) for 1 minute or more, until solution is extremely frothy.

Add gin, simple syrup, raspberry liqueur, and bitters. Shake hard with ice. (Alternatively, blend with a milk frother for 20–25 seconds to build a nice foam.)

Place ice from Collins ice mold or ice cubes in tall Collins glasses. Pour solution over ice. Refrigerate for about 2 minutes to somewhat solidify foam.

Top with a slow, steady pour of soda water until foam rises 2–3 centimeters above rim of glass.

Dutch Pilot

Rabib Rafiq

Velvet Falernum, a Barbadian sugar cane liqueur infused with lime, almonds, cloves, ginger root, and other spices, is a Tiki bar classic and key to West Indies "swizzle" cocktails, which were traditionally mixed with one part sour, two parts sweet, three parts strong, and four parts weak (water). In his twist on the swizzle, Rabib Rafiq shakes together half an ounce of Velvet Falernum (he makes his own, but you can usually find John D. Taylor Velvet Falernum at a good liquor store) with an ounce and a half of cannabis-infused gin and half an ounce of Leopold Brother's Michigan Tart Cherry Liqueur, a handcrafted spirit made from Montmorency cherries, for a bracing cocktail. The spice-rich Velvet Falernum brightens the tart citrus and cherry without overwhelming the gin and its botanicals. Golden Goat, a sweet, spicy sativa hybrid, plays well in this cocktail.

Serves 1

THC per serving: ✿

1½ ounces Cannabis Gin Tincture (recipe on page 113)
½ ounce Leopold Brother's Michigan Tart Cherry liqueur
½ ounce Velvet Falernum
½ ounce lemon juice
rosemary sprig
shaker
strainer
5.5-ounce glasses
ice

Put all ingredients in shaker. Add ice. Shake vigorously until cold.

Strain into 5.5-ounce glass.

Garnish with rosemary sprig.

Internal Combustion Collins

Rabib Rafiq

When it was first published in Jerry Thomas's *The Bartender's Guide* in 1876, the Tom Collins called for five or six dashes of sugar syrup, juice from a small lemon, one large wine glass of gin, and two or three lumps of ice. The cocktail took its name from a popular hoax of telling people that a fictional Tom Collins had said terrible things about them. A century and a half later, hoaxes have gone digital and cocktails have gone craft. Rabib Rafiq's Tom Collins reaches far beyond a wine glass full of sweet gin with lemon and even beyond craft. Rabib combines an ounce and a half of cannabis-infused gin, half an ounce of cannabis-infused simple syrup, three quarters of an ounce of lime juice, and half an ounce of green Chartreuse, an herbaceous French liqueur, for a cocktail that delivers a tingly, whole-body high. Rabib's cocktail combines two cannabis infusions with two strong spirits, and it's potent. Pay attention to the infusions you use, as your brain might not like dealing with sativa, indica, *and* alcohol. Infusing the syrup and gin with a heavy indica such as spicy Afghani makes this a serious nightcap. A zesty sativa such as Lamb's Breath lightens the mood.

Serves 1

THC per serving: 🌿

1½ ounces Cannabis Gin Tincture (recipe on page 113)

¾ ounce lime juice

½ ounce green Chartreuse

½ ounce Cannabis Simple Syrup (see recipe on page 119)

shaker

strainer

Collins glass

ice

Combine all ingredients in shaker half filled with ice cubes.

Shake well.

Strain into Collins glass almost filled with ice cubes.

Garnish with lime.

Cannabis Coconut Mojito

Andie Leon

Developed in Cuba centuries ago, the mojito is a drink made from rum, sugar, lime, and mint. The word *mojito* derives from the African word *mojo,* which means to cast a little spell. Ernest Hemingway brought mojitos from Havana to Key West, Florida, in the 1950s, but the cocktail was a sleeper until it showed up in the 2002 James Bond movie *Die Another Day.* Since then, the mojito has been showing up on cocktail menus worldwide, in delightful variations from frozen to dirty (made with raw sugar). Andie Leon makes her refreshing version with two ounces of cannabis-infused light rum and two ounces of coconut rum, coconut palm sugar, coconut water, and coconut milk. She crushes the lime, mint, and coconut palm sugar into two highballs using a wooden pestle (you can use the back of an ice cream scooper if you don't have a pestle), then fills the glasses with ice and pours in the rums and finishes with a splash of coconut water and a splash of coconut milk. Coconuts are a delicious source of fiber, vitamins, minerals, and amino acids, giving Andie's mojito a nutritional boost. For her simple rum infusion, Andie combines an eighth of an ounce of cured, decarboxylated cannabis flowers with a 500-milliliter bottle of light rum, which is more adaptable to infused flavors than dark rum, and lets it sit for at least a week.

Serves 2

THC per serving: ↘

1 fresh lime, cut into small pieces

10 mint leaves, no stems

2 tablespoons coconut palm sugar

2 ounces cannabis-infused light rum

2 ounces coconut rum

ice cubes

splash of coconut water

1 young coconut

½ cup of light coconut milk or coconut cream

2 young coconuts or 2 teaspoons dehydrated unsweetened coconut flakes

wooden pestle or ice cream scooper

2 highball glasses

Divide lime, mint, and coconut palm sugar evenly into 2 highball glasses.

Grind with a wooden pestle or ice cream scooper for approximately 30 seconds for each glass.

Fill glasses with ice and pour 1 ounce of cannabis-infused rum and 1 ounce of coconut rum into each.

Add a splash of coconut water and a splash of coconut milk. If you're using fresh coconuts, scoop out about 2 teaspoons of flesh and add a teaspoon to each glass (or add a teaspoon of coconut flakes to each glass).

Mix thoroughly. Serve.

Twentieth of April

Rabib Rafiq

Bitters, herb, and spice infusions with a bitter herb such as gentian root or wormwood as the base have received full new-darling treatment in recent years, with restaurants and mixologists making their own and cottage producers handcrafting batches flavored with everything from Jamaican jerk to *Lapsang Souchon.* Rabib Rafiq's mix of three different bitters with an ounce and a half of cannabis-infused gin, half an ounce of cannabis-infused simple syrup, and three quarters of an ounce of lime juice sticks to the classics. Angostura aromatic bitters is a floral gentian root-based tonic developed for soldiers' stomach ailments in General Simon Bolivar's Liberation Army in 1824, named for the Venezuelan city Angostura (now *Ciudad Bolivar*) but now made from a closely guarded combination of forty-seven herbs in Trinidad. Peychaud's Bitters was first bottled by a Creole apothecary in New Orleans from a secret family recipe brought over from Haiti in the 1830s, and bitters made from dried-bitter orange peels has been around since the nineteenth century (it was in the first martini, and Angostura makes one). Together, the three tarts up the botanicals from cannabis-infused gin and simple syrup while tempering the lime's acidity for an artful balance of bitter, sour, and sweet that's far too easy to drink. Rabib serves this cocktail in a champagne coupe, the broad, shallow glasses often used to serve champagne at weddings. You can use a martini or cocktail glass if you don't have coupes.

Serves 1

THC per serving: ☘

1½ ounces Cannabis Gin Tincture
(recipe on page 113)
¾ ounce lime juice
½ ounce Cannabis Simple Syrup
(recipe on page 119)
10 dashes Angostura bitters
5 dashes orange bitters
5 dashes Peychaud's bitters
shaker
strainer

Fill shaker ⅔ full with ice.
Place all ingredients in shaker and shake until cold.
Strain into champagne coupe.

Green Rush

Rabib Rafiq

Matcha, a fine green powder from *camellia sinensis* leaves, has been used in Japan since Buddhist monks began using it to help them sit meditation in the twelfth century. Matcha contains a moderate amount of caffeine along with L-theanine, amino acids that relax the mind, and chlorophyll, the bright green pigment that increases oxygen in the blood and detoxifies the liver and intestines. Rabib Rafiq likes matcha for all the reasons the monks did, including its astringent, full-bodied flavor. In this cocktail—a spin on one of Rabib's favorites called the Speak Low, created by Singo Gokan of the Angel's Share bar in New York—he combines matcha, cannabis, rum, and sherry for calm focus, euphoria, and bold taste. Rabib shakes a half gram of matcha with an ounce and a half of *rhum agricole* (rum made with sugar) and Lactart (lactic acid, available online at www.artofdrink.com) without ice to build a nice foam (like the foam after a tea master whisks matcha during tea ceremony), then gives it another shake with a half ounce of cannabis-infused simple syrup, a half ounce of sherry, and ice. When he has the time, Rabib blends the rum and matcha using a Japanese tea ceremony bowl and bamboo whisk; when he's in a hurry, he froths it in a Bodum milk frother. Rabib balances the matcha and cannabis's grit with Ron Zacapa 23, a smooth oak-aged rum distilled from virgin sugar cane honey, and intensely sweet Pedro Ximenez dessert sherry. He garnishes it with a strip of apricot peel, but you can use an apricot wheel or a grapefruit peel. The caffeine in matcha could throw people over the edge when combined with alcohol and THC. Warn guests that this cocktail is a trifecta.

Serves 1

THC per serving: ↘

- 1½ ounces Ron Zacapa 23 rum (or any high-quality aged *rhum agricole*, made with sugar)
- ½ ounce Pedro Ximenez sherry
- ½ ounce Cannabis Simple Syrup (recipe on page 119)
- 3–4 drops Lactart (lactic acid, available at www.artofdrink.com)
- ½ gram matcha powder
- apricot peel
- milk frother or shaker
- strainer
- rocks glass
- ice
- large ice cube

Put rum, matcha powder, and lactic acid in milk frother or shaker.

If using a frother, pulse for about 20–25 seconds, moving the frother up and down to let air get into the mix, until you build a good foam.

If dry shaking, place lid on tightly and shake well for at least 30 seconds.

Add sherry, simple syrup, and ice. Shake for no longer than 15 seconds.

Strain into a rocks glass with a large ice cube.

Garnish with apricot peel.

Lemon Lavender Champagne

Grace Gutierrez

Floral, bright, and bubbly, Grace Gutierrez's summertime champagne cocktail elevates any occasion to a celebration. Grace makes a cannabis and lavender simple syrup by breaking up cured cannabis flowers with her hands (she leaves the stems) and combining them with sugar, water, lavender, and vegetable glycerin, a sugar alcohol used to extract botanicals. Grace stirs together the simple syrup with fresh lemon juice and quality champagne for a mildly potent cocktail that's perfect for weddings and garden parties. You can use a half to three-quarters of a gram of cured cannabis flowers instead of a full gram for the simple syrup to make the cocktails less potent; Grace warns that making the simple syrup with more than two grams will ruin your party. She infuses the simple syrup with an uplifting sativa for brunch and a potent indica for an end-of-the-day refresher. As enticing as lavender can be, resist the temptation to use more of the mint than the recipe calls for. Too much lavender makes the cocktail taste soapy.

Serves 8

THC per serving: ✺

½ cup water

½ cup granulated sugar

1 gram cured cannabis flowers, broken up

¼ cup dried or fresh lavender flowers

1 teaspoon vegetable glycerin (available at health food stores)

16 tablespoons fresh-squeezed lemon juice

1 bottle champagne

garnishes such as lemon peel twirls, lemon wedges, or lavender sprigs

white wine glasses

fine mesh strainer

cheesecloth

To make a simple syrup, heat water and sugar until sugar is dissolved. Raise heat and bring to a boil. Stir in cannabis. Let simmer on medium-high heat for 20 minutes, covered.

Add lavender and vegetable glycerin to syrup. Boil another 5 minutes, stirring every minute or so. Remove from heat and let cool.

Line strainer with cheesecloth and pour simple syrup through to strain out cannabis and lavender solids. Squeeze cheesecloth and compost plant matter.

For the cocktail, combine 2 tablespoons lemon juice and 2 tablespoons infused lavender simple syrup into an 8- to 12-ounce white wine glass. Fill the rest of the glass with your favorite champagne.

Garnish with a lemon peel twirl or a lemon wedge and lavender sprig.

RESOURCE GUIDE

FOR GROWING

Organic Cannabis Consulting

Permalos Consulting

www.permalos.com

Sustainable cannabis cultivation using the ethics and principles of permaculture

Regenerative Design Institute

www.regenerativedesign.org

Permaculture design courses and resources

Cannabis Seeds

303 Seeds

www.303seeds.com

Some of the world's finest medical cannabis seeds

Aficionado Seeds

www.aficionadoseeds.com

Boutique seed collection specializing in heirloom genetics bred in California's Emerald Triangle

Dynasty Seeds

www.dynastyseeds.com

Seed company dedicated to providing stable, medicinal cannabis strains

Gage Green Group

www.gagegreen.org

A network of connoisseur cultivators and herbalists

Pacific Northwest Roots
www.pacificnwroots.com
Genetics of the Pacific Northwest

Sin City Seeds
www.homeofthedank.com
Dedicated group of cannabis breeders striving to produce one-of-a-kind genetics

FOR PROCESSING/STORAGE

Ball Jars
www.ball.com
Ideal for short- and long-term preservation of herbs and other plant material

Cannador
www.cannador.com
Humidification box designed for short- or long-term cannabis storage

CVault
http://thecvault.com
Curing and storage containers

Essential Extracts
www.essentialextracts.com
Extraction bag system for cold water, mechanical separation of essential oils

Fresh Headies
www.freshheadies.com
Multi-task filtration bubble bag system for solvent-free extraction of essential oils

Trim Bin
www.harvest-more.com
Two-bin tray system for trimming herbs

FOR COOKING

MagicalButter
www.magicalbutter.com
Micro-processing machine that makes cannabis extractions

FOR LEARNING

Books

Cannabis: A History, by Martin Booth (Picador, 2005)

Cannabis: Evolution and Ethnobotany, by Robert Connell Clarke and Mark D. Merlin (University of California Press, 2013)

Gaia's Garden: A Guide to Home-Scale Permaculture, by Toby Hemenway (Chelsea Green Publishing, 2009)

One Straw Revolution: An Introduction to Natural Farming, by Masanobu Fukuoka (NYRB Classics, 2009)

Organic Marijuana Soma Style: The Pleasures of Cultivating Connoisseur Cannabis, by Soma (Quick American Archives, 2005)

Sepp Holzer's Permaculture: A Practical Guide to Small-Scale, Integrative Farming and Gardening, by Sepp Holzer (Chelsea Green Publishing, 2011)

Teaming with Microbes: The Organic Gardener's Guide to the Soil Food Web, by Jeff Lowenfels and Wayne Lewis (Timber Press, 2010)

The Intelligent Gardener: Growing Nutrient-Dense Food, by Steve Soloman (New Society Publishers, 2012)

Websites

Bubbleman's World
https://www.youtube.com/user/BCbubbleman
Invaluable resource for making and using bubble hash and dry sift

Cannabis Cheri
http://www.cannabischeri.com/
Cooking, lifestyle, news, shopping

Cannabis International
www.cannabisinternational.org
Resource for the dietary and medicinal study and use of cannabis

Cannabis Maven
http://cannabismaven.com/
Business and social trends

The Cannabist
www.thecannabist.co/
News and lifestyle coverage of cannabis scene

The Cannabis Kitchen
www.the-cannabis-kitchen.com
News, information, tutorials, lifestyle

Cook With Herb
www.cookwith herb.com
Tutorials, DVDs, news

Culinary Cannabis
www.culinarycannabis.org
Recipes, tutorials, supplies, news

Erowid
www.erowid.org/plants/cannabis
Educational nonprofit organization

Ganjasana
www.Ganjasana.com
Resource for cannabis plant medicine yoga

The Hemp Connoisseur
http://www.thcmag.com/
Environmental, economic, and health benefits of cannabis and hemp

Hempista
www.hempista.com
Health and wellness, fashion and lifestyle

Holistic Cannabis Network
www.HolisticCannabisNetwork.com
Integrative nutrition and cannabis

JackHerer.com
http://www.jackherer.com/
Cannabis and hemp news and information

Leafly
www.leafly.com
News and advocacy site that connects medical cannabis patients with strains and dispensaries (also a phone app)

Leaf Science
www.leafscience.com
News and facts about cannabis

Medicine Hunter
www.medicinehunter.com/cannabis
News and insight about cannabis

The Stoner's Cookbook
http://www.thestonerscookbook.com/
Recipes, tutorials, shopping

Weedmaps
https://weedmaps.com/
Connecting cannabis patients to discuss and review dispensaries and doctors

Weedist
www.weedist.com
A community of cannabis connoisseurs

WikiWeed
www.wikiweed.com
Articles and information about cannabis (public is encouraged to contribute)

ADVOCACY AND INFORMATION
Americans for Safe Access
www.safeaccessnow.org
Ensures safe access to cannabis for therapeutic uses and research

Cannabis Consumers Union
http://cannabisconsumer.org/
News and advocacy

Council on Responsible Cannabis Regulation
www.unitedpatientsgroup.com
Cannabis information for medical cannabis patients

Hempology.org
http://hempology.org/index.html
The study of hemp and cannabis

Marijuana Policy Project
www.mpp.org
Working to increase public support for non-punitive, non-coercive marijuaa policies

National Organization for the Reform of Marijuana Laws
www.norml.org
Founded in 1970 to move public opinion to legalize the responsible use of cannabis by adults and to serve as an advocate for consumers

NORML Women's Alliance
http://normlwomensalliance.org/
Nonpartisan coalition of socially and geographically diverse women for cannabis law reform

Project CBD
www.projectcbd.org
Defending whole plant cannabis therapeutics

Safer Alternative For Enjoyable Recreation
http://archive.saferchoice.org/
Envisioning a society in which cannabis is regulated and treated similar to alcohol

Hemp
Hemp Industries Association
http://www.thehia.org/
Nonprofit group representing interests of hemp industry

North American Industrial Hemp Council
www.naihc.org
Advocating for US farmers to be allowed to grow industrial hemp

Rocky Mountain Hemp Association
http://rockymountainhempassociation.org/
Supporting the growth and development of all aspects of the hemp industry

CERTIFICATIONS

Clean Green Certified

www.cleangreencert.com

Third-party agricultural certification program that supports sustainable practices and environmental stewardship

Organic Cannabis Association

www.organicca.org

Organic standards for cannabis cultivation

TRAVEL

Bud And Breakfast

www.budandbreakfast.com

Cannabis-friendly lodging

Bud + Breakfast

www.budandbfast.com

Cannabis-friendly lodging and hospitality company

The Travel Joint

www.traveljoint.com

Leader in cannabis tourism, bringing the best hotels, restaurants, nightlife, entertainment, and places to purchase legal cannabis

GLOSSARY

Cannabidiol (CBD) A primary cannabinoid in cannabis that doesn't bind to CB1 receptors, where psychoactive effects are triggered, and can mute THC's psychoactive effects.

Cannabinoids Active chemical compounds in cannabis that plug into cannabinoid receptors in the human brain. Cannabinoids deliver powerful antioxidants and can shift neurological and physiological patterns.

Clone Specially selected cuttings from a "mother" cannabis plant that grow into full-size offspring.

Cola Clusters of female cannabis flowers that can grow up to a foot and more in length.

Cultivar A variety or strain of cannabis originating in and persistent under cultivation.

Decarboxylation The process of heating cannabis to break off THC-A's and CBD-A's carboxyl radicals, activating THC and CBD and making cannabis more potent.

Dispensary An establishment that sells cannabis. In states where adult-use cannabis is legal, medical dispensaries generally operate separately from "recreational" dispensaries (the cannabis industry prefers the term "adult-use").

Extraction Substance made by extracting cannabinoids from cannabis using a fat or solvent.

Fan Leaf Large iconic leaf with long pointy fingers on the outside of the plant. Fan leaves contain very little THC but, depending on the cultivar, can be high in CBD.

Flower Egg- or conical-shaped cluster of blooms on cannabis plants that grow up to several inches long. Sometimes referred to as "bud" or "nug."

Hash Extracted and concentrated resin from the cannabis plant.

Hemp Non-psychoactive cannabis subspecies used primarily for food, fiber, and high-CBD medicine.

Hybrid Cultivar made from breeding two different plants. (Hybrids can be accidental or intentional.)

Indica Type of cannabis plant with dark, rounded leaves and tight flowers. Indica delivers a cozy, hibernating all-over body effect for most people.

Infusion Substance created by extracting chemical compounds from cannabis in a fat or solvent.

Kief Concentrated resin glands that have been separated from the plant using dry, solvent-free methods.

Landrace Cultivar with pure genetics that's indigenous to a particular geographic region.

Marijuana Grow Operation A place where cannabis is grown legally, also known as a "grow op."

Sativa Type of cannabis with long, pointy, light green leaves and fluffy, fruity flowers. Sativa delivers a bright, uplifting euphoria that many people appreciate for daytime use.

Sugar Leaf Small resin-coated leaves trimmed from colas during harvest, often used in cooking. Also known as "trim."

THC Tetrahydrocannabinol, the active ingredient in cannabis that gives it psychoactive effects.

Tincture Infusion made by dissolving cannabis in alcohol.

Terpene Pungent oil produced in cannabis resin that interacts with cannabinoids in the human body to modulate the effects of THC and regulate dopamine and serotonin.

Trimming Process of manicuring cannabis flowers to remove sugar leaves.

Trichome Hair with crystal-like resin glands on cannabis leaves, stems, and calyxes where most cannabinoids and terpenes reside.

ACKNOWLEDGMENTS

Robyn Lawrence

The chefs—**Leslie, Mike, Scott, Joey, Andie, Rowan, Donna, Catjia, Herb, Lucie, Grace, Emily**—are this book's heart. Their collective wisdom is mighty, and their hearts are generous. **Povy Kendal Atchison** brought this book to life, literally and in imagery. **Rabib Rafiq** provided insight into herbal infusions well beyond cocktails. **Chris Kilham** spent hours and traveled miles to make sure a plant he loves was represented accurately and honestly. **Matt Davenport** showed up again and again—and again—and made it right. The food stylists—**Hadiya Brown, Catjia Redfern, Lucie Lazarus**, and **Alex Looby**—turned recipes into art. **Chuck Norris** whipped up photo-ready cocktails like the pro he is (*mahalo!*). Early readers were much more than readers. Insight from **Rick Kauvar, Scott Davenport, Zoe Helene, Karen Phillips, David White, Stacey Halyard, Stefanie Breslin, Veronica Trau, Stacey Lawrence, Rachael Carlevale,** and **Tracey Henry** made all the difference. **Tracey Henry** showed up like an angel at exactly the right time. **Rachael Carlevale**'s tenacity and enthusiasm gave this book juice. **Rich Kauvar**'s and **Zoe Helene**'s belief gave it sails. **Nicole Frail** was patient and a joy to work with. **Jane West** and **Wanda James** took time out of historic work for the cannabis industry—and women in the cannabis industry—to contribute. **Lori Tobias** and **Suzanne Gerber** tapped their vast networks and gave counsel. A shout-out to the seed companies and growers who supplied beautiful photos of beautiful genetics. **Stacey Lawrence** crunched numbers (sorry, really, just one last time….) and, along with his sister, **Cree**, put up with having a writer (who still feels guilty about missing the Crossroads tournament) for a mom. **Dennis Crawford** was a guide, butter and oil maker, recipe tester, supporter, and friend, always amused by what it took to make this happen.

Povy Kendal Atchison

I'd like to thank **Robyn Lawrence**, one of the best writers with whom I've had the pleasure to work with for more years than I can count. **Sandra Dallas** gave me the book publishing bug at a mere age of 16 along with encouragement and constant support. **Danielle Egan-Miller,** I can't believe you took me as one of your clients. You fought like hell for me and treated me like a rock star. Photographer **Sheri Giblin**, if it weren't for you I never would have learned food photography. You literally showed me the light. **Karin**, thank you for your keen knowledge, advice and wisdom. **Mr. Bob** and **Dana** for always having my back. And to my **husband** and **son**, thank you for putting up with all of the late photo shoots and messy kitchen.

CONVERSION CHARTS

METRIC AND IMPERIAL CONVERSIONS

(These conversions are rounded for convenience)

Ingredient	Cups/Tablespoons/Teaspoons	Ounces	Grams/Milliliters
Butter	1 cup=16 tablespoons= 2 sticks	8 ounces	230 grams
Cream cheese	1 tablespoon	0.5 ounce	14.5 grams
Cheese, shredded	1 cup	4 ounces	110 grams
Cornstarch	1 tablespoon	0.3 ounce	8 grams
Flour, all-purpose	1 cup/1 tablespoon	4.5 ounces/0.3 ounce	125 grams/8 grams
Flour, whole wheat	1 cup	4 ounces	120 grams
Fruit, dried	1 cup	4 ounces	120 grams
Fruits or veggies, chopped	1 cup	5 to 7 ounces	145 to 200 grams
Fruits or veggies, puréed	1 cup	8.5 ounces	245 grams
Honey, maple syrup, or corn syrup	1 tablespoon	0.75 ounce	20 grams
Liquids: cream, milk, water, or juice	1 cup	8 fluid ounces	240 milliliters
Oats	1 cup	5.5 ounces	150 grams
Salt	1 teaspoon	0.2 ounces	6 grams
Spices: cinnamon, cloves, ginger, or nutmeg (ground)	1 teaspoon	0.2 ounce	5 milliliters
Sugar, brown, firmly packed	1 cup	7 ounces	200 grams
Sugar, white	1 cup/1 tablespoon	7 ounces/0.5 ounce	200 grams/12.5 grams
Vanilla extract	1 teaspoon	0.2 ounce	4 grams

OVEN TEMPERATURES

Fahrenheit	Celcius	Gas Mark
225°	110°	¼
250°	120°	½
275°	140°	1
300°	150°	2
325°	160°	3
350°	180°	4
375°	190°	5
400°	200°	6
425°	220°	7
450°	230°	8

"Let food be thy medicine and medicine be thy food."
—Hippocrates

INDEX